REV. DR. SCOTT'S WORKS.

DANIEL:

A MODEL FOR YOUNG MEN.

Published by ROBERT CARTER & BROTHERS, New York.

THE WEDGE OF GOLD;

Or, ACHAN IN EL'DORADO.

Published in San Francisco, and also by the Presbyterian Board in Philadelphia.

TRADE AND LETTERS:

THEIR JOURNEYINGS ROUND THE WORLD.

Delivered before, and published at the request, of the "Mercantile Library Association of San Francisco." New York: CARTERS.

THE GIANT JUDGE;

Or, SAMSON THE HEBREW HERCULES.

Published in San Francisco, and also by the Presbyterian Board in Philadelphia.

ESTHER;

THE HEBREW-PERSIAN QUEEN.

By Rev. W. A. SCOTT, D. D.
OF SAN FRANCISCO.

"The Historical matters of Scripture constitute as it were the bones of its system; and its spiritual matters are its muscles, blood vessels and nerves. As the bones are necessary to the human system, so Scripture must have its historical matters. Those expositions are the safest which keep closest to the text."—*Bengel.*

SAN FRANCISCO:
H. H. BANCROFT & CO.
1859.

O'MEARA & PAINTER, PRINTERS.

DEDICATION.

Mothers and Daughters of the Pacific:

To you I beg leave respectfully to dedicate this humble attempt to explain and illustrate the wonderful history of the orphan Hebrew maid of Shushan, who became Queen of Persia. And I do so because I firmly believe the mightiest human power on earth, for good and for evil, is lodged in woman's hand:—

"*They who rock the cradle, rule the world.*"

And I also believe that the Sacred Scriptures alone, of all writings ancient or modern, have fully comprehended and rightly understood woman's mission, and truthfully and properly represented her in her true place. As it was by a woman our race fell, so it is by woman mankind are to be elevated and saved. The great Saviour of the world was born of a woman, and one of the most lovely and hopeful sights on earth is a woman beneath the cross with the Word of God in her hand, learning her duty and acquiring the graces which fit her for her high mission in the world.

Woman's calling and rights are much talked of in our day, but I am fully persuaded that it is from the Bible, and not from new platforms, that we are to learn what they really are; and that not so much from precepts, as from examples. The Bible does not explain whether woman is equal or superior to man—does not dogmatize on her social or domestic condition, but straightway tells us how she was created, and for what purpose, and then illustrates her mission by giving brief notices of how a few remarkable mothers and wives fulfilled their vocation, from the days of the patriarchs to the apostles. This is true "philosophy teaching by example."

To you, therefore, to whom Providence has chiefly committed the great moral power of moulding into shape the minds and manners, and consequently the eternal destinies of the millions that are soon to have their home on this coast, is this volume most respectfully dedicated.

CONTENTS.

CHAPTER I.

PERSIA PAST AND PRESENT.

CHAPTER II.

THE MEGILLOTH ESTHER.

CHAPTER III.

THESE HEBREW RECORDS CREDIBLE.

1A

CHAPTER IV.

POINTS TO BE PROVEN.

CHAPTER V.

SUSA AND HER KING.

CHAPTER VI.

THE FEAST AND THE DIVORCE.

CHAPTER VII.

ESTHER CHOSEN QUEEN.

CHAPTER VIII.

ESTHER CROWNED QUEEN.

CHAPTER IX.

THE JEW AND THE AMALEKITE.

CHAPTER X.

HAMAN'S REVENGEFUL PLOT.

CHAPTER XI.

MORDECAI IN SACKCLOTH.

CHAPTER XII.

THE QUEEN INTERCEDING.

CHAPTER XIII.

THE BANQUET AND THE SLEEPLESS KING.

CHAPTER XIV.

THE ROYAL HONORING.

CHAPTER XV.

HAMAN'S FALL AND DEATH.

CHAPTER XVI.

THE LAW OF RETRIBUTION.

CHAPTER XVII.

THE COUNTER-DECREE ISSUED.

CHAPTER XVIII.

THE PICTURES TO BE STUDIED.

CHAPTER XIX.

THE DAY OF SLAUGHTER.

CHAPTER XX.

THE LIVING MONUMENT.

CHAPTER XXI.

FLOWERS FROM THE TOMB.

INTRODUCTION.

THERE is no more powerful auxiliary to the pulpit than the PRESS. The intellectual and moral stimulus of editorship, instead of being a loss to a pastor's charge, are both to them and to the world preëminently useful, if his writings are successful in advocating the truth. I see not how a pastor's efficiency is impaired by habits of close study, as far as his health and pastoral visitings will allow, whether his studies are devoted to manuscripts that are never published or to regular authorship. For even if he does not publish, the habit of study, which is rarely acquired and pursued without the use of the pen, is a very great blessing to his hearers; and if he publish the results of his study in an acceptable manner, then his influence may be extended from a thousand to fifty thousand, and instead of preaching to a congregation of a few hundred members, he may preach to a whole continent for many generations. No man, however great his genius, has a right to serve the Lord in the sanctuary with unbeaten oil. The pastor after God's own heart is one that feeds the people with knowledge and with understanding—full of faith and of the Holy Ghost, and mighty in the Scriptures—showing unto the people out of the Scriptures the way of salvation through Christ. Oh, that the vast harvest-field that lies all around us, already ripe for the sickle, was filled with a great multitude of such servants of the Most High!

So great is my confidence in the English version, that I

have not knowingly departed from it in a single instance in the examination of the history of Esther. I do not remember to have met with any discussion as to the merits of the translation of Esther in our version, compared with the translation of the other historic books; but it seems to me to be an exceedingly correct and happy version. There are but few words that could possibly be improved. The only change I have introduced in the translation is to omit the division into chapters and verses, which, though of great convenience for reference, is often a marring of the force and beauty of the text, especially in the historical parts of the Old Testament and in the Epistles. My reverence for our English version is equalled only by my regard for the originals, which are our standard of faith and manners.

I do not believe, as a modern poet says, that the Holy Bible is "good Michael's Scripture," and that "history is the Devil's Scripture." No, the Bible is the word of the Lord, and history is but a record of how He governs the world. The great Bengel has truly said, that the "true commentator will fasten his primary attention on the literal meaning, but never forget that the spirit must equally accompany him; and at the same time, we must never devise a more spiritual meaning for Scripture passages than the Holy Spirit intended." But as from every point in the circumference of a circle, we may imagine straight lines converging to a centre, not one of which is exactly coincident with another, so in all the books of the Old Testament, I find either types, or promises, or prophecies, or national events, or personal narratives, that all point to the Church of God under the Great Messiah; and so, in expounding the Old Testament Scriptures, by searching out cotemporary and subsequent histories, and bringing together things new and old, from far and near, for the purpose of comprehending these Old Testament Scriptures, our great object always is to make the Messiah appear as He really is, the Redeemer of the world. I have attempted always in interpreting the Word of God, to follow the rule of Bengel: "Put nothing *into* the Scriptures, but draw everything *from* them, and suffer nothing to remain hidden that is really *in* them." I do not, however, understand it to be the duty of an expositor of the Word of God, to go through it selecting only "the berries and leaving the rest as fit only for the pruning hook;" but to take all the Scriptures together and just as they are, and to explain Scripture by Scripture, and that remembering the character of his audience, he will endeavor to have the true text, restore and defend it, then exhibit the meaning and force of the language employed, explain the circumstances under which the portion he is considering was uttered or written, and in a word, as far as possible, he will try so *to enlighten his hearers that they may be in a condition to understand the Scriptures similar to that of the hearers of the Prophets and Apostles themselves.* The Church of God in the days of the Prophets, and of Jesus Christ and his Apostles, did not require annotations, illustrations, Bible dictionaries, geographies of the Holy Land, and maps and descriptions of the birds, beasts and flowers of the country, nor of the manners and customs of the people. These were all familiar to them; they were immersed in the knowledge of local and national histories and customs, as they were in the atmosphere of the Holy Mountains. Accordingly, in the first ages of the Church, we have no commentaries, but the preaching was expository and homiletic. If Paul is in the synagogue, his text is out of the Hebrew Scriptures; and his argument is to show that, according to the Scriptures, Jesus is Christ. If he is on Mars' hill, his text is the Athenian altar *to the unknown God*, and his proofs and illustrations are from Greek authors and from the works of the Supreme Being. What are dead languages to us were living tongues to them, and the knowledge of their times, which we have to acquire by much study, was their common patrimony. The most learned men of our day are hardly as well acquainted with some of the idioms, proverbs and local customs, some knowledge of which is necessary to the elucidation of the Bible, as the children of the Church were in the days of the Prophets and of the Apostles. It takes much study therefore to put us on the same platform to hear the early teachers of religion, that their hearers occupied.

It is my firm conviction—a conviction that has fixed itself more and more deeply in my mind, year after year, that the best, and indeed the only way to resist successfully the extremes of error, fanaticism and rationalism, to which we are exposed, is to give more heed to the word of God. The Old Testament ought to be read with more simplicity and humility, and with a greater disposition to rely upon its statements, and to apply its truths to ourselves. The Old Testament is not a mere Hebrew ritual, nor a mere political hand-book of the ancient Jews. It is as much a part of the word of the living God as is the New Testament, and we are to study it as well as the New Testament, if we desire to know the will of God. The want of the Church, in our day, is earnest faith; and this is wanting, in part, because the Old Testament is not studied, and its meaning clearly apprehended. While we have the history of God's chosen people in the Old Testament, their national characteristics, and fortunes, do not exhaust its meaning. The God of the Bible is just as near to America as to Western Asia. The living God is as near to us as He was to Abraham and Moses, although His presence is not manifested in the same way. As the canon of Inspired Scripture is closed, so we are not to look for new, nor other revelations, neither by visions, voices, nor dreams, nor angels, nor spirits, nor internal illumination; neither to add to, nor even to explain to us the Bible. But the government of God is as *actual* in our day as in the days of Moses—as real over Americans as over the Hebrews—though, for obvious reasons, the form, or symbol, of its manifestation is different. We ought then to study the lives of Bible men and women, not as men and women in a book, or in a picture gallery, that were painted from fancy, but as real men and women like ourselves—and not as profiles, but as full-faced human beings. I do not understand the rationale of Bible narratives as stripping them of their supernatural, or Divine and theological adjuncts. These narratives are true histories, and were written by holy men of old, as they were moved thereto by the Holy Spirit. The men and women of the Bible are made known to us by their doings, and, as we look at the pictures, without requiring the name to be written below, we are made to feel, by the clear light that falls upon them from above, that they are true pictures, and inimitably executed. There is a dramatic power in the performances of Bible penmen that no mere human artist ever possessed. And this dramatic power consists, in part, in selecting a man—a common man—a man not distinguished, so far as we can see, by any peculiar gifts above his fellows—a man who seems to be flesh and blood—agitated with the same passions, hopes and fears, as ourselves—and yet, to bring this human, material, sinful man, so livingly before us, that while we feel that he is indeed an individual of the earth, earthy, that yet he is more than an ordinary man—he is a sample man—a teaching man—a representative man—a man set forth by the spirit of God to illustrate the Divine displeasure at sin, or the Divine goodness. If I do not succeed in revealing, as I would in my Bible readings and expositions, the thought that here possesses me, still, I am perfectly sure, there is a grand purpose in God's plan in having revealed to us so large a portion of saving truth in biographies. And I am more and more convinced, that one great cause of the modern growth of fanaticism and infidelity, is to be found in the departure of so many teachers from the custom of reading and expounding the word of God. It is worthy of serious consideration, whether there is not, and to what an extent, in our day, in the topical, metaphysical preaching of many, and in not a few of our popular tracts and treatises on practical and experimental religion, theological essays, religious tales, and pious novels—which are worse than "the pious frauds of the dark ages"—a dangerous tendency to draw away the public mind from the Book of God. Far be it from me to undervalue good books. Rather let us thank God for the genius, learning, talent, enterprise and wealth that have been employed in the publication of religious works; but, I submit it as an humble *monitum*, or inquiry, whether the frequent religious meetings, the cramming of the Lord's day, and the tendency of the popular religious literature, of our day, is not toward a substituting of tracts and books, and newspapers *about* religion, for the *Book of the Lord*, which, in itself, combines, in the utmost plentitude and purity, all that is serviceable to the health of the soul. How much better, for one truly serious, and anxiously inquiring the way to be saved, to read the word of God itself, and then get down on his knees, in his closet, and bow his soul as well as his body, as Paul did, when it was said of him, "behold he prayeth," and thus plead with God for the enlightenment of his Holy Spirit, rather than to read a whole bundle of human tracts, or listen to a studied narrative of his neighbor's conversion in a public meeting. There is no handbook for revivals like the inspired history of remarkable Bible conversions. For family reading, and catechising on the afternoon of the Lord's day, the hot-house system, now so much in vogue, is a poor substitute. For the family, and the place of business, the church and the world, there can be no substitute for the Bible. It is our only hope. The history of Christianity shows that it has always flourished most when it is just let alone by Cæsar. It seeks not promotion, but simple protection from the State. And history now shows, that the first step in the church from the Bible, is a step toward error. In the measure that we neglect, depart from, or substitute any other writings in the place of the Holy Scriptures, in precisely the same measure we throw open the gates to the enemy. It must be remembered, as a highly significant fact, that our Lord contented himself, in his solitary combat with the devil, and completely foiled him, in all his assaults, by simply saying: *It is written.* And if the "It is written" of his day, that is, Moses and the prophets, was sufficient, how much more ought we to rely upon the whole Bible?

Whatever candid readers may think of the manner in which this volume is written, I apprehend they will all agree that the history of ESTHER is one of the most beautiful and interesting books of the Old Testament. These pages are not the result of undisturbed literary leisure. Very far from it. They have been written under the pressure of arduous pastoral duties—

under the weight of the anxious soul-consuming cares that belong to a large congregation, in a new State, and in the first years of a great commercial city. That they are perfect, the author would be the last man to believe. No one can feel more sensibly than he does that imperfections attach to all his efforts, both from the press and the pulpit. If, then, it is asked, Why are they published? the answer is, partly because the work has been called for by friends, whose wishes the author did not feel at liberty to disregard; and, partly, because, as heretofore, so now, he is desirous of doing all he can toward the promotion of a sound Christian literature on this coast. "To do good," says Lord Bacon, "is the true and lawful end of aspiring. Merit and good works is the end of man's motion, and conscience of the same is the accomplishment of man's rest; for, if man can be a partaker of God's theater (or workshop,) he will be a partaker also of God's rest."

It may be proper here also to say, that I have complied with the wish of those who requested these lectures to be published, (that they should be published just as they were delivered,) as far as it has been within my power to recall and write out, from my manuscript notes, the precise language and illustrations used from the pulpit, with the following exceptions, namely, that the lectures are divided into chapters, which are shorter; and a part of what was delivered in the last lecture is inserted in the fourteenth chapter, because it seemed to belong rather to that part of the history. And, as in the great overland journey across our continent, the way is unequal—there is a variety of mountains and valleys, long and short stations, high hills and wide plains, and dark mountain gorges—so, also, is the Volume of Inspiration. And, as in the overland route, similar views are often presented, repeating the visions already past, and yet not the same; so here, in the following pages, there may seem to be repetitions, not so much of words as of ideas. If so, the reason is to be found, *first*, in the fact, that I have endeavored to follow the order and method of the sacred narrative itself, and to present the thoughts and lessons thereon just as they started up before me, taking the pictures of the way just as they came to hand. I could have avoided this, if I had thought it best to do so; but as it was my wish to follow the divine method, as far as I could, in presenting and explaining and vindicating the laws, the Word and the ways of the Lord, and as similar events are repeated in the text, so similar lessons are taught. *Secondly*, it has, also, just been said, that it was deemed best to publish these discourses, as nearly as possible, word for word, just as they were delivered from the pulpit, and as their delivery extended through several weeks, and was, in part, before different audiences, so some repetition was necessary, and, partly for the same reason, is still retained. And I am the more reconciled to have it so, from the fact that this is the Bible method, not only in Esther, but generally—namely, to teach little by little, line upon line, and precept upon precept. As it is pleasant to the traveler to have a change of scenery, rather than to have all the mountains together, and then all the hills, and then nothing but a wide plain; just so it is in history, the pictures are always changing and always repeating themselves, and yet they are not the same.

The errors and skeptical objections which it is hoped this volume may refute, or remove from the minds of candid inquirers after truth, are not always enumerated, nor the names of their advocates and the titles of their works given. This has not seemed to be necessary. All opinions and objections as far as I know are fairly represented, but the size of the volume and many other reasons forbid their full elaboration. I do not see that in order to know the right way to a place, we must first hunt out and explore, by a personal survey, all the tracks and by-ways that lead away from it. It may be that some of my readers are in happy ignorance of the errors I have tried to refute; if so, they will not perceive my allusions, nor is it necessary they should. On the other hand, those who are acquainted with them will be able I hope to understand the refutation offered. As to the truth of some of the quotations used in this volume from old authors and from the reports of the Royal Asiatic Society, and other readings of monuments, I have only to say with Pliny, "Penes auctores sit fides." While I believe them to be reliable and substantially correct, I beg that the authors themselves may be held respectively responsible. And while I have freely used all the authors within my reach that afforded me what I considered reliable help in explaining the sacred text, yet as far as I know, all due acknowledgments are made in the body of the work, and as far as my knowledge goes, this is the only volume of the kind offered to the public on the Book of Esther. Indeed one reason why, in my humble publications, I have selected such subjects as "The Wedge of Gold," "Samson, the Giant Judge," and the *Hebrew-Persian Queen*, is that these portions of our holy writings seemed to be almost overlooked. As Truth is of too noble and holy a nature to be forced upon mankind, I have only to add as one before me has done: "Pray, place the Holy Scriptures, kind Reader, before you on the desk of your heart, and acquaint yourself with the WHOLE matter, before you arrive at a decision." "Happy is he that speaketh in the ears of them that will hear." God Almighty bless all the readers of this volume. Amen.

W. A. SCOTT.

SAN FRANCISCO, 10th March, 1859.

CHAPTER I.

PERSIA PAST AND PRESENT.

"And see—the Sun himself!—on wings
 Of glory up the East he springs
 Angel of light! ————
  Where are the days, thou wondrous sphere,
 When IRAN, like a sun-flower turned
 To meet that eye where'er it burned?
  When, from the banks of BENDEEMEER
 To the nut-groves of Samarcand
 Thy temples flam'd o'er all the land?
 Where are they? ask the shades of them
  Who, on CADESSIA's bloody plains,
 Saw fierce invaders pluck the gem
 From IRAN's broken diadem."—*Lalla Rookh.*

THE wars of Persia with Greece, the lives of Oriental princes, and tales and illustrations of the manners of the East a long time ago, are a part of the early studies of our boyhood, and a never failing source of amusement to an enlightened mind, through all the periods of life down to old age. Even the loftiest strains of poetry in our holy prophetical books—the noblest outpourings of Hebrew song are about the people who lived on the Tigris and the Euphrates more than two thousand years ago. And even now, it is found after centuries for research and examination, and after the wonderful discoveries of Botta, Layard, Rawlinson and others, that the Hebrew Scriptures are the best guide to the East—that the minutest allusions in the Bible to the habits of the people of Bible lands, and that even the details of their wars and religions, and customs, given by the father of profane history, are so accurately told that the history of the inhabitants of those countries in the present day, written from actual observation, varies in but few things from that of Herodotus.

In our day, the long sleep of Oriental literature is broken—never again to be resumed. Its untombed records have assumed a place, in historic value, above the classic glory of Greece and Rome. The scholar, the antiquarian, and the interpreter of ancient records, have vast treasures of priceless worth now opened to them that were hidden for ages. The fall of Constantinople somewhat retarded Oriental studies by the consequent revival of Greek learning, which was followed by the invention of printing in the West. The tendency of the attention given to Greek literature, and of printing, was to lay aside the learning of the East as fabulous, or valueless. But, for the last three centuries, European travelers and scholars have been diligent in those researches that have so happily resulted in our present attainments.

As we are desirous of becoming acquainted with some of the most remarkable personages, and some of the most extraordinary events of ancient Persia, a brief reference to its legendary history seems necessary to enable us to form something like a correct opinion concerning its institutions. All men of letters have admired her poets, *Jami, Hafiz, Saadi* and *Firdusi;* but

Persia has been admired for something more than her poets. Alexander the Great intensely coveted her dominions, not so much because she was the favorite country of the imagination, as because she was wealthy and powerful. The legends of the golden egg, and like fancies, do not solve the great question, why Alexander marched his armies across her territory. Was it then to revenge Greece for Persian invasions before his day? or was it merely to imitate the exploits of Achilles, whom he greatly admired, and whose history he diligently studied? No. I believe his was a nobler ambition—an ambition as justifiable as that which inspired Napoleon, when he invaded Egypt and dreamed of an Oriental empire—an ambition in every way as justifiable as that of the English in the conquest of India, or of China—the very same in substance that now moves all the great powers of Europe, and the United States, to seek an extension of their influence over the populous regions of the East, namely: to carry European, that is, as it was called in Alexander's day, *Greek enterprise* into Asia, and thereby awaken its decaying kingdoms, and stimulate them to trade and civilization. No doubt he wished, at the same time that he was thus arousing them, to make them develop the riches of their country, and doubtless, also, he was quite willing, as a conqueror, to take the lion's share, but in as honorable a way as is practiced in our day. That such views were entertained by him is proven from his enlarged ideas of trade, and his building of cities and highways of travel and commerce.

These remarks are made, not for the purpose of indorsing the wars of Alexander the Great, but because it seems to me, justice has rarely been done to his genius and policy. Many cities were founded by him and the clearness of his foresight and the soundness of his judgment are seen in their continuance to this day as great seats of trade. And so great is the popularity of his name even in our times that many of the tribes of the East, claim to be his descendants. He was a Pagan, and did many very wicked things, but in his desire to possess Persia, and to advance into India from the west, he has been often imitated, and has his successors in our day among several Christian crowns. Persia was the scene of some of his greatest exploits. Chinghis-Khan and Timur-lane also led their plundering hosts over the same mountains and plains. Roman Emperors and generals and Moslem Kaliphs were in their day familiar with its cities and fortresses and battle-plains. As in Spain, first civilized by the Phenicians and long possessed by the Moors, we find Pagan, Roman and Eastern customs long obsolete elsewhere turning up at every step in the cabinet and in the campaign, in the palace and in the house, field and church; so it is in Persia. It is in Persia as much—perhaps more than in any other land that we find in our day ancient customs preserved with the greatest tenacity—especially such as are referred to in the Bible. The mountain-ranges and rivers and physical features of Persia are now as they were when Alexander conquered her and Xenophon wrote his classic chapters. No canals have been dug, no railroads built, and the posts are inferior to those of Cyrus. And the manners of the people are less changed than in any other oriental nation. The throne of the Shah is shorn indeed of some of the bright beams of the ancient dynasties of Persia, but still it recalls the glory of Cyrus, and the power of Darius and Sapor. "In Egypt," says "The Modern Traveller," "the intrusive Turk or Mamlouk, the degraded Copt, or the miserable Fellah, are dwarfed beside the gigantic monuments of the past, and hardly appear to belong to a scene where art and nature seem alike eternal and MAN is nothing; in Persia it is the living scene, the faded yet still imposing pageantry, the various tribes, and the diversified traits of human character that chiefly occupy attention, and by these faithful transcripts of the former ages it is that the imagination is transported far back into the past.*

Although Persia, in her earliest ages, seems to have altogether wanted the poet historian, she was not wanting in royal scribes. These secretaries, *Mirzas*, as they are called in modern times, were constantly with their kings—at feasts and councils, and on the field of battle. It was their duty to note down at the time his words, and make a record of his deeds. A similar custom prevailed among most Asiatic nations. The Mogul conquerors had their scribes. The great Hyder Ali used to appear in public surrounded by forty secretaries. Such records doubtless were the chronicles deposited at Babylon, Ecbatana, and Susa. The personal anecdotes and private conversations preserved by Herodotus, are probably a fair specimen of these records. They were not designed to be a history of the empire, nor of the people, but of the court. Herod, vii. 100, vi. 98; viii. 96, and Ezra, vi. i. Esther, vi. i. We shall have occasion to speak of them again.

---

*Vaux's Nineveh and Persepolis.

The great historic poets of Persia are Mirkhond and Firdusi, and Khondemir, son of Mirkhond. Their memorials of the empire are partly from traditions, and partly from records, and are very valuable as exponents of the inner life—the thoughts, manners and customs, of their forefathers. They tell us that the ancient name of Persia was *Iran*, and that ten tribes were united in composing its first inhabitants. According to Mohammedan writers, the founder of the Pischadian dynasty the first monarch of Persia was Kaiomurs, the son of Yasan Asam, the grandson of Noah. And that he was a long time subject to the Magicians, but at length emancipated himself from their tyranny, by the aid of tigers, panthers and lions. The famous Jamshid, his nephew, succeeded his son Hoshung, who was his immediate successor. The legends concerning Jamshid are numerous and curious. They suit for an epic rather than for a sober history. As a history of Persia, however, beyond Cyrus, we have nothing better than the fabulous annals of Jamshid and his successors.

Impenetrable obscurity reigns over the early history of Persia. Most of the early Persian writers have so mixed up their history with tales of griffins, monster giants and fairies, that no sober or reliable account can be gathered from their writings. According to some of them, several of the first kings of the dynasty which they call the Pischadian, reigned from five hundred to one thousand years each. The order of its rise seems to be Iran, Turan, and then Assyria, and then a second Persian dynasty of the Kaianites, and then Media, under Cyaxares, and then Persia proper under Cyrus the Great. Xenophon traces the pedigree of Cyrus up to Perses, who gave name to the country.

The first name by which Persia is known to us in the Bible is *Elam*, Gen. xiv. 1, which is to be regarded as identical with Kurdistan and Khuzistan. The date of the events spoken of in Genesis is thought by Vaux and others to be contemporary with the beginning of the Assyrian and Babylonian empires. Balkh, (Bactra,) the capital of Kaiomurs, is considered in the East as the oldest city on the globe. It is called *Omm-al-belad*, the mother of cities. From the time of Abraham, when Elam was a kingdom, to Isaiah, nothing occurs in sacred history that belongs especially to Persia. Isaiah, however, speaks of the Elamites as a warlike nation, "bearing the quiver," xxii. 6. And this account agrees exactly with what Strabo says of the mountaineers of Elymais. Jeremiah (xlix. 34, 39) foretells the overthrow of Elam and its subsequent recovery, which history records as fulfilled.

The hero of Firdusi is Rustam, but Sir John Malcolm labors with great zeal to show that the *Kai-Khosru* of this poet is Cyrus the Great. This is probably correct; and the poem itself, *Shah Nameh*, is a wonderful illustration of how the fragments of history may be embalmed in poetry. The fragments from which he composed this work were in Pehlvi, and are interspersed with incidents and exploits belonging to the history of China, India and Turan, while there is no allusion to the kings of Assyria, Egypt or Babylon. The traditions of the East say that Cyrus' mother was a Jewess, and on that account he was so favorably inclined to that remarkable people. For some four centuries the Romans called the rulers of Persia by the name of Khosrus or Chosroes, that is, Cyrus. The *Kai* occurring so often in the history of ancient Persia, means *King;* and is succeeded by *Shah* in our day.

The order of the empires that rose on the Tigris and the Euphrates is after this manner: The Assyrian, Chaldean and Medo-Persian, the Greek, Roman and Saracen, which was succeeded by the Persian kingdom of our own day. The Assyrian empire, of which Nineveh was the chief city, was probably founded by Nimrod. It unquestionably goes back to a very early period after the flood. The area of the Persian dominions in Esther's day was the seat of the great empires of Daniel's visions, which, as to time and manner, rose to power and passed away with an astonishing conformity to his predictions.

But little is known of Median history. The Medes are believed to have been an intelligent and wealthy people long previous to the Persian conquest. Their government was despotic, but the etiquette and strictures of their court remarkable. Cyrus the Great, who is to be regarded as the founder of the Persia of history, made Media, by forcible seizure, a part of the Persian empire. His dominions occupied the regions of all the older empires of that part of the globe that had preceded him. The period of our *Hebrew-Persian* Queen is about 500 years before the birth of Christ, and lies between the famous battle of Marathon and the retreat of the ten thousand Greeks. Postumius and Furius being consuls at Rome. The Chaldean monarchy, the lion empire of the Hebrew prophet, has past away. All comes to pass in its day just as Daniel sees and describes it standing on the banks of the river Ulai (Eulæus of the Greeks). Medes and Persians,

Greeks and Romans, take their places in history precisely according to the prophet's assignment, just as if they were pieces played by an invisible master on the Chess-board of the Universe. The two-horned ram of Daniel signified the Medo-Persian kingdom. And the proof is complete that Persia was represented at first by a ram. This is seen in ancient coins and from the sculptures on the pillars of Persepolis. Ammianus Marcellinus expressly says that "the King of Persia wore a ram's head of gold, set with precious stones, instead of a diadem." And it is also abundantly in proof, that as Persia was represented by a *ram*, so was Macedonia by a *goat*, and both these symbols agree with Daniel's vision. The story is that the first colony of Macedon were directed to take a goat for a guide and that they were to build a city, wherever the leading goat halted his flock, which they did, and called it Ægeæ, from Ægus, a goat, and hence the people called themselves Ægeadæ, and hence we have the name *Ægean* for the sea that washed their coast. Ancient Macedonian monuments contain this figure, and at Persepolis the subjection of the Macedonians to the Persians in the reign of Amyntas is recorded by representing a Persian as holding a goat by the horn. And in the Florentine collection there is a gem with an engraving which was probably made after Alexander's conquest of Asia, representing the Persian *ram* and the Macedonian *goat* united, that is, the two heads are conjoined.

If you visit Khuzistan, a province of the Persia that now is, you will see the kingdom of ancient Susiana. In the first years of Cyrus, this country was governed by his friend and ally, Abradates, but, at his death, it was incorporated with the Persian monarchy. Should you ever travel through it, you will find the northern part of it hilly, while the central portion of it is a great plain, the greater part of which is very fertile, but the southern and eastern part is chiefly a sandy desert, or extensive morasses. The banks of the rivers, in the southern and eastern portions, are capable of cultivation. Rice, indigo, wheat, barley, poppies, dates and sugar cane are raised. The climate is considered remarkably healthy; so much so, that the inhabitants of the surrounding provinces resort to it when sick, just as the old Roman invalids used to go to Egypt. The winters are mild, and the springs proverbially the delight of the earth. In the summer the heat, however, is so intense that the people spend the day in subterranean chambers, and sleep on the house tops, in the open air, at night. The chief trade of Shuster is in opium, indigo and sugar. Opium is produced here in great quantities from the large and beautiful Oriental poppy. The sugar of the country is very fine, and produced in a considerable quantity. The luxuriance of the sugar cane, and the excellence of the manufactured sugar is so great that the province is said to have its name from its staple commodity—Khuzistan, that is, *sugar country*.

The animals of this country are jackals and hyenas, which are very numerous, and their nightly howlings a great annoyance. Antelopes and gazelles are numerous, and the winged songsters are the same that are found in southern Europe. Locusts, all sorts of lizards and insects, and venomous reptiles are found in great abundance. This is the country, also, of the camel and of the wild ass, the wild boar and the lion. "The wild ass of the wilderness that snuffeth up the wind at her pleasure," is a beautiful creature, and so swift in her native wilds that she can be caught only by relays of horses and dogs.

It is foreign to my present purpose to dwell on the history of Persia from the death of Esther to the defeat of the Persians by the Arabs on "the bloody plains of Cadessia," where Iran's ancient diadem was broken, or to speak of Persia under the Saracens, and of her emancipation from them, and her present dynasty of Shahs. This belongs properly to the general historian and to the political writers of the great Powers of Europe and Asia, who are all struggling to get the ascendancy in Persia, just as heirs intrigue for a dying man's estates. Of the Tartars, the Seljukian Turks, Turkomans, "the white sheep dynasty," of Hassan, Hussein, Gengis-Khan, Nader Shah, "the great Moguls," "the terrible Afghans," Irak, Shiraz, Bagdad and Mosul, and of the fight between the British lion and the Russian bear for the vineyards of the Persian Naboths, I shall say nothing. Sure I am, however, as the poet says, that

> "All regions, revolutions, fortunes, fates
> Of high, of low, of mind and matter, roll
> Through the short channels of expiring time,
> Or shoreless ocean of eternity,
> In absolute subjection"———

to the mandate of Him who setteth up one and casteth down another, and doeth His will on earth and in the armies of heaven.

Happy then that people whose God is the Lord. Happy the nation that trusts in the Great Disposer of human events, amid the ever-changing scenes of time. In an empire so vast and so populous as that of the great king Ahasuerus, there were many large cities, of which little beyond their names, or the simple fact of their having once existed, is now known. It is difficult, and has, in fact, been done only in a few instances, to identify the mouldering remnants of cities that are scattered over the vast tracts of Persia, with the names of the cities described in the ancient history of that country.

But the same thing is true of the mighty cities of Egypt, Babylon and Greece. And is there not a day coming when the mighty cities of our times shall be as these mighty cities of old now are? "A school boy's tale, the wonder of an hour." The reins of the Universe however are in the hands of the same Supreme Ruler that governed the world when Ahasuerus reigned from India to Ethiopia. The hand of God is just as truly in the modern as in the ancient history of Persia. There is a God that judgeth in the earth in America, just as much as in Asia. His eye and his laws are just as much over London and San Francisco, as they ever were over Babylon and Susa. It is just as true now, as when Mordecai was made Grand Vizier, that "there is a reward for the righteous." We have then a personal interest in keeping the commandments of our God, for in keeping of them there is great reward. And we have a deep personal interest in escaping from the wrath to come! Let us then well consider the great question of the poet:

That day of wrath, that dreadful day,
When heaven and earth shall pass away,
What power shall be the sinner's stay?
How shall he meet that dreadful day?

When shivering like a parched scroll,
The flaming heavens together roll!
When louder yet, and yet more dread,
Swells the high trump that wakes the dead:

Oh! on that day, that wrathful day,
When man to judgment wakes from clay,
Be thou the trembling sinner's stay,
Though heaven and earth shall pass away.

Sir Walter Scott.

CHAPTER II.

THE MEGILLOTH ESTHER.

"——— Hast thou ever heard
Of such a book? the author, God himself;
The subject, God and man; salvation, life
And death—eternal life, eternal death."

* * * * *

"Read and revere the sacred page; a page
Where triumphs immortality; a page
Which not the whole creation could produce;
Which not the conflagration shall destroy;
In Nature's ruins not one letter lost;
'Tis printed in the mind of gods forever."

There is a remarkable people scattered over the world who have preserved their identity and national rites and festivals without having any home or any nationality on the face of the earth. Wherever they are found, from pole to pole, whether of fair complexion, as in Europe, or bronzed as in Asia, or "dark as any Ethiop" in Africa; whether speaking Russ, Polish, German, Spanish, Italian, Hindoo, or Arabic or English, they all observe an annual feast at which the following narrative is read, just as Americans read the Declaration of Independence on the *Fourth of July.* The Megilloth Esther, as they call the sacred roll which is read at the feast of Purim,

"*Is not* a theologic tract
To prove with Hebrew and with Arabic
If Job be allegory or a fact,
But a true narrative, —————"

of what happened to their fathers many years ago in the land of their captivity. The original is in Hebrew, and has been preserved with great care and fidelity. The following is the most faithful, elegant, and in every way the best translation that has yet been made of it into English. It was made in the early part of the seventeenth century by some of the best scholars then living, at the special command of a great and learned king of England, who had been educated by a Scotch pedagogue of great celebrity:

THE MEGILLOTH ESTHER.

Now it came to pass in the days of Ahasuerus, (this is Ahasuerus which reigned from India even unto Ethiopia, over an hundred and seven and twenty provinces:) that in those days, when the king Ahasuerus sat on the throne of his kingdom, which was in Shushan the palace, in the third year of his reign, he made a feast unto all his princes and his servants; the power of Persia and Media, the nobles and princes of the provinces, being before him: when he showed the riches of his glorious kingdom and the honor of his excellent majesty many days, even an hundred and fourscore days. And when these days were expired, the king made a feast unto all the people that were present in Shushan the palace, both unto great and small, seven days, in the court of the garden of the king's palace; where were white, green, and blue hangings, fastened with cords of fine linen and purple to silver rings and pillars of marble: the beds were of gold and silver, upon a pavement of red, and blue, and white, and black marble. And they gave them drink in vessels of gold, (the vessels being diverse one from another,) and royal wine in abundance, according to the state of the king. And the drinking was according to the law; none did compel: for so the king had appointed to all the officers of his house, that they should do according to every man's pleasure. Also Vashti the queen made a feast for the women in the royal house which belonged to king Ahasuerus.

On the seventh day, when the heart of the king was merry with wine, he commanded Mehuman, Biztha, Harbona, Bigtha, and Abagtha, Zethar, and Carcas, the seven chamberlains that served in the presence of Ahasuerus the king, to bring Vashti the queen before the king with the crown royal, to show the people and the princes her beauty: for she was fair to look on. But the queen Vashti refused to come at the king's commandment by his chamberlains: therefore was the king very wroth, and his anger burned in him.

Then the king said to the wise men, which knew the times, (for so was the king's manner toward all that knew law and judgment: and the next unto him was Carshena, Shethar, Admatha, Tarshish, Meres, Marsena, and Memucan, the seven princes of Persia and Media, which saw the king's face, and which sat the first in the kingdom;) what shall we do unto the queen Vashti according to law, because she hath not performed the commandment of the king Ahasuerus by the chamberlains? And Memucan answered before the king and the princes, Vashti the queen hath not done wrong to the king only, but also to all the princes, and to all the people that are in all the provinces of the king Ahasuerus. For this deed of the queen shall come abroad unto all women, so that they shall despise their husbands in their eyes, when it shall be reported, The king Ahasuerus commanded Vashti the queen to be brought in before him, but she came not. Likewise shall the ladies of Persia and Media say this day unto all the king's princes, which have heard of the deed of the queen. Thus shall there arise too much contempt and wrath. If it please the king, let there go a royal commandment from him, and let it be written among the laws of the Persians and the Medes, that it be not altered, That Vashti come no more before king Ahasuerus; and let the king give her royal estate unto another that is better than she. And when the king's decree which he shall make shall be published throughout all his empire, (for it is great,) all the wives shall give to their husbands honor, both to great and small.

And the saying pleased the king and the princes; and the king did according to the word of Memucan: for he sent letters into all the king's provinces, into every province according to the writing thereof, and to every people after their language, that every man should bear rule in his own house; and that it should be published according to the language of every people.

After these things, when the wrath of king Ahasuerus was appeased, he remembered Vashti, and what she had done, and what was decreed against her. Then said the king's servants that ministered unto him, Let there be fair young virgins sought for the king; and let the king appoint officers in all the provinces of his kingdom, that they may gather together all the fair young virgins unto Shushan the palace, to the house of the women, unto the custody of Hege the king's chamberlain, keeper of the women; and let their things for purification be given them: and let the maiden which pleaseth the king be queen instead of Vashti. And the thing pleased the king; and he did so.

Now in Shushan the palace there was a certain Jew, whose name was Mordecai, the son of Jair, the son of Shimei, the son of Kish, a Benjamite; who had been carried away from Jerusalem with the captivity which had been carried away with Jaconiah king of Judah, whom Nebuchadnezzar the king of Babylon had carried away. And he brought up Hadassah, (that is, Esther,) his uncle's daughter: for she had neither father nor mother, and the maid was fair and beautiful; whom Mordecai, when her father and mother were dead, took for his own daughter.

So it came to pass, when the king's commandment and his decree was heard, and when many maidens were gathered together unto Shushan the palace, to the custody of Hegai, that Esther was brought also into the king's house, to the custody of Hegai, keeper of the women. And the maiden pleased him, and she obtained kindness of him; and he speedily gave her her things for purification, with such things as belonged to her, and seven maidens which were meet to be given her, out of the king's house: and he preferred her and her maids unto the best place of the house of the women. Esther had not shewed her people nor her kindred: for Mordecai had charged her that she should not shew it. And Mordecai walked every day before the court of the women's house, to know how Esther did, and what should become of her.

Now when every maid's turn was come to go in to king Ahasuerus, after that she had been twelve months, according to the manner of the women, (for so were the days of their purifications accomplished, to wit, six months with oil of myrrh, and six months with sweet odors, and with other things for the purifying of the women;) then thus came every maiden unto the king; whatsoever she desired was given her to go with her out of the house of the women unto the king's house. In the evening she went, and on the morrow she returned into the second house of the women, to the custody of Shaashgaz, the king's chamberlain, which kept the concubines: she came in unto the king no more, except the king delighted in her, and that she were called by name.

Now when the turn of Esther, the daughter of Abihail the uncle of Mordecai, who had taken her for his daughter, was come to go in unto the king, she required nothing but what Hegai the king's chamberlain, the keeper of the women, appointed. And Esther obtained favor in the sight of all them that looked upon her. So Esther was taken unto king Ahasuerus into his house-royal in the tenth month, which is the month Tebeth, in the seventh year of his reign. And the king loved Esther above all the women, and she obtained grace and favor in his sight more than all the virgins; so that he set the royal crown upon her head, and made her queen instead of Vashti. Then the king made a great feast unto all his princes and his servants, even Esther's feast; and he made a release to the provinces, and gave gifts, according to the state of the king. And when the virgins were gathered together the second time, then Mordecai sat in the king's gate. Esther had not yet shewed her kindred, nor her people, as Mordecai had charged her; for Esther did the commandment of Mordecai, like as when she was brought up with him.

In those days, while Mordecai sat in the king's gate, two of the king's chamberlains, Bigthan and Teresh, of those which kept the door, were wroth, and sought to lay hand on the king Ahasuerus. And the thing was known to Mordecai, who told it unto Esther the queen; and Esther certified the king thereof in Mordecai's name. And when inquisition was made of the matter, it was found out; therefore they were both hanged on a tree: and it was written in the book of the Chronicles before the king.

After these things did king Ahasuerus promote Haman the son of Hammedatha the Agagite, and advanced him, and set his seat above all the princes that were with him. And all the king's servants that were in the king's gate, bowed, and reverenced Haman; for the king had so commanded concerning him. But Mordecai bowed not, nor did him reverence. Then the king's servants which were in the king's gate, said unto Mordecai, Why transgressest thou the king's commandment? Now it came to pass, when they spake daily unto him, and he hearkened not unto them, that they told Haman, to see whether Mordecai's matters would stand; for he had told them that he was a Jew. And when Haman saw that Mordecai bowed not, nor did him reverence, then was Haman full of wrath. And he thought scorn to lay hands on Mordecai alone; for they had shewed him the people of Mordecai; wherefore Haman sought to destroy all the Jews that were throughout the whole kingdom of Ahasuerus, even the people of Mordecai.

In the first month, (that is, the month Nison,) in the twelfth year of king Ahasuerus, they cast Pur, that is, the lot, before Haman, from day to day, and from month to month, to the twelfth month, that is, the month Adar.

And Haman said unto king Ahasuerus, There is a certain people scattered abroad and dispersed among the people in all the provinces of thy kingdom; and their laws are diverse from all people; neither keep they the king's laws; therefore it is not for the king's profit to suffer them. If it please the king, let it be written that they may be destroyed; and I will pay ten thousand talents of silver to the hands of those that have the charge of the business, to bring it into the king's treasuries. And the king took his ring from his hand, and gave it unto Haman, the son of Hammedatha the Agagite, the Jews' enemy. And the king said unto Haman, The silver is given to thee, the people also, to do with them as it seemeth good to thee. Then were the king's scribes called on the thirteenth day of the first month, and there was written according to all that Haman had commanded unto the king's lieutenants, and to the governors that were over every province, and to the rulers of every people of every province, according to the writing thereof, and to every people after their language; in the name of king Ahasuerus was it written, and sealed with the king's ring. And the letters were sent by posts into all the king's provinces, to destroy, to kill, and to cause to perish, all Jews, both young and old, little children and women, in one day, even upon the thirteenth day of the twelfth month, which is the month

Adar, and to take the spoil of them for a prey. The copy of the writing for a commandment to be given in every province was published unto all people, that they should be ready against that day. The posts went out, being hastened by the king's commandment, and the decree was given in Shushan the palace. And the king and Haman sat down to drink, but the city Shushan was perplexed.

When Mordecai perceived all that was done, Mordecai rent his clothes, and put on sackcloth with ashes, and went out into the midst of the city, and cried with a loud and a bitter cry; And came even before the king's gate: for none might enter into the king's gate clothed with sackcloth. And in every province whithersoever the king's commandment and his decree came, there was great mourning among the Jews, and fasting, and weeping, and wailing; and many lay in sackcloth and ashes.

So Esther's maids and her chamberlains came and told it her. Then was the queen exceedingly grieved; and she sent raiment to clothe Mordecai, and to take away his sackcloth from him; but he received it not. Then called Esther for Hatach, one of the king's chamberlains, whom he had appointed to attend upon her, and gave him a commandment to Mordecai, to know what it was, and why it was. So Hatach went forth to Mordecai, unto the street of the city, which was before the king's gate. And Mordecai told him of all that had happened unto him, and of the sum of the money that Haman had promised to pay to the king's treasuries for the Jews, to destroy them. Also he gave him the copy of the writing of the decree that was given at Shushan to destroy them, to shew it unto Esther, and to declare it unto her, and to charge her that she should go in unto the king, to make supplication unto him, and to make request before him for her people. And Hatach came and told Esther the words of Mordecai.

Again Esther spake unto Hatach, and gave him commandment unto Mordecai: All the king's servants, and the people of the king's provinces, do know, that whosoever, whether man or woman, shall come unto the king into the inner court, who is not called, there is one law of his to put him to death, except such to whom the king shall hold out the golden sceptre, that he may live: but I have not been called to come in unto the king these thirty days. And they told to Mordecai Esther's words. Then Mordecai commanded to answer Esther, Think not with thyself that thou shalt escape in the king's house, more than all the Jews. For if thou altogether holdest thy peace at this time, then shall there enlargement and deliverance arise to the Jews from another place; but thou and thy father's house shall be destroyed; and who knoweth, whether thou art come to the kingdom for such a time as this?

Then Esther bade them return Mordecai this answer, Go, gather together all the Jews that are present in Shushan, and fast ye for me, and neither eat nor drink three days, night or day: I also and my maidens will fast likewise: and so will I go in unto the king, which is not according to the law; and if I perish, I perish. So Mordecai went his way, and did according to all that Esther had commanded him.

Now it came to pass on the third day, that Esther

put on her royal apparel, and stood in the inner court of the king's house, over against the king's house; and the king sat upon his royal throne in the royal house, over against the gate of the house. And it was so, when the king saw Esther the queen standing in the court, that she obtained favor in his sight: and the king held out to Esther the golden sceptre that was in his hand. So Esther drew near, and touched the top of the sceptre. Then said the king unto her, What wilt thou, queen Esther? and what is thy request? it shall be even given thee to the half of the kingdom. And Esther answered, If it seem good unto the king, let the king and Haman come this day unto the banquet that I have prepared for him. Then the king said, Cause Haman to make haste, that he may do as Esther hath said. So the king and Haman came to the banquet that Esther had prepared.

And the king said unto Esther at the banquet of wine, What is thy petition? and it shall be granted thee: and what is thy request? even to the half of the kingdom it shall be performed. Then answered Esther, and said, My petition and my request is: If I have found favour in the sight of the king, and if it please the king to grant my petition, and to perform my request, let the king and Haman come to the banquet that I shall prepare for them, and I will do to-morrow as the king hath said.

Then went Haman forth that day joyful and with a glad heart: but when Haman saw Mordecai in the king's gate, that he stood not up, nor moved for him, he was full of indignation against Mordecai. Nevertheless, Haman refrained himself: and when he came home, he sent and called for his friends, and Zeresh his wife. And Haman told them of the glory of his riches, and the multitude of his children, and all the things wherein the king had promoted him, and how he had advanced him above the princes and servants of the king. Haman said moreover, Yea, Esther the queen did let no man come in with the king unto the banquet that she had prepared but myself; and to-morrow am I invited unto her also with the king. Yet all this availeth me nothing, so long as I see Mordecai the Jew sitting at the king's gate.

Then said Zeresh his wife and all his friends unto him, Let a gallows be made of fifty cubits high, and to-morrow speak thou unto the king that Mordecai may be hanged thereon: then go thou in merrily with the king unto the banquet. And the thing pleased Haman; and he caused the gallows to be made.

On that night could not the king sleep, and he commanded to bring the book of records of the chronicles; and they were read before the king. And it was found written, that Mordecai had told of Bigthana and Teresh, two of the king's chamberlains, the keepers of the door, who sought to lay hand on the king Ahasuerus. And the king said, What honour and dignity hath been done to Mordecai for this? Then said the king's servants that ministered unto him, There is nothing done for him. And the king said, Who is in the court? (Now Haman was come into the outward court of the king's house, to speak unto the king to hang Mordecai on the gallows that he had prepared for him.) And the king's servants said unto him, Behold, Haman standeth in the court. And the king said, Let him come in. So Haman came in. And the king said unto him, What shall be done unto the man whom the king delighteth to honour? (Now Haman thought in his heart, To whom would the king delight to do honour more than to myself?) And Haman answered the king, For the man whom the king delighteth to honour, Let the royal apparel be brought which the king useth to wear, and the horse that the king rideth upon, and the crown-royal which is set upon his head: And let this apparel and horse be delivered to the hand of one of the king's most noble princes, that they may array the man withal whom the king delighteth to honour, and bring him on horseback through the street of the city, and proclaim before him, Thus shall it be done to the man whom the king delighteth to honour. Then the king said to Haman, Make haste, and take the apparel and the horse, as thou hast said, and do even so to Mordecai the Jew, that sitteth at the king's gate: let nothing fail of all that thou hast spoken. Then took Haman the apparel and the horse, and arrayed Mordecai, and brought him on horseback through the street of the city, and proclaimed before him, Thus shall it be done unto the man whom the king delighteth to honour.

And Mordecai came again to the king's gate. But Haman hasted to his house mourning, and having his head covered. And Haman told Zeresh his wife and all his friends every thing that had befallen him. Then said his wise men and Zeresh his wife unto him, If Mordecai be of the seed of the Jews, before whom thou hast begun to fall, thou shalt not prevail against him, but shalt surely fall before him. And while they were yet talking with him, came the king's chamberlains, and hasted to bring Haman unto the banquet that Esther had prepared.

So the king and Haman came to banquet with Esther the queen. And the king said again unto Esther on the second day of the banquet of wine, What is thy petition, queen Esther? and it shall be granted thee: and what is thy request? and it shall be performed, even to the half of the kingdom. Then Esther the queen answered and said, If I have found favor in thy sight, O king, and if it please the king, let my life be given me at my petition, and my people at my request: For we are sold, I and my people, to be destroyed, to be slain, and to perish. But if we had been sold for bondmen and bondwomen, I had held my tongue, although the enemy could not countervail the king's damage.

Then the king Ahasuerus answered and said unto Esther the queen, Who is he, and where is he, that durst presume in his heart to do so? And Esther said, The adversary and enemy is this wicked Haman. Then Haman was afraid before the king and the queen.

And the king arising from the banquet of wine in his wrath went into the palace garden: and Haman stood up to make request for his life to Esther the queen: for he saw that there was evil determined against him by the king. Then the king returned out of the palace garden into the place of the banquet of wine; and Haman was fallen upon the bed whereon Esther was. Then said the king, Will he force the queen also before me in the house? As the word went out of the king's mouth, they covered Haman's face

And Harbonah, one of the chamberlains, said before the king, Behold also the gallows fifty cubits high, which Haman had made for Mordecai, who had spoken good for the king, standeth in the house of Haman. Then the king said, Hang him thereon. So they hanged Haman on the gallows that he had prepared for Mordecai. Then was the king's wrath pacified.

On that day did the king Ahasuerus give the house of Haman the Jews' enemy unto Esther the queen. And Mordecai came before the king; for Esther had told what he was unto her. And the king took off his ring, which he had taken from Haman, and gave it unto Mordecai. And Esther set Mordecai over the house of Haman.

And Esther spake yet again before the king, and fell down at his feet, and besought him with tears to put away the mischief of Haman the Agagite, and his device that he had devised against the Jews. Then the king held out the golden sceptre toward Esther. So Esther arose, and stood before the king. And said, If it please the king, and if I have found favor in his sight, and the thing seem right before the king, and I be pleasing in his eyes, let it be written to reverse the letters devised by Haman the son of Hammedatha the Agagite, which he wrote to destroy the Jews which are in all the king's provinces: For how can I endure to see the evil that shall come unto my people? or how can I endure to see the destruction of my kindred?

Then the king Ahasuerus said unto Esther the queen and to Mordecai the Jew, Behold, I have given Esther the house of Haman, and him they have hanged upon the gallows, because he laid his hand upon the Jews.

Write ye also for the Jews, as it liketh you, in the king's name, and seal it with the king's ring: for the writing which is written in the king's name, and sealed with the king's ring, may no man reverse. Then were the king's scribes called at that time in the third month, that is, the month Sivan, on the three and twentieth day thereof; and it was written according to all that Mordecai commanded unto the Jews, and to the lieutenants, and the deputies and rulers of the provinces which are from India unto Ethiopia, an hundred twenty and seven provinces, unto every province according to the writing thereof, and unto every people after their language, and to the Jews according to their writing, and according to their language. And he wrote in the king Ahasuerus' name, and sealed it with the king's ring, and sent letters by posts on horseback, and riders on mules, camels, and young dromedaries: Wherein the king granted the Jews which were in every city to gather themselves together, and to stand for their life, to destroy, to slay, and to cause to perish, all the power of the people and province that would assault them, both little ones and women, and to take the spoil of them for a prey. Upon one day in all the provinces of king Ahasuerus, namely, upon the thirteenth day of the twelfth month, which is the month Adar. The copy of the writing for a commandment to be given in every province was published unto all people, and that the Jews should be ready against that day to avenge themselves on their enemies. So the posts that rode upon mules and camels went out, being hastened and pressed on by the king's commandment. And the decree was given at Shushan the palace.

And Mordecai went out from the presence of the king in royal apparel of blue and white, and with a great crown of gold, and with a garment of fine linen and purple: and the city of Sushan rejoiced and was glad. The Jews had light, and gladness, and joy, and honor. And in every province, and in every city, withersoever the king's commandment and his decree came, the Jews had joy and gladness, a feast and a good day. And many of the people of the land became Jews; for the fear of the Jews fell upon them.

Now in the twelfth month, that is, the month Adar, on the thirteenth day of the same, when the king's commandment and his decree drew near to be put in execution, in the day that the enemies of the Jews hoped to have power over them, (though it was turned to the contrary, that the Jews had rule over them that hated them;) The Jews gathered themselves together in their cities throughout all the provinces of the king Ahasuerus, to lay hand on such as sought their hurt: and no man could withstand them, for the fear of them fell upon all people. And all the rulers of the provinces, and the lieutenants, and the deputies, and officers of the king helped the Jews; because the fear of Mordecai fell upon them. For Mordecai was great in the king's house, and his fame went out throughout all the provinces: for this man Mordecai waxed greater and greater. Thus the Jews smote all their enemies with the stroke of the sword, and slaughter, and destruction, and did what they would unto those that hated them. And in Shushan the palace the Jews slew and destroyed five hundred men. And Parshandatha, and Dalphon, and Aspatha, and Poratha, and

Adalia, and Aridatha, and Parmashta, and Arisai, and Aridai and Vajezatha, the ten sons of Haman the son ofHammedatha, the enemy of the Jews, slew they; but on the spoil laid they not their hand. On that day the number of those that were slain in Shushan the palace was brought before the king.

And the king said unto Esther the queen, The Jews have slain and destroyed five hundred men in Shushan the palace, and the ten sons of Haman; what have they done in the rest of the king's provinces? Now what is thy petition? and it shall be granted thee: or what is thy request further? and it shall be done. Then said Esther, if it please the king, let it be granted the Jews which are in Shushan to do to-morrow also according unto this day's decree, and let Haman's ten sons be hanged upon the gallows. And the king commanded it so to be done: and the decree was given at Shushan; and they hanged Haman's ten sons. For the Jews that were in Shushan gathered themselves together on the fourteenth day also of the month Adar, and slew three hundred men at Shushan; but on the prey they laid not their hand. But the other Jews that were in the king's provinces gathered themselves together, and stood for their lives, and had rest from their enemies, and slew of their foes seventy and five thousand, but they laid not their hands on the prey. On the thirteenth day of the month Adar; and on the fourteenth day of the same rested they, and made it a day of feasting and gladness. But the Jews that were at Shushan assembled together on the thirteenth day thereof, and on the fourteenth thereof; and on the fifteenth day of the same they rested, and made it a day of feasting and gladness. Therefore the Jews of the villages, that dwelt in the unwalled towns, made the fourteenth day of the month Adar a day of gladness and feasting, and a good day, and of sending portions one to another.

And Mordecai wrote these things, and sent letters unto all the Jews that were in all the provinces of the king Ahasuerus, both nigh and far, to establish this among them, that they should keep the fourteenth day of the month Adar, and the fifteenth day of the same, yearly, as the days wherein the Jews rested from their enemies, and the month which was turned unto them from sorrow to joy, and from mourning into a good day: that they should make them days of feasting and joy, and of sending portions one to another, and gifts to the poor. And the Jews undertook to do as they had begun, and as Mordecai had written unto them; because Haman, the son of Hammedatha, the Agagite, the the enemy of all the Jews, had devised against the Jews to destroy them, and had cast Pur, that is, the lot, to consume them, and to destroy them; but when Esther came before the king, he commanded by letters that his wicked device, which he devised against the Jews, should return upon his own head, and that he and his sons should be hanged on the gallows. Wherefore they called these days Purim, after the name of Pur. Therefore for all the words of this letter, and of that which they had seen concerning this matter, and which had come unto them, the Jews ordained, and took upon them, and upon their seed, and upon all such as joined themselves unto them, so as it should not fail, that they would keep these two days according to their writing, and according to their appointed time every year; and that these days should be remembered and kept throughout every generation, every family, every province, and every city; and that these days of Purim should not fail from among the Jews, nor the memorial of them perish from their seed. Then Esther the queen, the daughter of Abihail, and Mordecai the Jew, wrote with all authority, to confirm the second letter of Purim. And he sent the letters unto all the Jews, to the hundred twenty and seven provinces of the kingdom of Ahasuerus, with words of peace and truth, to confirm these days of Purim in their times appointed, according as Mordecai the Jew and Esther the queen had enjoined them, and as they had decreed for themselves and for their seed, the matters of the fastings and their cry. And the decree of Esther confirmed these matters of Purim; and it was written in the book.

And the king Ahasuerus laid a tribute upon the land, and upon the isles of the sea. And all the acts of his power and of his might, and the declaration of the greatness of Mordecai, whereunto the king advanced him, are they not written in the book of the Chronicles of the kings of Media and Persia? For Mordecai the Jew was next unto king Ahasuerus, and great among the Jews, and accepted of the multitude of his brethren, seeking the wealth of his people, and speaking peace to all his seed.

CHAPTER III.

THESE HEBREW RECORDS CREDIBLE.

————— Precious Bible!
"When yonder spheres sublime ————
Pealed their first notes to sound the march of time,
Thy joyous youth began: but not to fade—
When all the sister planets have decayed;
When wrapt in flames the realms of ether glow,
And Heaven's last thunder shakes the world below;
Thou, pure, unsoiled, shalt o'er the ruins smile!"

It is a remark of the late venerable *Dr. Alexander* that, "there never has existed upon earth a nation whose history is so deserving of our attention as that of the Jews." This is certainly true, for they are and always have been a peculiar people. An extraordinary providence has always been exercised toward them.

Up to the carrying away into the Babylonish captivity, the history of the ancient Jews is contained in their sacred books, but subsequent to that event, we have nothing concerning them but fragments; and of these the Book of Esther is one of the most valuable .During the period of their history between their captivity and the coming of Christ, many important prophecies were fulfilled; and in the days of Ezra, Nehemiah and Esther, we find the origin of the moral condition and of the political and ecclesiastical state of things that prevailed when Christ was born. A knowledge of Hebrew history for five hundred years immediately preceding the Advent is necessary to understand the New Testament.

It is not, then, merely because the Book of Esther is an interesting and true picture of the Persian court for thousands of years, but also because it is a chapter—a very remarkable chapter—of God's dealings with his people, and of his care for his church, that we invite you to study it. But our Chronicles of Ahasuerus, Esther and Mordecai, are they of canonical authority? I answer, we have the same authority for believing that the Book of Esther belongs to the Hebrew canon that we have for Ezra, Nehemiah, or any of their historical books. It is found in Hebrew just as we find them. For although several of the proper names of this book are of *Persian* origin, there is scarcely a doubt among scholars that it was written originally in Hebrew. Foreign names are found in the writings of Moses and in Daniel, as well as in other parts of the Old Testament, but no one denies on that account that Hebrew is their original. The Book of Esther is not found in Arabic, nor in any other ancient Oriental language, but the Hebrew, Syriac and Chaldee. Ancient copies differing more or less from each other, and from the Hebrew text, are found in Greek and Latin. The Chaldee copy, as given in the *London Polyglott*, contains five times more than the Hebrew text, but the book, as we receive it, has always been considered as a part of the canon of their holy writings by the Jews. And as they were remarkably careful to preserve their sacred writings, and jealous of any change or interpolation, the presumption is very strong in favor of the authenticity of this book. The ancient Jews were made the keepers of the Oracles of God, and if they had not been true to this trust, our Lord and his apostles would certainly have charged them with neglect or corruption. But this they did not do. Our Lord reproved them for misinterpreting and for rendering of none effect the commandments of God by their traditions, but never with having been unfaithful in preserving the sacred text.

There is some difference of opinion, both among ancient and modern writers, as to the author of the Megilloth Esther. A majority, both of Hebrew and Christian interpreters, both ancient and modern, ascribe it to Mordecai. The Rabbins generally, and Clemens of Alexandria, tell us that Mordecai was its author. Some say it was composed by the great Synagogue. Others have attributed it to the high priest Joachim. This was the opinion of Philo, the Jew. Augustine thinks it was written by Ezra.* A few think that ix: 20, 23, prove it to have been the joint composition of Esther and Mordecai; but this reference is not conclusive proof of this, for the passage seems to speak, not of this memoir or history of Esther, but of the circular letters that were sent throughout the empire, or, at least, of them chiefly.

Some Christian writers have doubted its claim to a place among canonical Scriptures; but their objections do not merit a labored reply. It may be true there is no prophecy in this book—that it is not quoted in the

*De Civ. Dei., lib. xviii: C. 36.

New Testament—that there is no mention in it of any of the names or attributes of Jehovah, nor even of prayer or sacrifices to Him. But the singular fact that the name of God does not occur in the book, does not seem to me to have authorized some of the fathers to reject it from the canon. It is certainly one of the most striking illustrations of a superintending Providence to be found in any of the sacred narratives. And may not this omission have been designed? Perhaps the purpose was to prove to the Gentiles the fact that the God of the Jews was the Supreme Ruler of the universe, without exciting their prejudices by making a display of His name. The narrative tells its own story, and carries with it its own evidences. It implies clearly and necessarily the existence and presence of the God of Abraham. The Hebrews have never denied its authenticity. They esteem it everywhere, I believe, even to this day, as one of the best of their holy writings. They call it, by way of eminence, *Megillah* that is, THE VOLUME. And some of them believe that whatever destruction may attend their other sacred writings, that the Pentatuch and the *Megilloth Esther* will always be preserved by a special Providence. They have always placed it on a level with the law of Moses. The Jewish celebration of Purim, to commemorate their deliverance from the massacre intended for them by *Haman*, historically proven to have had its rise at that time; and its observance, from that time to the present day, by the Jews in every part of the world, is one of the simplest and strongest proofs that can be given of the truthfulness of its historical statements.

It were certainly difficult to show how a national festival like *Purim* could have arisen, if it does not perpetuate a reality. Historically, we have just as much proof of the truth of the history of the Book of Esther, as we have of the truth of the subject-matters commemorated in the anniversary of the American Declaration of Independence. There is nothing in the history itself that shows it to be a fiction, or a mere invention of a novel writer. Queen Esther's history is an oriental romance, and yet it is a literal truthful history.

And as Mordecai was a man of God, and a principal actor in the history which this book records, and in every way a fit person to write it, I see no reason to hesitate in ascribing it to his pen. It may have been revised by Ezra. The six additional chapters found in the Vulgate, and received as canonical by the Greek and Latin churches, are not extant in Hebrew, nor do they contain internal evidence of authenticity, and consequently they are not received by Protestants as a part of the sacred canon. They seem to have been compiled by Hellenistic Jews, and are to be considered of no more value or authority than so many pages of Philo Judæus or Josephus. The *Apocryphal books,* though not admitted by us to a place among the Holy writings which we believe were given by Divine Inspiration, are nevertheless worthy of our attention. They are generally supposed to be the productions of Alexandrian Jews. As ancient Jewish documents before the coming of Christ,—as a collection of traditions or fragments of history, and of lessons on prudence and morality, and sometimes of piety, they "are all curious, and some of them extremely valuable." They are particularly useful as helps to elucidate the phraseology of the New Testament.

But may we rely on the facts stated in the *Megilloth Esther?* And are we able to understand it? Is it an intelligible history? Happily for us, we have various independent and numerous sources from whence to draw materials by which to satisfy ourselves that the Megilloth Esther is a true narrative, and by which to show that it is intelligible to us. In the *first* place, we have the ancient versions. It is not necessary here to describe at length the ancient versions that have been made of the Holy Scriptures, but as our pages are not designed for learned or professional readers, it seems to be necessary to give a brief notice of those versions that are referred to in this work for illustrations and proofs of the narrative. The chief versions to which we refer, are the Septuagint, Vulgate, Chaldee Versions, or Targums, and the Talmud.

After the Hebrew ceased to be a living tongue, and especially after the spread of Christianity, both Jews and Christians desired translations of the Hebrew Scriptures into the prevailing languages, and these translations, of course, soon assumed the place of the original Hebrew text. Some of these versions were made directly from the Hebrew, others were versions from versions. Thus the Septuagint or Alexandrine version was made directly from the Hebrew text; but the Latin Christians made their version from the Septuagint, and, in the fourth century, that was superseded by the Vulgate, which is Jerome's version of the Septuagint using the Itala as the basis.

The *Septuagint* is the work of some seventy learned Jews, who, by order of Ptolemy Philadelphus, about 280 B. C., translated the Hebrew, from the best manuscript text that could be obtained, into the Greek and adding some from Greek manuscripts not found in Hebrew. The immediate object is said to have been to obtain a good copy of the writings of Moses, for the celebrated Alexandrine Library.

The Latin Bible, known as the *Vulgate*, is so called, because it was made from the Greek, which was then the *vulgata*, common or popular tongue. The *Vulgate* was the first book ever printed, and, by the decree of the Council of Trent, in 1545, if I am not mistaken, is the authorized standard version of the Catholic Church. The first copy with a date was printed at Mayence, 1462.

The Targums, or Chaldee versions, are allowed to be the works of Hebrews, living in the Holy Land and in Babylon, at different times, from about 150 years before Christ to the eighth or ninth century of our era. The name Targum is from the Chaldee, to *translate*, and means *translation*. They are sometimes, however, but improperly, called paraphrases, for there is nothing about them paraphrastic. Some of our Lord's quotations from the Holy Scriptures seem to have been made from the Chaldee. The more ancient Targums are among the best translations that have been made. The latter are not of so much value. There are eleven of them in all, the chief of which are, the Targum of Onkelos, of Jonathan, of Pseudo Jonathan, and of Jerusalem.

The *Talmud* is a Hebrew work, containing the doctrines, religion and morality of the Jews. Its authority among them is equal to or greater than the Hebrew Scriptures. The name is from *lamad*, to teach, and means pre-eminently their *traditional doctrines*. There are two works known by this name: The Talmud of Jerusalem, and the Talmud of Babylon. The Talmud of Jerusalem is said to be the work of Rabbi Jochanan, about 300, A. D., and was designed for the Jews of Judea. It is composed of two parts, the *Mishna* and the *Gemara*. The *Mishna* is a collection of traditions gathered by the doctors and put together in this body, lest they should be lost. The *Gemara* again is a collection of illustrations of the *Mishna*, or a supplemental commentary upon it. These two constitute the Talmud of Jerusalem. The Talmud of Babylon consists of the *Mishna* of Judah the holy, and of a *Gemara*, collected or composed about 400, A. D., as is believed by Rabbi Asa of Babylon. It was designed chiefly for the Jews in Babylon and on the Euphrates. I believe this Talmud is generally preferred to that of Jerusalem. I have heard that it is a common saying among the Hebrews, that the Bible is water, the *Mishna* wine, and the *Gemara* hypocistis. They say the Talmud contains the things taught to Moses by God himself, who taught them to Aaron and his sons, and they to the Elders of Israel, and they to the prophets and the members of the great Synagogue, who communicated them to the Rabbis, who composed the Mishna and Gemara. Horne on the Scriptures and Bible Dictionaries, will enable you to pursue this study, if you are so inclined. The works also of *Philo Judæus*, a noble Jew of Alexandria, about A. D. 40, contain many curious treatises that are of much importance in illustrating the language, phraseology and sentiment of the New Testament. The writings of *Josephus*, a learned

Jew of the priestly line and of royal descent, are too well known to need any description. He was born about thirty years after the Advent, and was alive in A. D. 96, but it is not known when he died. Though I believe Josephus is not a popular author among the Jews, and has been often severely criticised, still his works must be regarded as of great value to Biblical students.

Secondly. All the sources of Persian history now opened to scholars are found to corroborate the Megilloth Esther in every possible way. These sources, so far as the period of our history is concerned, may be said to consist of the old traditions of Persia embodied in the poets we have named, and the works of Herodotus, Xenophon, Ctesias, Arrian, Josephus, and Strabo; and the fragments incidentally recorded in the sacred books of the Jews. Xenophon, Ctesias and Arrian were eye-witnesses of the last days of the Persian empire. Ctesias was a resident of the Court of Cyrus the Younger, but all that we have of the twenty-three books which he wrote then, are some fragments preserved in Photius. He was a medical man. The most reliable sources are the Oriental discoveries of our own day, especially for information concerning the sacred scriptures.

In the Asiatic Journal, xii. vol., Major Rawlinson has given a most interesting memoir of the Persian Inscriptions from Behistun. The Major, now Sir Henry Rawlinson, has, in public lectures and by drawings and numerous models, taken from the sculptures now in the British Museum, repeatedly pledged himself to adduce by most abundant coincidence the authenticity of the Holy Writings. He says the Inscriptions go back to about 2,000 years before Christ, and that from every part of Assyria a multitude of inscriptions have been deciphered, which confirm in the minutest details the pages of Scripture, and explain many passages hitherto obscure.

These readings are particularly interesting as to the signification and derivation of names, and also as to "The earliest connection of the Chaldees and Indians, and the Babylonian mythology; the ethnology and geography of the Assyrians; the historical records, all are illustrated; in every case, there is an entire agreement with the Bible. The lecturer inferred, from his studies, that the Book of Job belonged to a time about 700 before Christ. In the inscriptions there is a period of nearly a thousand years, without mention of Judea, but during that period, there was no inducement for intercourse between the Assyrians and the Jews. The visit of the Queen of Sheba to Solomon was verified. So, the wars between Sennacherib and Hezekiah. There were four distinct captivities of the Jews. Some inscriptions referred to the time of Nebuchadnezzar; others threw light on the existence and actions of Belshazzar, who was joint king with his father, Minus, and who shut himself up in Nineveh."

CHAPTER IV.

POINTS TO BE PROVEN.

"Look through the world which all about you lies,
The noisy town, its common, daily life,
Flushed with coarse passions, hot with selfish strife,
The crowded street, the dens of VICE and WANT,
The gilded halls where Pride and Fashion flaunt,
And from their mingled threads, the grave, the gay,
Weave, if you will, the Epic of to-day."

1. We hope to be able to show as this wonderful roll is unfolded before us, that we should be thankful to the Jews for their *Megilloth Esther*. It is a true history of persons and events in a remarkable period of the Church of God. The adversaries of Revelation delight in pressing the objection that our Sacred Writings contain contradictions. The argument is this: An account or story, say they, is not to be believed, the narrators of which give contradictory statements about it; the sacred writers give contradictory accounts of some of the things of which they write; therefore they are not to be believed at all. Now the same argument applied to Xerxes, Cyrus, or Alexander, would prove that such men never lived. Archbishop Whately has applied the argument with great force in his "Historic Doubts,"

concerning Napolean Bonaparte. The argument stands thus: A story is not to be believed, whose reporters do not agree in their statements concerning it: the historians of the life of Napoleon do not agree in their reports: therefore, the story of his life is not to be believed. The same process of argumentation would prove there never was such a battle as that of Bunker (Breed's) Hill, nor of New Orleans, for some of the historians of the wars and of the times of the actors in these battles, have omitted to mention them at all, or have made contradictory statements concerning them. It is not agreed, for instance, whether *cotton* bales were used by General Jackson at the battle of New Orleans or not. This argument would prove that no such persons as Washington or Jackson ever lived.

It is the more important to attend, also, to the fact that our position is very different from that of the heathen. The inquiry that naturally arises in the mind of a Chinaman, or of any Pagan, when Christianity is proposed to him, is not, *What are the objections to Christianity?* but, *Why should I receive it?* The very reverse is the ordinary process among ourselves. Being brought up in a Christian country, and not unfrequently without inquiring into the reasons of our faith —in fact, without being stimulated to seek for reasons for believing it, till we find it controverted; and when it is controverted, then we find ourselves answering objections to, rather than seeking for evidences in support of Christianity. This is manifestly giving the opponents of Revelation a great advantage. For it is plain that a child can ask a question that seven wise men cannot answer, or propose a difficulty concerning some familiar thing that a score of philosophers cannot explain. It is not necessary to be able to solve satisfactorily all the objections that are alleged against the doctrines of Revelation, before we receive it as the Word of God. This would be as if a man must be a natural philosopher, and skillful enough to explain the process of breathing and all the apparatus made therefor before he could inhale the air; or be able to analyze his bread and explain the whole process of eating and of digestion and assimilation *before* he should be allowed to eat. And surely this is a process but few will be able to realize. The true view of this point is, that *there may be truth—truth supported by irreffragable arguments, and yet, at the same time, be obnoxious to apparent objections, numerous, plausible and by no means easily answered.* Dr. Johnson has stated this point in this way:. "There are," says he, "objections against a *plenum* and objections against a *vacuum;* but one of them must be true. And sensible men, really desirous of discovering truth, will perceive that reason directs them to examine, first, the argument in favor of that side of the question where the first presumption of truth appears." The case, then, stands in the manner following: We have books which we call Sacred. The first thing is to examine their authority and the evidences that support it. Then we may hear objections; but if the proofs that the Bible is the Word of God are sufficient, then, even if there are objections not easy if at all susceptible of solution, still we are bound to receive it as the Word of God. When the Gospel was first preached, Jews and Gentiles demanded to know on what grounds its claims rested.* They asked themselves, each one, Why should I embrace it? Not what are the objections to it? So in regard to the Bible, we believe the difficulties are greatly overstated. The objections are magnified. Many of them are only apparent. Patience, candor and intelligence may remove them, or explain them. But, if not, we have reasons for believing the Bible to be the Word of God, *in spite* of all the objections to it that its opponents have ever been able to produce. And as reasonable, accountable beings, we are bound to hold to it as the Word of God, until we are furnished with something better.

Where books and newspapers are not generally circulated, the people are much under the influence of oral teachings. In older times, among all nations, story tellers were an influential class of instructors. The people of the East have always been remarkably fond of story telling. The Arabian Nights, Persian tales of Genii, and all their literature is proof of this. The chief points of Abraham's life, and of Isaac and Jacob, of Joseph and Moses, and of Joshua, David and Solomon, live on their lips to this day. The names are sometimes changed altogether, and generally a little modified, and Ishmael and Esau are usually made greater heroes than Isaac and Jacob; and many a weary evening is beguiled away in the Arab's tent by the story of Hebrew patriarchs and kings. Rebekah's marriage with the son of the great Shiekh, *Abou Ibrahim, El Halil*, and the story of Joseph, of Daniel,

---

* Whately, in several of his very able works, and Dr. Hawkins, in his work on Tradition, have some excellent thoughts on this subject, and presented much more fully than can be done here.

and of Susannah and Hadassah, are almost as well known among the wandering children of the deserts of Asia and Africa, (though they are neither able to read nor write,) in their essential points, as they are to our Sunday school classes. From this there are two lessons to be learned: *First,* That God graciously consulted for the preservation of revealed truth by committing His oracles, in times past, to Orientals, and not to any of us Western peoples, nor to a race resembling us. The language of the Hebrews, its idioms and structure, and their geographical position and national relationships, and peculiar formation of mind, fitted them pre-eminently to receive and preserve for mankind until the fullness of time for their manifestation, the Divine communications, made from the beginning, to patriarchs and prophets for the benefit of the human race. *Salvation is of the Jews.* They were God's reservoir of saving truth. And the second lesson is, that we owe a great debt of gratitude to God and to our country—to our parents and friends for our privileges, literary and religious. We have the word of God in all its essential purity, both in the original and in translations and versions, so that we may all hear of the wonderful things of God in the tongue with which we were born.

2. We expect to be able to show that true happiness is to be found in putting our *trust in Providence.* The whole story of Esther "is like a transparency hung before the Pavilion of the Almighty, through which his counsels shine, and his unerring hand is invisible." The whole book illustrates the fact that Providence

has a life plan for every individual, and works out that plan in the use of the ordinary events of life.

We shall find a providence in this history touching the ancient Church of God worthy of special remembrance. It is both natural and strange that any of the Jews should have preferred to remain in exile after the decree of Cyrus permitting them to return to their own land, and to the enjoyment of their own peculiar religious services at Jerusalem. As they built houses and planted vineyards in the land of their captivity, and prayed for the prosperity of their conquerors and masters, it is not strange they should have become attached to their Persian homes; but it is strange that any of those that belonged to Abraham's posterity should have become so indifferent to the great promises that were yet unfulfilled as to seem to abandon them, and give up their distinctiveness as a nation, made peculiar and separated from all other peoples. Such, however, was the fact. While some returned, many were content to remain. Nor are the Jews we find throughout the Persian empire to be supposed as belonging only, if at all, to "Those trackless fugitives, the lost Ten Tribes." They were also of the house of Judah and Benjamin. But the God of their fathers neither failed to protect those that returned to the Holy Land, nor those that remained behind in Persia. Nor are examples of eminent piety and zeal for their religion wholly wanting either among those that returned with Nehemiah and Ezra, or among those that remained on the Euphrates.

The two prominent agents raised up at this time for the preservation of the church are *Mordecai* and *Esther*, by whom God worked out a "glorious deliverance from one of the most mournful, imminent and universal dangers of total destruction that ever had threatened the Jewish church." The providence of God in raising up a Hebrew maid to be the Queen of Persia, and in overthrowing Haman for his iniquity, and in rewarding Mordecai for his piety and integrity, is wonderful. The piety and wisdom of Esther and Mordecai are not, however, so super-eminent as to obscure the dealings of a most gracious sovereignty. The virtues of the instruments do not render any the less conspicuous the mercy and power of God toward his ancient people in their captivity and voluntary exile. The sovereign goodness of God toward his church is seen sometimes in using the heathen to afflict it, and then in overturning them and in making their perdition subservient to the advancement of his truth. Jehovah is King in all the earth. He maketh the wrath of man to praise him, and the remainder of wrath he restraineth. A poet has well said, in teaching us to recognize God's providence, that

"If pestilence stalk through the land, ye say,
This is God's doing;
Is it not also His doing, when an aphis creepeth on a rose-bud?
If an avalanche roll from its Alp, ye tremble at the will of Providence:
Is not that will concerned when the sear leaves fall from the poplar?"

"Let all those that seek thee rejoice and be glad in thee: let such as love thy salvation say continually, The LORD be magnified. But I am poor and needy;

yet the LORD thinketh upon me: thou art my help and my deliverer; make no tarrying, O my God." Prov. xl. 16, 17. "Are not five sparrows sold for two farthings, and not one of them is forgotten before God? But even the very hairs of your head are all numbered. Fear not therefore; for ye are of more value than many sparrows." Luke xi. 6, 7.

3. We expect to be able to show from the testimony in this case that it is not only God's plan to work by means, but often to surprise his people by unexpected deliverances, and by bringing great results out of small beginnings. The greatest events in human history have been generally produced by apparently insignificant causes, and because of their *quiet might*, they have awakened at first but little interest. The greatest powers of nature are silent and invisible. The power of gravitation, what is it? Who hath seen it? The lightning and the dew how powerful, and yet how impalpable! The ruins of a city, are they not the fruits of a spark? And if a noble mind is wrecked, is it not the result of a wrong impression recieved in the nursery, or of some insidious falsehood imperceptibly imbibed and left to take root and grow strong and work out the ruin, before its poison was detected? The turning point of Washington's life—the decision that made him the Father of his country, was it not his regard for his mother? Joseph and Moses, Daniel and Mordecai, illustrate the value of right principles implanted in the youthful mind by parental affection and piety. One could not yield to the most seductive temptation, because to do so would be a sin against God; another refused the

honors of an empire, then the greatest on earth, and chose to suffer poverty and persecution with God's people, because of the faith in which he had been brought up. And Mordecai and Daniel, captives in the most licentious and luxurious heathen cities on the globe—far from home and from all parental oversight—and great favorites with the Courts of Babylon and Persia, never forgot their education, nor brought reproach upon their mothers' catechism or their fathers' faith. The impressions made on their young hearts by their Hebrew parents were indelible. The beauty, power and fascination of the most splendid heathen courts could not efface them. The fiery prophet Elijah is another illustration of the effectiveness of silent influences. The solemn thunder came rattling from the desert clouds, the hurricane came sweeping over the rocks and riven mountains of granite and porphyry, filling the air with clouds of sand—the rocking and crashing march of the earthquake, and the blinding flame of the lightning—all failed to reach his heart. God was not in the wind, nor in the fire, nor in the earthquake. It was when the Lord spake to the prophet "in the still small voice," that his heart was opened and his stubborn soul was conquered. *Mother*, sow the seed. *Father*, instill the principle. And cry to God, mightily both of you, and far away, and many days hence, the seed will grow, the principle will live, and your God will be the God and everlasting portion of your children. The waving harvest is all from seed cast into the ground with mingled hopes and fears. The rolling river springs from brooks among the hills, whose tiny fountains an infant's hand could turn aside.

"That yew tree of a thousand years was once a little seed;
And Nero's marble Rome, a shepherd's mud-built hovel:
A speck is on the tropic sky, and it groweth to the terrible tornado.
An apple, all too fair to see, destroyed a world of souls!
A tender babe is born—it is Attila, scourge of the nations!
A seeming malefactor dieth—it is Jesus, the SAVIOUR OF MEN."

Tupper.

CHAPTER V.

SUSA, AND HER KING.

"——— Susa, by Choaspes' amber stream
The drink of none but kings."
Par. Reg. II.

SOMETIME between the famous battle of Marathon, and the celebrated retreat of the ten thousand Greeks under Xenophon, say about five hundred years before the angels sang "Glory to God in the highest, and on earth peace, good will toward men," the great king Ahasuerus sat on his throne, in the royal city of Susa, and made a feast to all his princes and servants. But so uncertain is human fame—so evanescent all earthly glory, that it is difficult to know who this same great king Ahasuerus was. Almost every Medo-Persian king, from Cyaxeres I down to Ochus, or Artaxerxes III, has, in turn, been identified by some interpreter of ancient records as the Ahasuerus of Esther. Some of the uncertainties that surround us, in Persian history, may be anticipated, when we remember the curious fact that, up to this time, I believe, no trace whatever is found of the name of Xerxes in the Persian records. It is probable, as his father reigned sixty years, that the period of his government has been confounded with that of his father, *Gustasp*. If so, it is a remarkable instance of the uncertainty of enduring fame. If a monarch, that led such armies as Xerxes did, has failed to perpetuate his name in the history of his own country, who can expect to live in the memory of mankind? If it be correct that Gustasp was his father, and that his reign is merged into his, then his name, in the Persian annals, is not Xerxes, but Isfunder, the father of Artaxerxes Longimanus. Perhaps all agree that the name *Ahasuerus* of the Hebrews and Romans is the same as the *Artaxerxes* of the Greeks, and the *Ardsheer* of the Persians. *Ardsheer*, or *Ardashir*, signifies, according to some, "the lion of the camp"—Sir John Malcolm says, "the Prince of the earth;" and Grotefend says, "the great warrior." The whole name, in Persian, is *the long-handed Ardsheer*, which corresponds exactly to Artaxerxes Longimanus, that is, Artaxerxes Long-arms—his arms are said to have been so long, that when he stood upright, like Rob Roy, the ends of his fingers reached below his knees. It was at the court of this long-armed prince that the famous Themistocles found refuge as an exile, and where he is said to have learned the Persian language in one year. Thucy. lib. I: 138. If this is correct, it is a proof that the Greek and Persian languages were much alike, which is as we should expect, if they are descendants from one common mother, the Sanskrit, as our best scholars tell us. See Vaux., p. 116.

Some say, *this Ahasuerus* was Xerxes the Great, the terror of Greece—so Jahn, Scaliger and others. The learned Scaliger identifies as proof of this, Xerxes' queen

Hamestris with Esther. But how can this be, when Xerxes had a son by Hamestris that was marriageable in the seventh year of his reign? And the similarity urged between the names is more than counter-balanced by the striking dissimilarity of their characters. Queen Hamestris was as much unlike Queen Esther as the name Xerxes was like the name Artaxerxes.

Usher says, Ahasuerus was *Darius Hystaspes*, and that Atossa, his wife, was Vashti, and Artystona was Esther. Now, if Herodotus is correct, and all the Archbishop's reliance is upon the Greek writers of Alexander's age, and following, this Artystona was a daughter of Cyrus, and could not therefore have been Esther. And again, Atossa bore several daughters and four sons to Darius, *after* he was king; but, according to the Bible, Vashti was divorced in the *third* year of the king's reign. She could hardly, therefore, have been the mother of four sons and several daughters in three years; and, moreover, Atossa retained her influence over the king to his death, and gained the crown for her son, Xerxes. Atossa then could not have been Vashti, nor Darius Hystaspes, Ahasuerus. No doubt the difficulty of fixing the identity of *Ahasuerus* has been enhanced from the fact that the same name has been given to two other Persian kings in the Bible—to Cambyses, the son of Cyrus, in Ezra iv.: 6; and to Astyages, king of the Medes, and father of Cyaxares, Dan. ix.: 1, neither of whom can be identical with the Ahasuerus of Esther. Dr. Kitto properly concludes that the real alternative is between Xerxes the Great and Artaxerxes Longimanus; but, it seems to me, the reasons which he assigns in favor of Xerxes are not at all satisfactory. See his Cyclo. Bib. Lit. The extent of the king's dominions, and the luxurious habits of the court, and the condition of the Hebrews, and the favor shown to them, apply equally well to either of the Persian monarchs named, so that no decisive proof can be had to this point from the internal evidences of the book of Esther. If anything can be gathered from the history of Esther at all, bearing on this point, it is in favor of Artaxerxes Longimanus, whose favor toward the Hebrews we may conclude was owing to the influence of Mordecai and Esther.

Josephus, and the apochryphal books, and the Septuagint, and, I believe, the learned generally, have agreed that *this Ahasuerus* was Artaxerxes Longimanus, son and successor of Xerxes. So Drs. Prideaux, Hales, Gray and many others. The reasons, briefly, in favor of this opinion, are:

1. The high authority of Josephus and of the authors who hold this opinion.

2. Though, as I have stated before, Persian chronology is but little more than a mass of confusion, if not of contradictions, still, as far as we can understand it from contemporary records, the time of *Artaxerxes Longimanus* is more fully in harmony with the events recorded in our history than of any other Persian king.

3. There are, it seems to me, insuperable difficulties in receiving the Xerxes of the Greeks as the husband of Esther, or of admitting any other Persian king than Artaxerxes Longimanus, as the Ahasuerus of the Bible. And yet I believe the tendency of scholars,

at the present moment, is to make Xerxes the Great the Ahasuerus of the Megilloth Esther. The argument for Xerxes, from the reading of the name by Grotefend and Champollion, is, however, more than counterbalanced by the readings of Rawlinson and the investigations of Malcolm, which, so far as they seem to throw any light on the subject, are in favor of Artaxerxes Longimanus. It will be remembered, in this connection, also, that Ahasuerus, like Cæsar, Pharaoh, Louis or George, was common to several kings, and may be regarded as a title rather than a name.

Ahasuerus reigned *from India even unto Ethiopia.* So varied was the climate of Persia, and so extensive its limits, that the younger Cyrus was correct, though a little boastful, in saying to Xenophon: "My father's kingdom is so large that people perish with cold at one extremity, while they are suffocated with heat at the other." The great extent of the dominions of the Persian kings may be learned from the great numbers and the great diversities of national costumes found in their armies. Herodotus says that, in their infantry and cavalry and marine were no less than *fifty-six* different nations. The empire was the largest under Artaxerxes Longimanus, the Ahasuerus of the text. It was greater than that of Assyria, Chaldea, and greater than the Median. It extended as far west as Greece; north to the Euxine and Caspian, and south to the interior of Africa. Literallly "from India even unto Ethiopia." Xenophon's account of the extent of the Persian empire confirms the text in a striking manner. The terms of boundary are almost identical. He says, the great and glorious kingdom of Cyrus was bounded by the *Red Sea*, and on the south by *Ethiopia*, and on the north by the Euxine, and on the west by Cyprus and Egypt. Cyrop. lib. viii. The time had been when the Cilicians, Egyptians, Phenicians, Syrians and the forefathers of the Persians themselves had all been subjects of Nineveh, but long before the return of the Hebrews from Babylon, Nineveh had fallen, and Assyria and Media, as separate kingdoms, had ceased to exist, and the Persian empire was supreme, from the Indus to the Hellespont, and over all Arabia and Egypt, to the heart of Africa. In the days of Daniel, we find Cyrus and Darius reigning over one hundred and twenty provinces; but it were an easy thing for the successor of Xerxes to add seven more, which would make the number of king Ahasuerus. The Russian empire, in our day, consists of *fifty-four* governments, but these governments cover an area much more extensive than the one hundred and twenty-seven provinces of Persia. And who can tell how many provinces Her Majesty, Queen Victoria, reigns over?

And now that we are "acquaint" with the king and know something of his empire, let us look at his capital and palace. *Shushan the palace*, according to the Septuagint, means *Shushan the city*. This is the Hebrew also, and is no doubt correct, for it was the city that was called Shushan, and not the palace. The three great capitals of ancient Persia were Ecbatana, Babylon and Susa. It is believed that Susa is the same as Shushan, and that the Shus, or Shuster of our day, represents the Susa of the text. The name, according to some, is Pehlvi, signifying "delightful," and was given to the city because of its exceeding pleasantness of situation and climate. Others say the name Susa signifies "Lily," and that the city was so called, on account of the great profusion of this beautiful flower, that clothes the surrounding plains, interspersed with a great variety also of sweet scented plants. Strabo is extravagant in his descriptions of the beauty of this city—a city which he says is "most worthy to be praised." He says also that the plains around were so fertile that they produced "two hundred fold." Aristotle also refers to Susa as "a most wonderful city," and says, "its palace shines with gold, amber and ivory." It was the favorite residence of Cyrus, and believed to have been preferred to Babylon by all the Persian kings. Its gardens and surrounding plains were once filled with oleanders, pomegranates, dates, lemons, oranges, or covered with "golden seas of corn," while the distant view was bounded by snow-clad mountains, somewhere amongst which the remains of Noah's ark are buried. A thick forest of tamarisk, poplar and acacia, skirt the plain around the ruins, which are a cover for lions, wolves, foxes, boars, porcupines, jackals, lizards, serpents, francolins and partridges. Mr. Loftus' chapter on Susa is well worth the attention of all Biblical readers. See pages 335–348.

The early history of Susa is almost unknown to us, but it must have had a beginning, though that beginning is lost in the dim shadows of the past. From the early history of Abraham we have learned that Elam was a kingdom in his day, and it is almost certain that the kingdom of Chedorlaomer was founded by Elam the son of Shem; and from Ezra iv.: 9, we see that the

Elamites were a dependency of Persia; and Daniel tells us, viii: 2, that Shushan was the palace city, and that it was in the province of Elam. From all of which we conclude that the Elam of the Bible, the Elymais of the Greeks and Romans, and Susiana, are one and the same. Some make Susa identical with Cush. Herodotus does indeed tell us that Susa was built by that Ethiopian Memnon, who assisted king Priam in defending Troy, and that at one time the city was called Memnonia, after its founder. Persian annalists say it was founded by Hoshung, the grandson of Kaiomurs, a king of the early Pischdadian dynasty. I know not how to reconcile these discrepancies. I cannot tell which is the true account. They are hardly however all correct. But they serve to prove its early antiquity and greatness. Its magnificence is also to be inferred from its representation upon the embroidered pallium, or shawl of Alcisthenes of Sybaris, described in Aristotle's Memorabilia. See Loftus, p. 336.

Herodotus distinguishes the Eastern Ethiopians of Asia from the Western Ethiopians of Africa, by the straight hair of the former and the curly hair of the latter. Herod., Book vii: 69, 70. And in the Odyssey, *Homer* speaks of a divided race of men—some at the extreme west, and others at the extreme east. i: 22. From this and other testimony it is concluded that the Eastern Ethiopians of Herodotus and the Chaldeans of the Bible are one and the same, and that the seat of the empire of the Memnon who aided Priam against the Greeks at the siege of Troy was Susa, which after him was called Memnonium. This Memnon is styled an Ethiopian. The recent readings of the primitive cuneiform inscriptions of Susa and Mugeyer render it probable that the Chaldeans were a colony from Egypt. The same ideas of astronomy that were held by the Egyptians prevailed in ancient Babylonia.

Rawlinson also explains another matter relating to Belshazzar, which is of great importance. According to the Bible, this king promised Daniel that he should be made "*third* ruler in the kingdom," if he should succeed in interpreting the hand-writing. Why was he not made next to the king as Joseph was in Egypt? For the very good reason that Nabonidus and Belshazzar reigned *jointly;* and as there were two on the throne, if Daniel is raised to it, he would emphatically be "the *third* ruler in the kingdom." Truly there is no device nor knowledge against the Lord. His blessed word is a tried word, but precious and abiding. It never fails. To explain some difficulties that have been raised about the Shushan of Esther, and Daniel "in the palace which is in the province of Elam," it has been said there must have been two cities of this name in the province of Susiana, the one the *Shushan* of the Bible, in the mountains of Bakhtizari; the other, the Susa of the Greeks; and that it was to distinguish the one from the other that Daniel says "Shushan the palace." But this explanation is not necessary, and is not sustained by history. Josephus corroborates the Bible account. He states that Daniel built a famous castle at Susa, which was in a fine state of preservation in his own time.

We know that a palace has been discovered at Nineveh, in which are found a series of sculptures recording the conquest of Susiana, which, as artistic productions, are pronounced the *chef-d'œuvres* of all Assyrian sculpture. No other Persian city was equal to Susa for beauty of situation and salubrity of climate. It vied with Babylon in riches, and in the grandeur of its walls, temples, gardens, and state buildings. It was from this city Xerxes set out on his ill-fated expedition against Greece, and it was here he deposited the treasures he took from the City of Athens and from the temple of Delphi. It was here the vast treasures of Persia were kept. Alexander the Great found here *fifty thousand* talents of gold, probably equal to two hundred and seventy millions of pounds sterling, besides a large number of vessels of gold and silver, and jewels of very great value.

According to Arrian's expedition of Alexander, III. 16, there was a very strong citadel in Susa, and it once stood a terrible siege. Under the Sassanian kings Susa appears as a considerable city. In the third century it was a Christian See. Under its walls was fought a great battle by the Persians under Hormuzan, against the Moslem hosts, but from that day, it seems to have been lost from history. There is no reason to doubt, however, but that it has been identified. An account of the ruins at the present day, and of the evidences of its magnificent structures, columns, palaces, and gardens, is to be seen at length in Loftus, and the reports of the Royal Asiatic Society. Recent excavations at Susa, show that the pavement of the palace was formed of red, and blue, and white, and black marble, arranged in gorgeous Arabesque patterns of the different parts of the animals that Daniel saw in his visions, on the banks of the river Ulai, when this em pire was in in its glory, and according to the history in our text. It may be remembered also that among the sacred emblems found here is the *cross*—just as we find it among the Egyptians, more than a thousand years before Christ was born. The ruins of Susa cover some twelve miles square, extending almost to the bank of the Kerkhad, supposed to be the ancient Choaspes. The mounds are like those of Babylon, huge hillocks of earth and rubbish, broken bricks, and colored tiles. The largest one, according to our best authors, is one mile in circumference, and one hundred feet high. Near to it is another almost as large. The people of the country call them *the palace and the castle.* They are like the pyramids of ruins covering the site of Babylon, and believed to have been built of clay and tiles, and layers of brick and morter. Blocks of marble covered with sculptures, are often found by the Arabs, who search among the ruins for treasure; which they think is hidden there. They believe that it is in hopes of finding treasure that Europeans are so fond of digging up their old ruins. Major Rawlinson says he has identified the port and citadel of this ancient city. He states that the great mound is 165 feet high, and 1100 yards round the base, and 850 yards round the summit; and that on the summit there is a slab with thirty-three lines written in the cuneiform or arrow-headed character, and three Babylonian sepulchral urns are found embedded in the soil. He also says he finds there floorings of brickwork, and broken pottery, glazed tiles and kiln-burnt bricks. Large figures in the palace ruins are also found, resembling in every particular those lately discovered in the pavements of Egypt and Assyria. At the foot of the highest pyramid is the tomb of Daniel. Though the small building that now covers the spot is modern, there is no improbability but it marks the last resting place of the prophet.

It is true there is a contradiction in some of the copies of Josephus about the tomb of Daniel. In some his burying-place is made "Ecbatana in Media," but *Jerome*, professing to copy from *Josephus*, places it in "Susa in Persia." This proves that in his day his copy of Josephus had this reading, and we believe this to be the true one. For it appears from our best authorities that Daniel was governor of the province of Susiana under the king of Babylon; and we know he was highly honored by him, and that he "did the king's business at Shushan the palace." And Josephus says that the house which Daniel built for himself at Susa remained "in freshness and undiminished beauty at the time he wrote."*

But the glory of Susa—its beauty and wealth, its palaces and temples, are now mouldering masses. It is no uncommon thing for the traveler who visits the ruins of this once populous, powerful and "delightful city" to have to seek shelter at night from lions, hyenas and other beasts of prey, that now have their dwelling in the marble halls that were once radiant with the beauty of Persia, within the walls of the Mohammed Mosque—Tomb of Daniel.

The intelligent and pious traveler will find his greatest interest in these ruins to arise from the fact, that they mark the site of the great city that was once the scene of a most deeply interesting series of events that

* See Prideaux's Connexion, and Work of Sir R. R. Porter.

closely concerned the Church of God, and are still a proof of how he watched over his people and protected them in ancient times from destruction, though in captivity for their sins. Nor will he fail to ask himself, how are the mighty fallen! Kings and princes, proud oppressors and tyrants, may quaff the tears of their subjects and make music of their groans, and build thrones of human skulls, but they cannot be sure of their names enduring forever on earth, and much less may they expect to find favor for such things with the King of Kings. Only the pure in heart shall see God.

CHAPTER VI.

THE FEAST AND THE DIVORCE.

" The king was on his throne,
  The Satraps throng'd the hall,
A thousand bright lamps shone
  O'er that high festival !"

*   *   *   *   *   *

" I am a slave, a favor'd slave at best,
To share his splendor, and seem very blest ;
When wearier of these fleeting charms and me,
There yawns the sack,—and yonder rolls the sea.
What ! am I then a toy for dotard's play,
To wear but till the gilding frets away ?"

Byron.

We are now to attend a royal feast at the Palace of Ahasuerus in Susa. The Greek authors all agree that the Persians were remarkable for luxury and magnificence in their palaces and at their entertainments. Their resources were gathered by commerce from Greece and Spain, and the Islands of the Mediterranean. A trade had long existed between Tyre, Sidon and Palmyra, by caravans with Africa and Persia. They abounded in ebony, ivory, cotton, linen, wool, gold, spices and slaves. The Persians in the days of Esther were masters of all the wealth and trade that remained of the cities and empires that had existed before them, from India to Ethiopia. They used the cotton cloths of the Indus, the lion hides and leopard skins of Africa, the camels of the Arabs, and the chariots of the Libyans, Babylonians and Egyptians. Every traveler who visits the ruins of the early periods of the Persians, is struck with amazement at the grandeur, and size and magnificence of their royal residences. Heeren has a diagram of the sculptures that represent the festival hall, reception hall, and audience chamber, the king's house, queen's apartments, sanctuary and banqueting room of the kings of Persia. Imagination cannot picture a sight more imposing than the vast forest of the solitary, mutilated gigantic pillars, colonnades and obelisks of Karnak, and such, or but little, if at all inferior, was the style of the buildings of the Persian capitals. The royal garden pavilion at Ispahan, with its numerous columns and rich embroideries and hangings, may possibly give some idea of the *garden of the king's palace at Susa.* History records that on several occasions Persian kings have feasted as many as five thousand men at once, and at an expense of two hundred talents. So onerous was the expense of providing for Xerxes' table, that Herodotus relates that a poet of Abdera called upon the people to offer sacrifices with thanksgiving to the gods, that it was not the custom of Xerxes to take two meals in one day, for his dinner was as much as they could possibly provide for, and if he had taken a notion to have supper too, they would all have been utterly ruined. Lib. vii. It is in evidence then that the Persians were in possession of every thing required for such feasting and display as are described in our text. They had all sorts of musical instruments, and glass vessels, both cut and ground, mirrors, embroidery and tapestry of many kinds, and Hermione purple, and were acquainted with the use of iron and bronze, and had gold and silver and jewels in great abundance. Oriental luxury is proverbial, but especially that of the Persian kings. No eastern monarchs have ever surpassed, perhaps none have equalled them in show or grandeur, or pompous titles. "The great king," or the "king of kings," and divine honors were their recognized titles and dues. The well remembered line of Horace,

> "Persicos odi, puer, apparatus."
>
> "I tell thee boy, that I detest
> The grandeur of a Persian feast,"

well expresses the common feeling in his day in regard to Persian luxury and pride.

Dr. Russel, in his history of Aleppo, gives an elaborate description of an Eastern house and pavilion, which, in every particular, justifies the whole description of Ahasuerus' palace, as given in the Bible. Sir John Chardin also describes ruins at Persepolis in which were pillars, columns, and apartments, like those of the king's house at Susa. It is common, in the East, to extend a covering of canvass lined with calico, or striped silk, over the court yard where a feast is given, to keep off the sun. Such a custom, at entertainments, is often seen in Birmah, and in Calcutta. Indeed we have seen substantially the same thing at Sebastopol fetes, Fourth of July celebrations, and even at camp meetings. And in the Colisseum, or Flavian Amphitheater at Rome, one may see, to this day, the marks on the walls of the masts, or scaffolds, which were erected when that area was covered with an awning, as it was when their shows were exhibited to the people.

The precise occasion of Ahasuerus' feast is not stated. The Chaldee Targum says it was in commemoration of the suppression of a most dangerous rebellion. Others think that it was in honor of his having triumphed over his competitors for the throne — Artabanes and the Bactrians — or that it was in honor of his having quieted the disturbances that grew out of his father's assassination. Some think that it was intended to celebrate his victories in Egypt and Asia Minor. And others, to commemorate the dedication of Susa as one of the royal capitals. Whatever it was designed to commemorate, it was a proclamation that he was the absolute possessor of the vast Persian empire, and that he was at peace with all the world. And while it was commemorative of glorious achievements, it would serve also to animate his soldiers, gratify his officers and allied princes, and prepare them for future exploits. Men are but little more than children all their lives. If they are not engaged in war, they must have fetes and feasts. It is on this principle that fairs, fire companies and the like, besides their intrinsic utility, are of great use in working off surplus excitement, and so preventing social or civil disturbances. The French Emperor understands this subject well, and so did old Ahasuerus. Accordingly he made a feast worthy of himself, and of his empire. It was an extraordinary display of his wealth before his nobility and the princes of all the conquered provinces—pomp so extraordinary had never before been seen in the world—such rich canopies, gorgeous curtains, tall columns, and rich stuffs suspended in festoons, golden couches, tesselated floors, beds of gold and silver, overlaid or studded with gold and silver—divans such only as Orientals can make—a feast and a display compared with which all other feasts and pomps seem nothing better than famine and poverty. There was a whole world of food—meats and drinks—and that for half of the year for guests from far and near—from a hundred and twenty-seven provinces. It has been usual, in all ages, to celebrate victories and the accession of a new sovereign to the throne by acts of clemency and feasting. In China it is the custom to have three years of mourning on the death of an emperor, during which no public feasts can be held; but, at the expiration of this period, the succeeding monarch gives an *inauguration* festival of very great magnificence.

The feast of Ahasuerus was not like that of Belshazzer, Dan. v, to profane the sacred vessels, nor defy the God of the Hebrews, nor was it murderous like Herod's, nor like Mehemet Ali's feast of death to the Mamelukes. Nor was there any compulsory drinking, nor *mixed* dancing. The waltz was never known at a Persian court, nor would it be tolerated for a moment in any Oriental palace. *And the drinking was according to law; and none did compel: for so the king had appointed to all the officers of his house, that they should do according to every man's pleasure.* There was genuine politeness at the king's feast in regard to drinking. *It was according to law.* It was a Greek custom to compel every guest to keep the round or leave the company. The rule was *drink or be gone,* and surely the latter was far the safest and best. The Romans made some advance toward the politeness of the Persians in choosing a ruler of the feast. He was chosen by the casting of a dice, and called the *arbiter bibendi,* and his regulations were supreme. It was his duty to suit each guest with the wine he preferred, and to mingle water with the drink of a guest who was about to become too much excited. See Hor. Sat. lib. ii, and Latin poets. In health, man's best drink is a little water. But if advanced in life, or afflicted with oft infirmities and a weak stomach, like Timothy's, or if from the pressure of good society, wine as used, then true politeness, as well as morality and religion, forbids the absurd practice of urging people to drink, or to eat, what is not agreeable to them, or more than is to their taste. It is cruelty—it is diabolical to over persuade or allure a friend—especially a youth, into any excess, either of eating or drinking. We must be temperate ourselves, in all things, and do all we can to make others so also.

The length of this feast is not incredible. We have parallels. In modern times, we read of feasts in Persia continuing *one hundred and eighty days.* We read also of a Chinese Emperor, who frequently gave feasts that continued one hundred and twenty days. The apocryphal Judith says that Nabuchadnosor kept a feast at Nineveh for *a hundred and twenty days,* in honor of his victory over Arphaxed. And, according to Athenaus, lib. iv: 13, Deip. Ariamnes undertook to feast the whole Gaulish nation for a year, and did actually succeed in supplying them during a whole year with tents, meat and wine. The feast of king Ahasuerus was a double one. First, to the princes and nobles, for one hundred and eighty days, and *when these days were expired, the king made a feast unto all the people that were present in Shushan, both great and small, seven days. And also Vashti, the queen, made a feast for the women, in the royal house which belonged to king Ahasuerus.* There is no difficulty in our story, growing out of the polygamy and exclusiveness of the harem of eastern princes. For, though they had several wives, they had only *one queen.* The patriarchs and Hebrew kings had several secondary wives—concubines, who were really their wives—but only the children of one, the first wife, could inherit the birthright or the crown. David and Solomon had but one queen. The Sultan of Turkey may have ninety wives, but there can be but one *Sultana.* Nor is there any want of proof that ancient oriental queens were crowned, as Vashti and Esther were. The wife of Mithridates was strangled with her own diadem, which was fastened with white and purple bands around the head. But this was by no means the last time that a crown cost a head. They are always dangerous, but they were especially so to English queens, in the days of *Henry the Eighth.* Observe, also, that, according to oriental custom, Vashti feasts with her women in the female apartments, while the king feasts in the court of the royal gardens. Women did not mingle with the men in public as with us, except on some special occasions. The king held his feast in the *court of the gardens,* because no room was large enough, and because, in that climate, it was more pleasant. The Orientals are fond of gardens, and of feasting out of doors. "The sweet waters" of Asia and of Europe are favorite resorts for the ladies of Constantinople. These are public gardens, chiefly used for walking, smoking and eating. The ladies monopolize them, under the guardianship of eunuchs. Open courts are common in eastern houses. Such courts were often paved with colored marbles or painted tiles, and hence our *Mosaic,* that is, *Musive* work, for I believe it is admitted the Romans borrowed it from the Greeks, and the Greeks from the Asiatics; and if the Romans got it from the Etruscans and Latins, they learned it from the Egyptians.

To what extent the king's brain became wild with "wine and wassail," as the flashing goblet circulated, is not apparent. He was, however, seized with the desire to have the queen before him, with the crown royal—all in her jewelled robes and with her diadem on, *to show the people and the princes her beauty, for she was fair to look on.* No doubt he considered her the greatest treasure of his kingdom. He seemed to have designed to shut up the feast by the dazzling sight of the queen, arrayed in all her sparkling robes, so that his princely guests might go away, saying, King Ahasuerus is richer in the beauty and loveliness of his queen than in all the treasures of his one hundred and twenty and seven provinces. We have an instance from Herodotus that explains, in some measure, the king's command to bring in the queen. He tells us that, when seven Persians were sent to Amytas, a Grecian prince, and being hospitably entertained by him, as the Persians began to drink, they said to him: "Prince of Macedonia, it is a custom with us Persians, whenever we have a public entertainment, to introduce our concubines and young wives."

The *Targum's* rendering, that the king commanded to bring the queen into his presence, *naked,* is not at all probable, and seems to me to be positively contradicted by the text—*to bring the queen before the king, with the crown royal.*

But when *the seven chamberlains that served in the presence of the king* brought his command to the queen, did she appear before him? Astonishing! The *queen Vashti refused to come at the king's commandment by his chamberlains.* How can she justify herself for such disobedience? Perhaps she thought within herself, 'for more than six months the king has been carrying on this revelry, and I and my women have had our feasting among ourselves in our apartments. I am sure if the king were at himself, he would not have sent me such a commandment. It will not really honor him to gratify this foolish humor of his; and when he comes to sober reflection he will thank me for saving him from the disgrace of having made such an exhibition of me. It is not the king, but the wine that is in him, that sent the chamberlains to me with this extraordinary message. And as the wit is out when the wine is in, so also I fear all prudence is lost. There is no knowing what excesses are going on in the royal gardens—what insults may be offered to me. The king's commandment is unusual, unsafe, needless and immodest. I will not go.' Well, proud queen, we are astonished at your refusal. We sympathise with your modest and virtuous reflections, but we cannot approve of your disobedience. The king has not transcended his lawful power in sending for you. It is according to the laws and constitution of the empire. Nor has he commanded you to sin against your conscience as to any religious scruples. And have you well considered also that the wrath of a king is terrible—especially of a royal despotic husband? Do you remember that the blood once inflamed by strong drink is easily made to boil with rage, even toward those that were most tenderly loved but a few moments before? Do you think how you are mortifying his pride—eclipsing all his glory—in the presence of all the princes and people of his vast empire? Do you suppose, however much he loves you, that he can allow himself to receive such a slight, at such a time and before such a company, from *a woman*, even if she is his queen? You cannot suppose for a moment that the son of Xerxes and sovereign of such an empire can allow his nobles and guests to retire from such a feast, saying, "How poor and miserable a man is this great Ahasuerus. He may govern one hundred and seven and twenty provinces, but he cannot govern one woman. He rules an empire from India to Ethiopia, but he cannot rule his own bed-chamber."

I do not know queen Vashti's motives—I am not able to fathom her disposition. She was beautiful, and she was a queen* It is not at all strange, therefore, that she had a will of her own. The fair sex are seldom wanting in that. But I do not find any justification of

* *Vashti* is a Persian name, and signifies a *beautiful woman;* and the word translated *ladies*, in this history, is *Saroth*, our *Sarah*, and means princesses'

her disobedience, unless the king had commanded her to do something that was contrary to law, and was contrary to her sense of duty to God. But the records do not favor any such idea. We admire the queen's courage and modesty, for though beautiful she was not vain or bold; for if she had been she would not have lost such an opportunity of displaying her charms. And she must have been a woman also of great physical and moral courage, or she would not have given up so much grandeur, and incurred the risk of losing her head as well as her crown; for she could not have been ignorant of what would probably be the result of her refusal, and the wonder is that the royal counsellors were satisfied with taking away her crown. Her conduct could scarcely have been construed into anything short of treason, for as a Persian subject, how could she refuse obedience to the king? But I am unwilling to believe that Vashti is such a *rara avis in terris*—that a black swan is not half so rare a bird as many interpreters will have it. For there are many women who would surrender a crown rather than their character, and give up life itself rather than sin against their sense of right and duty. No mere prudery, however, can justify her disobedience. Unless it was a sin to obey, it was a sin for her to disobey. "It is not," says the pious bishop Hall, "for a good wife to judge of her husband's will, but to execute it; neither to go into a curious inquisition for the reasons of an enjoined charge, much less into a resistance; but in a hood-winked simplicity she must follow whither she is led, (even if it is to California,) as one that holds her chief praise to consist in subjection to her own husband."

Therefore was the king very wroth, and his anger burned in him—is an oriental phrase for intense anger. It occurs elsewhere in the Bible. But in the midst of his rage he determined to abide by the law, and by the judgment of those who knew the law, and what it became him to do in this emergency, for though possessed of supreme power, he was obliged by custom to consult the first men of the kingdom, which saw his face, and who knew the common law of the empire, and who could cite precedents and tell him how other kings had done in similar cases. And so it was that after consultation with the wise men which knew the times, for so was the king's manner, he made a law in the heat of passion which he would have been glad afterward had it never been made. The *wise men*, verse 13, were astrologers and magicians, such as were common in Egypt, Babylon, and the East—men who professed to be able to foretell future events, and to frame suitable laws for the government of princes and empires, by reading the past and the future from the stars. Vitringa thinks, and no doubt correctly, that these wise men were the historiographers of the empire—well versed in ancient history—so that they could tell the king what laws and customs had prevailed, and how kings were wont to do in such perplexing cases. According to Juvenal, Satire vi, the Orientals were so superstitious that they believed whatever came from the mouth of their astrologers issued from the fountain of Ammon. These *wise men* were his privy council. Consult chap. vi: 13. 1 Chron. xii: 32. Isa. iii: 2. Ezra vii: 14.

And Memucan answered. Orton thinks this youngest State counsellor was intensely selfish in his advice to the king—that he had more authority in the king's cabinet than he had in his own castle, and that, accordingly, he wished to make a great State affair of the queen's disobedience, that he might have a royal edict to deliver himself from domestic tyranny. His opinion seems to me, however, a poor piece of argument. The queen's conduct, in all other respects, seems to have been so dutiful, that no charge could be brought against her but this one act of disobedience; but from it he drew a general inference, that if the queen's disobedience was not resented, all the Persian ladies would follow her example, and there would be a general domestic insurrection throughout the empire. His associates were either so drunk that they did not understand his counsel, or were unable to give one of their own, or were so anxious to make the slavery of their harems still more perfect, that they all assented to it, and the king issued a decree accordingly. His argument ran from the greater to the less—if the queen herself is divorced for one act of disobedience, and loses her crown, much more must all wives of inferior rank submit to their lords. The nobles evidently fanned the flame of the monarch's wrath with a hearty good will. They wished a withering rebuke—a striking example to go from the throne—so that all their Mrs. Caudles—all their strong-minded wives might, at once, be made to obey implicitly their lordly humors. They persuaded the king that, unless he acted promptly and very decidedly, there would be daily revolutions in every household in his kingdom, and though they prevailed in having the decree issued, I have no idea they gained anything by it. There were, and there always have been, and, I presume, there always will be till the millenium, domestic as well as civil and national revolutions.

"Let there go, therefore," said they, "a royal commandment from the king, and let it be written among the laws of the Persians and the Medes, that it be altered not." So wise and so perfect did they esteem themselves, that they held that their laws could never be amended or repealed. This was ignorance equalled only by presumption. Stability in laws is, however, a great blessing, for frequent changes are almost as bad as no laws. With us, happily, it is a part of our Constitution and laws that they may be amended or repealed, in a constitutional and peaceful way. But with the Persians, if it was once entered in the records of the empire that Vashti was no longer queen, and that every man should bear rule in his own house, then there was no door open for dispute or change. In this royal decree against insubordination and Caudle-lecturing, there is much that is true and much that was tyrannical; but the decree itself was unnecessary and unwise. A modern annotator says, it is one of the most amusing things in all history to look at the king of Persia and his jovial compatriots—the sages of the greatest monarchy on earth—issuing a decree, in all the known languages of the day, *that every man should bear rule in his own house.* Doubtless, when this decree was published, there was an "inextinguishable burst of shrill merriment through every one of the hundred and twenty-seven provinces." As far, however, as this decree was proper, it was substantially nothing more than a Persian edition of the great Creator's will. The Persian's edict did not add anything to its authority. It originally came from God. It is a necessary and proper law. Common sense, from the foundation of the world, in every nation, even among savage tribes, has taught the necessity and propriety of a man ruling as head of his own household. The unalterable decree of the king of Persia is also the unchangeable law of Heaven. "Let every man love his wife as himself, and the wife see that she reverence her husband." Eph. v: 33. "Wives submit yourselves unto your own husbands, as it is fit in the Lord. Husbands love your wives, and be not bitter against them." Col. iii: 18, 19.

1. And does not this history teach us, *that the great law of domestic happiness is love?* No Persian decrees are required to execute the mandates of love, nor can any royal commandment make a household happy without it. Woman is man's other self. She is his greatest blessing and his chief joy, both in sunshine and in sorrow. Her society is necessary to correct his pride and selfishness, and to refine his manners and elevate his feelings and hopes. A palace as magnificent as that of the Czar without a woman is but a miserable garret, to shiver and freeze in, both as to body and soul. And a log cabin, with a true woman's love, is a palace worth more than that of king Ahasuerus. An English wit, (Jerrold,) says that tea with the flowers and scents of the warm East has exercised so great a social influence upon the masses of the English people, that it is not very easy to say too much in praise of it. It has civilized brutish and turbulent homes, saved the drunkard from his doom, and to many a mother given cheerful, peaceful thoughts, in a home that otherwise would have

been forlorn and wretched. But I fancy that in this rhapsody of the humanising mission of tea, he always included the refining influence of woman. For tea without her delicate hand and inspiring presence, is scarcely better than the miserable weed that rivals it in public favor. It is only when woman—"lovely woman," presides at the urn, surrounded by the olive plants of wedded love, that I can see in the stream of steam rolling from the kettle the fallen idols of the Pagan barbarism of the East tumbling down, and the beauteous temples of truth, freedom and piety, rising in their stead.

The true way for all queens to rule is to "stoop to conquer." Let their husbands call themselves as much as they please "the lords of creation," and let them seem to hold the reins, but it is theirs to tell them how to drive. This is the more excellent way. The dispute about the sphere of the sexes is as unphilosophical as it is unscriptural. It is God's will that man should be the head and woman the heart of society. If he is its strength, she is its solace. If he is its wisdom, she is its grace and consolation. And where there is the proper view of marriage, or of the sacred duties that God requires of husband and wife, there is no strife as to who shall govern. Both rule. The word of God is exceedingly plain on this subject. Domestic strife is always a great evil, but it becomes doubly so when it occurs *before* company, as happened with the king of Persia, and when professed friends come in and make bad worse. It is then the wound becomes incurable.

2. Let us learn to guard against all excesses, not only

in feasting and in the loss of time, but of feeling and passion. How inconsiderate, how rash, how sinful was Herod's oath and terrible decree against John the Baptist! And scarcely less wicked were the king's unjust and cruel proceedings against his wife. And because of unjust and sinful separations between husbands and wives our land mourneth, and our State has become a hissing and a term of reproach. I know not where to find language to describe the sin and evils of divorce as it prevails in our day. According to law marriage is merely a civil contract, but that does not allow us to forget the sacredness of the tie that binds husband and wife together, nor has any legislature the right to separate them, except as the word of God allows. The tendency of the age seems to remove all restraint upon marriage, which of course is contrary to good manners and morality, and contrary to the word of God.

If the king had not taken counsel of his own hot blood, and of his wise men under the influence of wine, he had not brought upon himself a world of trouble. A single word spoken in anger, or an act done under the excitement of the passions, may cause a lifetime of repentence. Constitutions are very differently constructed. Men's educations, temperaments and circumstances differ, but all should act calmly and intelligibly, and with great charity toward their fellow men. It was a maxim with General Jackson to take much time to deliberate—to think out the right resolution—but when once the resolution was taken, then to think only of executing it.

3. *How emphatic a lesson is here of human vanity!* The great monarch of such a vast empire is not able to

govern himself. And all the grandeur of half a year's feasting is spoiled by the disobedience of his queen. This was the dead fly in his pot of ointment. One hundred and twenty-seven provinces did not satisfy him. The whole earth was not enough for one for whose mortal remains less than two ells have long since been quite sufficient. The pride of displaying the riches of his empire was "a windy happiness" that could not fill his heart. No earthly portion can satisfy the human soul, for it was made in the image of God, and nothing but God in Christ can now make it happy.

Ahasuerus' feast was full and flowing and long, but it had an end, and where now is all its glory? And how much the better to-day is it with him and his courtiers that they had so long a revelry in the royal gardens! What does it matter that they had beds of gold and silver, and feasted and laughed, and passed along the jest and the song! Great was the confluence of peoples at the king's tables, but they are all gathered with a much greater assembly—the congregation of the dead, whose sisters are worms, and whose mother is corruption. Happy, and only happy, is he whose sins are forgiven, whose iniquity is pardoned, and who has a part in the resurrection of the just.

4. Alas! that so lovely a place as a garden should have been the scene of such revelry and sinning. A garden is associated with some of our holiest and saddest thoughts. Sin fastened on our race in a garden. It was in a garden the curse was pronounced, and there too the great promise of a Redeemer was given. And it was in a garden the Messiah entered the lists of mortal combat to bruise the old serpent's head. Our gar-

dens—would that we had many more of them—that their beauty and fragrance might lead us to adore the Creator, and to pour forth to Him amid his glorious works the grateful, cheerful homage of the heart. Instead then of making our gardens the scenes of sinful mirth and dissipation, as did the Persian king, let us make them oratories for pious breathings to heaven—let them give us thoughts of God and of the love and sufferings of his Son Jesus Christ. It is to Him we owe all our pleasures in the creatures and gifts of Providence, as well as the hope of eternal life. And so also let the garden be a preacher to us of our frailty. Verily at our best estate we are altogether vanity. We are like the grass that springs up in the morning, and is cut down and withered in the evening. Our days are few and full of sorrow. Our possessions and enjoyments here below, are passing away as the tender sighings of the evening breeze that passes over our garden plants. All our gardens of delight are in a vale of tears. O let us then send our affections up before hand to heaven, and fix them upon things at God's right hand, and so plant them in the Paradise above, that in due season, we may be transplanted ourselves from these low grounds of sorrow to the shores of a blissful immortality.

CHAPTER VII.

ESTHER CHOSEN QUEEN.

"*Sar.* I speak of woman's love.
Myr. ——————— The very first
Of human life must spring from woman's breast.
Your first small words are taught you from her lips,
Your first tears quenched by her, and your last sighs
Too often breathed out in a woman's hearing,
When men have shrunk from the ignoble care
Of watching the last hour."
Byron's Sardanapalus.

"In youth women are our idols, at a riper age our companions, in old age our nurses, and in all ages our friends."
Lord Bacon.

WE have learned something of Persia, past and present—as it was, has been and now is—so far as such brief historical items were thought to be conducive to the proper understanding of the Book of Esther and our better acquaintance with the condition of the Hebrews at the time of the Advent; and we have made a visit to Susa, and been introduced to the *king Ahasuerus,* and have contemplated his empire and his capital—the extent, riches and glory of his vast dominions, and were an invited guest with the princes of his one hundred and twenty-seven provinces, from India even unto Ethiopia, at the feast which he gave for one hundred and four score days, to show "the riches of his glorious kingdom and the honor of his excellent majesty." And then we visited the queen, feasting with her women in the apartments of the royal house that belonged to king Ahasuerus, and we saw how she received the king's command to appear before him "with the crown royal, to show the people and the princes her beauty." We have heard her haughty and firm refusal, and how the king was very angry, and how his cabinet advised her immediate divorce, and how it was done, and the king and all the sages of Persia and Media decreed, by a royal commandment that could not be altered, and how it was written and sent into every province and to every people, after their own language, *that every man should bear rule in his own house, and that all wives throughout all the empire shall give to their husbands honor, both to great and small.*

In these transactions there are some things commendable and some things very much to be blamed. It must have been a terrible mortification to the *great king Ahasuerus* at such a time, when he was showing his riches and the power of Persia and Media to his princes and servants, to be obliged to submit to such disobedience in his queen. "Is this the man of a thousand thrones?" What a pity that he who governed millions of men and reigned supreme over so vast an empire could not govern himself! His weakness is seen in his excessive indulgence in wine and in his vanity, and in giving such a command at such a time. As a king and as a husband, it was his honor and his duty to be a covering of the eyes to his wife, and not an exposer of her modesty. Gen. xx: 16. But in his seeking advice of his wise men there is something commendable. Despot as he was, he desired everything to be done according to law. The king, though excited with wine and exceedingly angry, and all-powerful, would not have anything done contrary to the usages and constitution of his empire. Absalom's folly is seen in the choice of his counsellors, and Napoleon's greatness of genius is seen in the fact that he could hear all his cabinet had to say, and gather up all the varied information they had to give, and then act independently upon his own judgment and without hesitation. As a general rule, it is true that *the greater the power the greater the need of advice lest it be abused, and yet the greater the danger, and the need of true courage to give it.*

Though we have admired the beauty, dignity and courage of queen Vashti, we have not been able to excuse her disobedience, as most interpreters have done. The record does not authorize us to find that her obedience would have been a sin against God, and therefore we cannot justify it. Her divorce, however, was hasty, cruel, and contrary to the will of God and to good morals. Nor is it long till the king has leisure to repent of what he had done in wicked haste. *When the wrath of the king was appeased he remembered Vashti, and what she had done, and what was decreed against her.* And no doubt now he would have been glad to receive her back again as his wife; but his counsellors knew very well if this was done it would cost them their heads; therefore, they said, "Let there be fair young virgins sought for the king, and let the maiden that pleaseth the king be queen instead of Vashti." "And the thing pleased the king, and he did so." Esther ii: 1, 4.

In the advice here given to the king we recognize the voice of the minister Memucan. You remember his plea for divorcing Vashti was that it was necessary in order that wives should be made to honor their husbands. The object proposed was a good one. Every man's house should be his castle, and every man should be *lord* of his own castle, and his wife and children should be in subjection to him. Good order in families undoubtedly lies at the foundation of a well regulated state. But husbands should be careful not to give unreasonable commands. They ought not to verge on ground that is in itself sinful to occupy. Nothing is more revolting to a refined mind than family quarrels or domestic bickerings. Domineering on the part of either husband or wife, is contrary to true refinement and to the spirit of christianity, and to the express words of the apostles. The consequences of such insubordination are well stated by Memucan. "If," says he, "wives despise their husbands, whom they ought to reverence, and contend for dominion over them whom they ought to obey, then there will be nothing but insubordination and strife, and the higher in society the case may be, that is an example, the greater will its influence be." Though this statesman-courtier had a very difficult and dangerous post to fill—that of interfering between a man and his wife, and of helping his Sovereign to forget his sorrow for abusing one queen by taking another, yet he seems to have had courage and skill quite sufficient for his difficult task. His advice was highly politic. The plan he proposed, while it would serve to ingratiate himself into the king's favor, by counselling him to follow his own humor in having a wife, it would gratify him also in relieving his grief for the loss of the old queen by the charms of a new one. Courtier-like, he was careful to be on the winning side. His incense was to the rising sun, not to the setting. Memucan would have been a fit counsellor for Henry *the Eighth.* Josephus, however, thinks well of him, and pronounces him an honest man, and sincerely desirous of promoting the public good by securing the ends of justice, which, as a politician in such a court, was not an easy work. Josephus also says that Ahasuerus was sincerely attached to Vashti, and would most gladly have forgiven this offense, if he could have done so according to law, or consistently with his dignity as the king of so great an empire. And no doubt Memucan seeing this disposition in the king, was the more urgent for immediate measures to get a queen instead of Vashti, for her return to favor would of course imply his ruin.

The measure proposed to the king for obtaining a queen instead of Vashti, is substantially the same that is used for replenishing the Harem or seraglio, to this day. The most beautiful throughout the land are bought or selected for the Harem, without regard to nationality, or any question as to the condition of their birth, whether high or low, free or slaves.

In the East the regulation of the harems of princes and rich men are substantially the same everywhere, and have been but little, if at all changed since the days of Solomon. Even the restriction of the Koran, allowing only four wives, has not produced much change, for it places no limit to the number of concubines or secondary wives. In Solomon's harem there were seven hundred women of high birth—"princesses,"—and three hundred concubines, making, exclusive of the female slaves of his establishment, which were no doubt very numerous, one thousand wives of the first and second classes. These wives and their attendants occupied apartments of their own, seldom or never seeing each other. Solomon's establishment then must have been very large. It is no wonder he had need for the gold of Ophir, and for the spices and gums and ivory of the whole world. But even great as his establishment was, we are not altogether without parallels. It has been stated that the late emperor of China had three thousand women in his seraglio, many of whom it is probable, he never saw. The usual number in the establishment of the great Moguls of India, was reckoned at a thousand. Sultan Selim is said to have had two thousand; the Sultan Achmed three thousand, and the *Persian* king Khosroes, who died A. D. 579, according to his historian had twelve thousand females in his harem. Our Bible word *concubine,* signifies a female occupying a middle condition between wife and slave. She lawfully belonged to her owner, and could claim his protection as a secondary wife, and could not have any other husband, no more than if she were his only wife. Oriental polygamy is altogether a different thing from the free love system of our day, and bad as it is, it is not so corrupting.

The females of an Oriental seraglio may be divided into three classes: *First,* The favorites, who, without the legal rights of wives, are considered as such of the first class. If one of these becomes the mother of a son who is acknowledged as the heir to the throne, then this mother (wife) is the sultana, and the sovereign and all his other wives must own her as the queen. This is the case with the Sultan of Constantinople. For it is a part of the state policy of Turkey that the Sultan can never marry, but may keep his harem filled with women who have no political or civil rights. They all enter his seraglio as slaves, and rise only in his favor as they have children or gain influence over him. But there can never be but one sultana at a time, and issue of no other can inherit the throne. The secondary wives, or concubines, are the *second* class; and the *third* class are called *Odaliks*, or as it is in French, *Odalisques*, which I believe is a Turkish word, signifying "slaves of the household." These are the female slaves of the establishment kept for the pleasure of the prince or great man. They ai to wait their time for promotion, and although it may and does not come to most of them, yet it is possible, and does happen to one and another.

In Persia the Shah marries, and usually contracts such alliances with ladies of high family, for the purpose of strengthening his hand. It was with this view that the great Zenobia, Queen of Palmyra, designed to wed one of her daughters with the son of the terrible Sapor of Persia, that she might the better provide against the growing power and eastern conquests of imperial Rome under Aurelian. It is true, however, that the Persian sovereigns both in ancient and modern times have been restless and dissatisfied with this restraint, and that they have sometimes raised to the highest honors such as have entered their harem as slaves. It has often happened in Persia and other eastern countries that other causes as well as giving birth to an heir to the crown have raised a favorite wife to sovereignty. And perhaps there is not in any history a more striking illustration of this, and at the same time one more appropriate to our subject, than Catherine *the First* of Russia, wife of Peter the Great. She was a Livonian peasant of the humblest origin, and taken prisoner at the sacking of a town in Peter's first war with Sweden, and afterwards became his wife, and for her great services to him and the army on the Pruth, when engaged against the Turks, was crowned with great pomp at Moscow, and succeeded, on the Czar's death, to the throne of all the Russias.* And if this is credible in the history of Russia in the sixteenth century, why is not the Book of Esther credible in the history of Persia five hundred years before Christ?

Now there lived, at this time, in the royal city of Susa, that is, Shushan, a Jew of the tribe of Benjamin, of the captivity in Babylon, whose name was Mordecai, and he had an uncle's daughter, whose father and mother were dead, whom he had taken for his own daughter, and brought up with great care and kindness. She was very beautiful—*was fair of form and good of counte-*

* Catherine was crowned in the Cathedral at Moscow in 1724, by the Archbishop of Novogorod, with the most imposing ceremonies and pomp. "Peter himself clothed her in the imperial mantle, and placed the crown on her head, and when she would have fallen on her knees he raised her. Thus she who was born in obscurity, and of unknown parents, was now decorated with the ornaments of imperial power as empress, and received such honors as were never before accorded to a wife by the sovereigns of Russia. Her Majesty was so much affected that she sank at the feet of the Emperor, which she would have embraced, but he raised her and reassured her confidence." *Fowler's Lives of the Sovereigns of Russia*, 1 *vol.*, *p.* 353.

nance, as it is literally in the text. Her parents called her *Hadassah*, that is, a *myrtle*; but, when she was introduced at court, the Persians, according to our Greek authors, called her *Esther*, that is, a *star*. The second Targum says, this name was given to her from the name of the star Venus, which, in Greek, is *Aster*. The fair Simoisius of Homer, whom "great Ajax sent," so tragically, "to the shades of hell," received his name from the river Simois, on whose banks he was born. Numerous instances occur in the Bible, and it was generally if not universally the case, among eastern people, to give names to their children expressive of some remarkable accidents connected with their birth. It is most likely, therefore, as the myrtle, in Persia, is one of the most delicate and beautiful of flowers, that Hadassah's parents considered her exceedingly beautiful at birth, and gave her this name because they thought her as beautiful as the myrtle in the land of their captivity. See Iliad iv: 549.

Now it came to pass, in the collecting of maidens, according to the king's decree, that Hadassah was brought to the king's house, to the custody of Hege, chief officer of the king's harem, and she pleased him, and he showed her special favors during the time of her purification. I think the Vulgate and Josephus must be in error in calling Esther Mordecai's niece; for she was the daughter of Abihail, the uncle of Mordecai, and was, therefore, as we should say, his *cousin*. This is the Hebrew. It is true, however, that terms of relationship are used with considerable vagueness in oriental languages, and even in some modern ones. This Hege was, no doubt, as the Septuagint, Vulgate, Targum and the Syriac all say, the king's chief eunuch. It is well known that such persons only have the custody of the harems of the East. *Hege* and *Hegai* are, doubtless, only variations of the same name.

The maids of honor appointed to Esther, and the style of her entertainment, as described in the text, may be illustrated from *Knoller's* description of a bridal procession and traveling equipage of a bride in Turkey. He says he saw one that had "eleven coaches full of young maidens attended by black eunuchs, and these were followed by twenty-eight virgin slaves, attired in cloth of gold and accompanied by twenty-eight black eunuchs on horse back and richly clad. And then followed two hundred and forty mules, loaded with cloth of gold, tapestry, satin, velvet and cushions, which are the chairs of Turkish ladies."

The things for their purification were oil of myrrh and sweet odors, as we learn from chap. ii: 12th verse. The myrrh was used six months, and then the sweet odors six months — making twelve months for the trial, lest the king should be imposed upon. There may also have been something of State in keeping the damsels so long in preparation, and something educational. The Orientals are proverbially fond of oils and odors, and the profusion indicated in the text gives us some idea of the luxury and sensual magnificence of the Persian court at that time. The king's taste was fastidious. The officers of his household thought six months' perfuming with the oil of myrrh necessary to make the skin soft and smooth, and six months of sweet odors to make the body vigorous, and to give it, in a hot country, an agreeable scent. Hege was, indeed, charmed with the Hebrew maid at first sight, and before the king saw her, his chief officer had decided she should be the queen. He accordingly gave her the best apartments of the Seraglio, and special attention to prepare her for the king.

In the tenth and eleventh verses of the *second* chapter, we find that Esther did not make known her people. Mordecai had told her not to show that she was a Jewess. The reason usually given for Mordecai's command does not seem to me to be correct. This reason is, that if she avowed herself a Jewess, she would have been pronounced a slave, and thrown out of the list of competitors at once. History does not sustain this view. Slaves were eligible to the harem, and still are in the East, and from being an odalisque may become a sultana. And besides, Esther was not a slave in any other sense than were all the Hebrews that had been transferred from the Babylonian empire to the Persians as captives. The true reason no doubt was that Mordecai wished to prevent the unnecessary raising up of any prejudice to her disadvantage—that she might have at least an equal opportunity with the rest. The knowledge that she was of the Hebrew race would have been against her. It was more expedient not to put her success in peril by unnecessary disclosures as to her nation. After her crown is more firmly settled, and she has a stronger hold on the heart of the king, then it may be safer to bring to light that she belongs to a despised race. I do not, however, see here any compromise of principle, nor any prevarication. Anything of this kind would have been sinful. For an untruth is never to be uttered, either by gesture or by silence—

no more than by words; but all truths are not suitable at all times. Nor is it necessary always to tell all that we know to be true. As no question was made about her parentage, or her religion, Mordecai told Hadassah not to volunteer to make any communications on the subject. This was a very different thing from telling her to deny her race and religion. He did not command her to tell a lie. Nor did she violate any law or sin against any moral obligation by not telling these things in advance. She sanctions no fraud, for her race and religion were no bar to her entrance into the harem, if known. And when duty calls, we find her avowing that she is a Jewess, and of the faith of Abraham. As no question was raised in gathering the fair virgins for the king's harem, as to their race or religion, so there was no deception practiced. Those who find fault with our record, and with Esther for entering the king's seraglio, and becoming the queen of a heathen king, overlook altogether the customs of those times and countries. The moment she entered the king's harem, she was elected to be his wife, just as Hagar was Abraham's secondary wife. She was a captive—a subject, and the will of the king was the supreme law. And the moment she was called to the king's seraglio, she was engaged to him, and when she was taken to his bed, she was married to him, as the secondary wives of the patriarchs were to them, and when she was crowned she was queen.

It is a common saying that all marriages are made in heaven, but that some how sometimes there is a mistake in their coming down to earth. Yet the Bible does certainly teach that a good wife is from the Lord, and that the way for young people to expect happiness in wedded life is to marry in the Lord. In this case it is easily seen that the God of Abraham is engaged in providing the great king of Persia with a wife. He is not indeed to be charged with the drunken revelry of the king, nor with Vashti's haughty disobedience, nor with the rash and heavy judgment of Memucan; yet it was His hand that gave incomparable beauty to this Jewess, and it was His spirit that gave her favor in the eyes of the keeper of the women, and caused her also to obtain favor in the sight of the king.

CHAPTER VIII.

ESTHER CROWNED QUEEN.

"And the king loved Esther above all the women, and she obtained grace and favor in his sight more than all the virgins; so that he set the royal crown upon her head, and made her queen instead of Vashti. Then the king made a great feast unto all his princes and his servants, even Esther's feast."
Esther ii: 17, 18.

As Vashti lost her husband and her crown at a feast, so it is with a feast and royal behests that Esther is proclaimed to have gained a husband and a crown, the very same that Vashti lost. The king seems desirous to show the courtiers and princes of all his provinces that, as they had seen his mortification and revenge on one queen, so they should see his victory and magnificence in crowning another younger and more beautiful. And he is determined the whole empire shall rejoice on account of her coronation. "And he made a release to the provinces, and gave gifts according to the state of the king." Verse 18. In our day, sometimes an amnesty is proclaimed, prisoners are released, debts forgiven, and political offenders pardoned, in honor of the birth of a prince, or the proclamation of peace after a terrible war, or in honor of the coronation of a sovereign. In like manner did Ahasuerus honor the advancement of Esther to the royal crown with a great feast, and by the remission of tributes. It is probable that a tenth, or some considerable amount of the custom money, was allowed the queen for her household, just as in Great Britain, where it is known as the *aurum Reginæ*, the queen's gold; and that, for the purpose of making her popular, this was remitted. Pilate was wont to show the clemency of the Roman Government by releasing a prisoner unto the people at the Hebrew festival. Herodotus expressly tells us that the Persian kings were accustomed to give their wives cities and provinces for the purpose of supplying them with different articles of dress; one was assigned for ornamenting the head and neck, another for robes, girdles, etc. The city of Anthilla was bestowed on one of the queens of Persia, to supply her with sandals. The meaning of the text is, that the revenues, which had been thus used, were remitted—not collected, in order that the people might be pleased with the new queen; and the king himself *gave gifts*—supplied the *pin money*, out of his own treasury *according to the state of the king*.

According to Hebrew tradition, Mordecai had been reduced in his circumstances by the captivity, but had retained the refinement and tastes of his former more opulent condition. His house was one of the best of his class in those days, situate by the river's side, and concealed from view by a grove of cypresses. In his garden were figs, olives, pomegranates and myrtle in such culture as showed his taste and industry. Being a man of wealth at home in Judea, he was himself well educated, and highly valued the institutions and learning of his father-land. He had devoted, therefore, the leisure of his retirement to study and the training of this Hebrew maiden, the orphan daughter of his uncle. And as soon as he hears of the decree to collect all the beautiful maidens for the royal seraglio, his heart bounded with joy. For he felt sure none were more charming than his lovely maid. Accordingly he flew with haste to her apartments to open up the subject. As he came near, offering many ejaculatory thanks and prayers from his heart, he heard Hadassah singing a mournful song from Jeremiah, and making her harp tell forth the sorrows and wrongs of her country. But when he entered he exclaimed, "cease my child, Israel is to be redeemed. The Lord will delight again in Judah." The glow on her cousin's face showed his joyous excitement. And as he relates what has taken place at the palace, and what is now to be done for a new queen, the sagacity of her sex penetrates, at a glance, all his ambitious hopes, and she sank down on the divan as a delicate flower faded from its rich color. And not until her wise kinsman has succeeded in persuading her that it is of the Lord, and that it is her duty to him and to her countrymen, and to Jehovah, does she consent to enter the list of candidates for the Persian crown. It was in answer to her kinsman's earnest appeal, somewhat after this style, that she yielded, "The God of our father," said he, "has chosen you as an instrument for the salvation of thy people. A Hebrew maiden on the Persian throne, and the horn of Judah is once more exalted. Jehovah calls thee, Hadassah, like Deborah, and like Judith thou shalt stand forth in our holy records as the Saviour of our people and our faith."*

The day she left her uncle's house for the king's harem was a trying hour. The last beral was spent in furnishing her with as becoming a wardrobe as possible. Her robes were flowing and graceful, as only an eastern maiden can show; "her dark hair confined with a lustrous band of diamonds, her large soft eyes full of thought, and her whole figure expressive of majesty of soul mingled with sweet gentleness." In the same harem were the beauties of Circassia and of Georgia, and of

"The isles of Greece! the isles of Greece
Where burning Sappho loved and sung."

Here were the bright-eyed houris from the hanging gardens of the Indus, and from the shores of the Caspian, and from Ethiopia, and from "Araby the blest;" all radiant with the smiles of hope. But the peerless beauty of the Hebrew maiden takes the eunuch by surprise. He at once shows her particular favor, and this was a prelude to her complete success. No doubt there was great emulation among the damsels of Persia who thought themselves, or whose friends thought them, fair enough to please the king. Every one hoped to become a queen. But "the king loved Esther above all the women; so that he set the royal crown upon her head, and made her queen instead of Vashti."

When Esther became queen, *then Mordecai sat in the king's gate.* That is, he was advanced to some kind of service—perhaps a kind of sub-porter of the

* This part of our story was beautifully told in the GLEANER of this city, by Rev. Dr. Eckman, of last year.

palace; and here, though faithful to his Hebrew faith, we find him diligent in business and remarkable for his fidelity to the king. True piety never interferes with a man's loyalty to his government. On the contrary, he is the truest friend to man who is the most faithful to his God. The fear of God and proper regard for our fellow men are always consistent. It happened, then, just as we should have expected, for as soon as Mordecai detected the conspiracy of the two chamberlains against the king's life, he informs Esther of it, and the king is saved. The best defence of a prince is the fidelity of his attendants. Standing armies, and life guards, and palace walls, and subterranean passage-ways from barracks to barracks, are no sure reliance. Nor does the chapter of rebellion, assassination, dethronement and exile, belong to any one age or nation. Russia and France up to the present moment are equal in such details to any of the older Oriental despotisms. No greatness, no care, no apparent popularity, is a perfect security against treachery or violence. The absolute king over millions, from India to Ethiopia, was not secure from the traitor's hand.

The story of this conspiracy against the king is briefly told: "In those days, while Mordecai sat in the king's gate, two of the king's chamberlains, Bigthan and Teresh, of those which kept the door, were wroth, and sought to lay hands on the king Ahasuerus. And the thing was known to Mordecai, who told it unto Esther the queen; and Esther certified the king thereof in Mordecai's name. And when inquisition was made of the matter it was found out; therefore they were both hanged on a tree: and it was written in the book of the chronicles before the king." Esth. ii: 21, 23. This account is confirmed by Josephus in every essential particular. He says the discovery was made by a Jew, who overheard the plot, and that he told Mordecai, and he told Esther, and Esther told the king in Mordecai's name; so that Mordecai's name was registered in the Chronicles as the discoverer of the conspiracy.

The Hebrew story of this conspiracy is that the haughty Vashti relented, and greatly desired to regain her crown and the king's favor, for that she tenderly loved him. And that this conspiracy was primarily intended to destroy Esther, by accusing her to the king, and charging her as its head, and that when she should be disgraced, then Haman who was in power, and who it is said was Vashti's brother, was to force the king to receive Vashti again, or if he refused, to kill the king, and assume the crown himself. It is easy to suppose at least that the anguish of the fallen queen must have been intense, and that she indulged the bitterest enmity toward her happy successor. Nor would it be surprising if she did attempt to regain her crown by intrigue and violence. From the subsequent developments of Haman's character, we are prepared to think that he was at the bottom of this conspiracy. The attempt on the king's life by his chamberlain, is no new event in the history of the East. The cause is not stated, but most probably they were creatures of Haman, who thought to make himself king by having Ahasuerus slain. The Targum says that they thought that Queen Esther was about to have them removed, and Mordecai put in their place; and that on this account, they intended to poison her and kill the king in his bed-chamber. And then with Haman on the throne they would have the first honors and greatest emoluments of the empire. How true it is, that

"Uneasy lies the head that wears a crown."

Happy, immeasurably happy, he, who though poor in this world, is rich toward God—an heir to a crown incorruptible, undefiled, and that fadeth not away, reserved in heaven, where neither treason, nor violence can reach it, nor shall any creature prevent the Lord, the righteous judge, from placing it on his head on the day of the revelation of the Lord Jesus.

Oriental princes in particular, carry their lives in their hands. Not a few of those who have been a terror in the land of the living have gone down to the pit slain. Bloody minded and deceitful men do not live out half their days. And not unfrequently the very moment they fancy themselves secure, they are surprised with sudden destruction. Treachery is a kind of murder that will out. Some bird of the air carries the voice, or some stone out of the wall whispers of the plot. Somewhere something miscarries, or some link in the long crooked chain breaks, or the friction causes the machinery to work so hard, that suspicion is awakened and conviction secured.

The traitors were hanged, but not by a mob. The king had *inquisition made of the matter.* Due investigation was made, their guilt was fully proven, according to law, and the history entered in the Chronicles of the king, with the particular record, that the name of the king's servant who had saved his life was Mordecai. The mode of the execution of these traitors, after lawful conviction, is not mentioned, but it is remarkable how law-abiding the king and court were. They knew nothing of the convenience of Judge Lynch's court. The words, *they were both hanged on a tree,* may mean, either that they were *hung* to a gallows of wood, or that they were *impaled,* that is, placed on the sharp point of a stake, set upright in the ground. This is a most dreadful kind of punishment. The sharp stake is forced through the length of the body, by pulling the legs down with great force. Sometimes the poor victim lives a considerable time, but, of course, in the greatest agony.

There is another incident connected with Mordecai that shows us something of the man's heart, while, at the same time, it proves the truthfulness of our history. *Every day* he walked *before the court of the women's house,* to know how Esther did, and what should become of her. This was while she was undergoing her preparation to come before the king. And it was natural for him, as he loved her as his own child, to feel anxious for her welfare, and as the apartments of the women were deemed so sacred, so inviolable, that it was a great crime even to inquire what was doing within them—so he lingered as near as it was lawful, to pick up whatever intelligence might be available of the condition and prospects of his beloved Hadassah. Chardin says, expressly, " A man may walk a hundred days, one after the other, by the houses where the women are, and yet know no more what is done there than at the farthest end of Tartary."

1. It were well for us to consider here what a model

girl we have found under the humble roof of Mordecai's house, in the land of their captivity. *The Hebrew maid in the royal Harem, in seeking to please the king, is a model for all who seek to advance rapidly in the world.* Kind, respectful, obedient to her foster-father, unostentatiously attentive to her private devotions, as a follower of the true religion, and, at the same time, careful not to neglect the preparations fit to be made for her coming before the king. There was no love of extravagance about her. She follows the wish of the chief chamberlain, and gives him as little trouble as possible, and grows every day in his esteem. And, for one in her situation, this was a great point gained. Her modesty and good sense make Hege's experience of great avail to her. Extravagance is not only a wicked use of God's bounty, but it is the sign of a little and trifling mind. But a proper regard for dress and the decencies of good society is commendable, and according to the Gospel. Extravagance is not only sinful, but is seldom successful. Modesty, virtue, amiableness of temper and true piety are the greatest charms in woman.

"It is the artless who catch the game."

2. *We see the effects of a good education.* Esther on the throne is still obedient to Mordecai. The precepts she has learned in her cousin's humble home she remembers at the great court. As queen, with the royal crown on her head, she is what Mordecai has made her. Hadassah—myrtle—let her be called forever, for in the court of the great king she does not forget the guide of her youth. The purple circlet on

her brow does not cause her to be ashamed of her poor kindred, nor to forget the commandments of the friend of her youth. She does still his commandments, *like as when she was brought up with him.*

We are not to suppose that in all this wonderful history there is anything like chance, or what people call mere luck. The agents were all free, but they were all hard workers. If Mordecai is tender and faithful, liberal and kind, his orphan ward was obedient, teachable and diligent. She reverenced him as a father, and with the crown on her head as Sultana of all Persia, she "did his commandments like as when she was brought up with him." Nor could the circumstances of her youth be considered as favorable. She was surrounded by idolaters—she was in danger of being led astray by evil associations, for as

> " Oft converse with heavenly habitants
> Hath cast a beam on the outward shape—
> The unpolluted temple of mind—
> And turned it by degrees to the soul's essence;"

so do evil associates destroy the soul.

A grateful remembrance by one in great authority of those that were his benefactors in the days of his obscurity, is always pleasing and worthy of praise. Accordingly we see Esther's nobility of mind in not being too much elated in her prosperity. Like Joseph, no court pomp could make her forget her poor kin and truest friends. There is always something hopeful in dutiful children. Reverence for the aged and the good argues an appreciation of excellence that we may hope will lead to a matured imitation. It was God's plan to make Esther's influence affect the fate of nations, and save his chosen people from the sword; but of all this she was ignorant in her early years. How, then, was she prepared for her mission? By first attending to the duties of her station as an orphan girl that was cared for by an excellent kinsman. David, by his fidelity to his flock of sheep as Jesse's shepherd son, leading them over the hills of Judea, and finding out the best pasture for them, and watching over them at night, was preparing himself for the throne of Israel. Act well your part in the lot God has given you, or you will never be prepared for a higher one.

Nor are you to suppose that Esther as an orphan girl had no sad moments—no fears, no misgivings about her success in life. She was not at any time filled with a prophetic spirit, nor endowed with power to work miracles. She was in her youth just like any other affectionate, well-behaved Hebrew maiden. Her days of trial she had to meet just as my fair young readers will have to meet theirs. The day she left her quiet home for the harem was a day she never forgot. And then how critical, how painfully trying, the day when she is to be introduced to the great king. But happily does she pass the ordeal. God so blesses her endeavors that she gains the favor of all who look upon her. She seemed to be a singular combination of all that was beautiful with all that was maidenly and becoming, so that when she passed from the hands of the chief officer of the harem to the royal presence, she beamed upon the king in all the brilliancy and softness of the evening star, and he at once said "This maiden shall be my queen, and Esther shall be her name."

"The soul that rises in us, our life's star,
Has had elsewhere its setting,
And cometh from afar.——
Heaven lies about us in our infancy."

3. In the discovery of the conspiracy and the entering on the records of the empire an account of Mordecai's distinguished services in saving the king's life, a good foundation is laid for Mordecai's advancement. Esther at least, is able now to prove that he whom she has appointed into the king's service is a man to be trusted. But there is no impatience—no over hastening in his case. There is no complaint that his remuneration is delayed. O that we could always *feel* that God's time is the best time—that patient waiting on the Lord is no delay. God's leisure is always most opportune. Mordecai's hour is set on the eternal dial. It is sure to come, and the intervening dangers and apparent drawbacks shall only make his honors the greater, and his experience of the loving kindness of the God of Jacob all the more precious. Young man from home—in a strange land—often have you been disappointed—often thought the golden prize within your grasp, but it escaped you—amid your long deferred hopes, remember Mordecai. He was for the moment apparently overlooked. But his reward came. Impatient young man—you think you rise to fame too slow. Your steps upward in your profession do not satisfy you, and yet you may be rising faster than you think, and much more surely than you could do in any other way. Think not of how you shall become great, but only of how you may do your duty in your place, whatever it is, in the most thorough and perfect manner.

Wellington in his campaigns did not stop to write letters proclaiming his heroism, nor of his becoming great; but only of giving the French a sound drubbing, and his greatness came of itself. *Impatient*, are you of doing your work and to make your mark in the world? Remember *Havelock*—young soldier—remember Havelock—"every inch," as Lord Hardinge said, "every inch a soldier, and every inch a christian." Toiling on fifty years, almost all of them spent under India's burning sun, panting for his work to do, and blanched and weary; yet the work Providence had assigned him came at last. He did it and died—nobly did it, and his soul sped its way to his God, and in every English home there is sorrow as for a father dead.

4. *God often cares for his people, when and in ways and means that they know not of.* Several steps, important steps, are here taken for the deliverance of the Hebrews in Persia from a danger that was near at hand and most imminent, but, as yet, not developed. The way is prepared to raise them up a friend, when they shall most need one, though, as yet, they know nothing of the danger, and such a friend as they should most need—the only one, speaking after the manner of men, that could really serve them effectively.

Speaking with reverence, history shows that God's plan is often out of our sight, but never out of his mind. An irreversible decree has gone forth, from the palace of Shushan, throughout the vast empire, that Vashti is no longer queen, and that every man must rule his own house, and may divorce his wife for disobedience, without regard to his tyranny or foolishness in giving his commandments. But whether this decree serves the king's passion, or Memucan's deeper policy, it is God's plan for bringing to the Persian throne a queen after his own heart, for the deliverance of the seed of Jacob. Haman, in his rage against the children of God's friend, Abraham, has not yet appeared on the stage; but in the *tableau* already exhibited, the sequel will show we have the means of his overthrow, and means, also, for the complete defeat of his murderous plot. The great king has peace and plenty, and considers himself established on his throne, and, for this reason, he prepares a most extraordinary feast. This feast gratifies his vanity and whets the appetite of his court and army for new conquests—but especially would he show his greatest gem, his beautiful queen; but she is disobedient, and, in his rage, she is divorced, and no law of the Medes and Persians can be repealed. The king, therefore, must have another queen, and the plan to obtain one is suggested by his ministry, who have their own schemes to advance, but, nevertheless, the plan introduces Hadassah, and the conspiracy against the king's life, that took place about the same time, serves to make a valuable record of her cousin's great services to the king. Here is a wonderfully numerous band working together, and every one—the conspirators shall I call them?—fulfilling his part, exactly at the right time. The great king, Ahasuerus, and the ravishingly beautiful queen Vashti; Memucan and his ghostly council of astrologers—the traitorous eunuchs and privy council—Mordecai and his lovely cousin: Her marriage and coronation, followed by Mordecai's fidelity in saving the king from death, and the queen the agent of communicating this to the king, and of having his name duly entered on the court journals as the deliverer of the king; but, as yet, though contrary to custom, no reward is bestowed, but that, however, is because Providence has a greater one in reserve than would now be given.

What an array have we here of lust and passion, of cross purposes—a variety of selfish views and schemes and passions; and yet God is working over and through, and by all, with a steady and fixed purpose to save his people, His Church. Promotion cometh neither from the east nor from the west; but from the Lord. He raiseth up one and casteth down another. There are indeed many devices in man's heart, *but the counsel of the Lord, it shall stand.*

5. Remember, my fair young readers, of this history of the model Hebrew maid and peerless queen, that you may all wear a crown more precious than ever adorned a Persian throne. Though each of the fair virgins gathered into the king's seraglio, hoped to become a queen, only one could succeed to that honor. But you may all gain the heavenly prize. O that you were all as ambitious of your espousals to the king of glory. What time! what quantity of myrrhs and sweet odors were consumed in preparing Esther for the king! How much more diligent and pains-taking should we be to secure a preparation for the presence of the glorious Majesty of heaven! But how can this be done? "Wherewith shall I come before the LORD, and bow myself before the high God? Shall I come before him with burnt offerings, with calves of a year old? Will the LORD be pleased with thousands of rams, or with

ten thousands of rivers of oil? Shall I give my first-born for my transgression, the fruit of my body for the sin of my soul?" Micah vi: 6, 8. How can man be just in the sight of God? If I wash myself with snow water, and make my hands never so clean, yet shall thou plunge me in the ditch, and my own clothes shall abhor me: For He is not a man, as I am, that I should answer him, and we should come together in judgment. Neither is there any days—man betwixt us, that might lay his hand upon us both. Job ix: 30, 33. After all the cleansing oils of our own tears and repentance, and the sweet odors of our own good works, we are altogether unholy and vile in the sight of God. It is only by free grace that we are saved. It is from Jesus Christ alone we can obtain the wedding garment. He is mighty to save.

And why, brethren, should we be afraid to die? Why should we live so much in dread of the grave? It is like Esther's baths of sweet perfumes, in which she lay for a time purifying herself with spices, that she might be reckoned fit to come before her lord the king. So in the grave our body is prepared to be rebuilt for our heavenly home. Earth and worms do but refine and purify our flesh, since our Lord himself past through the same way to glory, and left an enduring perfume there to animate the bodies of all his saints. "He is the resurrection and the life, whosoever believeth in Him though he were dead, yet shall he live."

CHAPTER IX.

THE JEW AND THE AMALEKITE.

"And when Haman saw that Mordecai bowed not, nor did him reverence, then was Haman full of wrath."
Esth. iii: 5.

"Happy the man who sees a God employ'd
In all the good and ill that chequer life;
Resolving all events, with their effects
And manifold results, into the will
And arbitration wise of the Supreme."
Cowper.

THERE is no explanation given in the text how it came to pass that the Hebrew maid found such favor in the sight of Hege, nor how it was that she so greatly pleased the king. But so it was, that the king loved her exceedingly, and she was married to him, and she became, by the will of the God of Abraham, SULTANA of the Persian throne.

But a new character is now introduced to us. "After these things did Ahasuerus promote Haman, the son of Hammedatha the Agagite." Esth. iii: 1.

Agagite, perhaps, descended from Agag, king of the Amalekites, who was spared by Saul but killed by Samuel; and it may be that his prejudices against the

Jews were hereditary. Agag was probably a common name for the kings of Amalek, as Abimelech was among the Philistines, and Pharaoh among the Egyptians. The meaning then, is, that Haman was descended from a kingly line—*atavis editus regibus*—and it is no wonder, therefore, that he had bad blood in him, for even in royal races the black drop of original sin which, according to Mohammedan theologians, and which even according to our orthodox catechisms, is in all men by nature, has been known to grow to an enormous size, and spread through the whole system. Haman's history proves that he was a worthy son of such sires. His inauguration as *Grand Vizier* did not, therefore, forbode any good to the Jews.

The events of the *third* chapter of Esther seem to have occurred about five years after the king's marriage with the Hebrew maid. The cause of Haman's promotion is not stated. His power, however, was very great. *His seat was above all the princes that were with him.* And the king's *servants*, that is, the officers of the court, as well as the porters or keepers of the gate, among whom was Mordecai, all *bowed and reverenced Haman*, except Mordecai; *but Mordecai bowed not, nor did him reverence.* Was this mere obstinacy? Was it insubordination, or was it required of him by his religion? It seems probable from the language used, and from the fact that the Persian kings sometimes exacted divine honors from their subjects, that something more than *civil reverence* or homage was demanded by Haman and refused by Mordecai. The usual word for mere civil respect is "kara," *to bow.* Mere politeness and official position required this from Mordecai, and this much Hebrew law enjoined. But Mordecai did not bow—lo yikara, *nor did he do him reverence:* velo yish tachaveh, *nor did he prostrate himself.*

The monumental history of the Nile and of the Euphrates and Tigris, abound with proof that Eastern kings received honors and homage as gods. How, then, could Mordecai, a Jew, with the laws of Moses before him, (Exod. xx, xvii: 14; Deut. xxv: 19,) and in the light of the history of his people, with a good conscience, render divine homage to a human being, and especially to a wicked man, and still more to an Amalekite, one of the race devoted to destruction? You remember the Hebrews had been expressly commanded to blot out this nation from under heaven, "as a thing accursed." That such was the ground of Mordecai's refusal, is clearly to be inferred from the *fourth* verse, where, when his fellow servants were urgent upon him to comply with the king's command, and, like them, do reverence to Haman, *he told them he was a Jew.* It was not, then, from a mere personal whim, prejudice, or freak of feeling, but from an all-powerful religious conviction that he acted. We have the same thing in Daniel, where the offense for which he was cast into the lion's den was his refusing to cease praying to the God of his fathers. In this instance, we find a good man obliged to differ from the majority of his companions and fellow officers. All the rest of the king's officers were exceedingly obsequious to the new favorite; but Mordecai, adhering to his principles with a bold and daring resolution, did not bow to him, nor do him homage. Among commentators there is some difference of opinion about Mordecai's conduct. Some praise and some condemn him. But, as I understand the history, Mordecai did right, and showed himself to be a man of true courage and heroic piety. The homage required was something more than the usual reverence or respect for a prime minister. The usual form of etiquette was well established and widely known. A royal decree, therefore, could hardly have been required to make it known to the servants of the palace, which was done in this instance — "for the king had so commanded concerning him." And, as we have just seen, the Hebrew intimates that the reverence here commanded was of an idolatrous kind. The divine adoration which the Persian monarchs received is, in fact, expressed by the very word here used for doing reverence: "Shachah" signifies *prostration*, such as is practiced in rendering the profoundest reverence that a man can pay to God, namely, "by lying down flat on the ground with the hands and feet extended, and with the mouth in the dust." This, then, was the kind of reverence that Mordecai refused to render to Haman, the Agagite Persian premier, and, in refusing this homage, we find him adhering to his religion. *He followed principle, not expediency.* His conduct resembles that of Joseph and Moses and Daniel and the three Hebrews in Babylon. They all remembered their catechism, which taught them to fear God, and not dare to sin against Him, by departing from principle on the plea of policy or expediency. According to Hebrew tradition and the Targum, Haman had set up a statue of himself, which every one that passed by was obliged to worship. The apocryphal additions to the Book of Esther, which, though not inspired nor of canonical authority, are, nevertheless, of some value as ancient fragments, embodying the ideas of remote times, inform us that Mordecai said, in his subsequent prayers to Jehovah: "Thou knowest that if I have not adored Haman, it was not through pride, nor contempt, nor secret desire of glory; for I felt disposed to kiss the footsteps of his feet gladly for the salvation of Israel; but I feared to give to a man that honor which I know belongs only to my God." Mordecai's principles and conduct were followed by the apostles, when they laid down and acted upon the fundamental principle of liberty, *that we must obey God rather than man.* The great and learned Olshausen, in his commentary on this text in Acts, has well said, that though "many enthusiasts and rebels have misapplied this principle to the defense of their insane or mischievous undertakings, * * * yet the highest freedom of a Christian maintains no conflict at all with his unqualified obedience to the civil government, even though it be an unrighteous one. He moves, in fact, with his old and new man, as it were, in a *two-fold world.* In the one character, he is placed in subjection to earthly relations, and, therefore, willingly gives to Cæsar what is Cæsar's; but, in the other, he is a member of the spiritual world, and, therefore, gives to God what is God's." The true doctrine, without question, is, that a Christian must obey the civil magistrate, except when obedience to him is clearly a sin against God. True piety is not rude. It is not built upon the ruins of good manners, nor of refined civilization; but it does teach us to govern ourselves by principles—principles taught by the Word of God and approved by our conscience, enlightened by his Word and Spirit. The Gospel, also, teaches us, both by precepts and examples, to be steadfast, unyielding, even unto death, in the profession and maintenance of truth.

As we shall hear of this old Hebrew again, let us take a good look at him, as we pass by the gate this evening. I could wish you would closely observe him, so that you may know him when you meet him again. He is not only a man of principle, but in his vindication of himself, he shows that he is not criminally indifferent to the good opinions of others—that he is not influenced by a mere fancy or whim, but is governed by a strong sense of duty. Will you observe him sitting at the king's gate, thinking of the past, and wondering how the great future, of which he had some undefined, almost unconscious prophesyings within, was to be developed. His piety and faith were of a simple, earnest kind. Though he did not see *how*, yet he was perfectly sure, salvation was for the Jews. And then his mind wanders to the palace, and he wonders how the new sultana wears her honors, and then he sternly questions his own heart, "Did I take sufficient pains, and use all the means to establish her youthful heart in the principles of our holy religion? Did I do all my duty to her, and will she be faithful to the God of Jacob, amid the splendor of this great heathen court? Does she ever think of me, and remember that, under God, she owes her education and crown to me? My post is now an humble one, but I am content with it. It is best; but, oh, that salvation were come for Zion, that Judah's horn were again exalted." His pious meditations would, doubtless, have continued much longer, but here comes the newly raised favorite of the king, ruffling past in great pomp, "and," as bishop Hall says, "when the sun shines upon the dial, every passenger will be looking at it; there needed no command of reverence, where Ahasuerus was pleased to countenance. All his subjects are willingly prostrate before this great minion of their sovereign, only Mordecai stands stiff, as if he saw nothing more than a man in that Agagite."

But yonder come his fellow servants of the palace; what have they to say? Why they say to him, *why transgressest thou the king's commandment?* And verily, aged man, why? Is it that all eyes may be turned upon you? It is true, indeed, that he is the observed of all observers, who does not go with the multitude, even though they go to do evil. Any one that dares to think and speak for himself is sure to be condemned by the many that he differs from; for his position and principles are a running commentary of condemnation upon them. It has ever been so, and perhaps it will always continue to be so; for it is not for the man that lives in the cellar to say what he sees who dwells on the house-top. Some men are before their times, and some men never catch up with the age in which they live; and some men have not moral courage enough to hear themselves breathe honestly and freely. We see this daily as to the press and the pulpit. Is not the daily bread of the printer put in jeopardy if his journal does not meet the popular taste? And have we not seen large bodies of business men combine to starve newspapers to death by withholding their patronage, unless the said papers would defend their conduct? And is it not true that if one pulpit has the courage to utter an honest opinion that does not happen to coincide with the rest of the pulpits, that then all the pulpits and papers that have neither capacity to understand nor the moral honesty to comprehend the poor dissenter, open their batteries upon him? Such proscription is tyranny, and it is a species of tyranny from which we are not yet emancipated. The tyranny of fanaticism and the cruelty of a vicious public sentiment are evils prevailing in our day, which every patriot must see and deplore.

And again his fellow-servants say: Friend Mordecai, consider well what you are going to do. Remember, it is not Haman merely, but his master, also, that you offend. Is it wise, then, for you to peril the forfeiture of your place and your life, upon a question of mere etiquette or courtesy? It is extremely impolitic and dangerous for you not to do homage to so great a prince. And besides, if you will not bow with us, then you will have to suffer alone. "Yes, friends," says he, "I have considered all this; and I am content to meet the consequences. It is not a mere question of courtesy. *I am a Jew.* My religion is, with me, a glorious reality. It forbids me to render divine honors to any human being, or to any creature. I must abide by my principles." And now, seeing they cannot change his purpose, his disobedience is construed into a malicious obstinacy; and his monitors fancy that they have been treated with contempt. It is usual for those who do not succeed in reforming or changing the opinions of others, to become their enemies. Even in giving a reproof, a friend is gained or lost. If the reproof is received, a friend is saved, but if it is spurned, a terrible enemy is made. As John the Baptist did not succeed in reforming Herod, his head was the price of his fidelity. So here, Mordecai's monitors feel slighted, and begin to hate the man whose courage they could not make quail—they, therefore, pick a quarrel with him, and as a revenge for his refusing to pronounce their shibboleth, they turn informers against him, and tell Haman how proud and stubborn the old Jew in the gate sat as he passed by. And so, the next time he comes along, he watches the Jew, and so do they, *to see whether Mordecai's matters would stand*—that is, whether he had courage to remain steadfast, and if he did, whether Haman would not strike off his head. Possibly, also, it was the habit of the Persian kings to excuse their Hebrew subjects from such acts of obeisance as they could not conscientiously render, and they wished to see now who was to prevail, the prime minister or the Jew. From the history before us, and also from that of Daniel, it seems probable that it was only when some special decrees were made for the benefit of some malicious or revengeful courtier, that the Jews were molested in their religion.

Mordecai's fellow-servants were not capable of understanding his principles. Cowards never apprehend the true character of a brave man. Little minds cannot see up into the magnanimity of a great and noble soul.

But it was not long till this proud Amalekite, with more pomp than usual, snuffing up the air as he walked, comes along by the gate, saying: "I'll see, myself, the man that refuses homage to the greatest prince of Persia." Aye, and so you shall, proud son of Hammedatha. You shall see him, and you will find him as inflexible as the marble statues and granite sphinxes that guard the city gate. Your eyes shall sparkle with fury as you see him sit quietly, without paying you the slightest homage. Nor will he even open his lips to you. He utters no threats, nor does he even show a frown; but his joints are not supple enough to bow. You may possibly break them, but you cannot make them bow to the dust before you. Death on the rack, or in any form your rage may inflict, is more easy to him than the bending of his old knees, that have never learned to bow, except to JEHOVAH alone.

1. But how does it come that we find a man of such integrity and strength of character, and loftiness of principle, here in Persia, a captive far from the home of his fathers? It comes in a very philosophic way. Mordecai is what his education has made him—Mordecai is the concrete word for all the influences that have been operating on him from his birth to this moment. And among these we are, doubtless, to find the teachings and example of his parents in the home of his youth, amid the hills of Judea. Parents—*especially the mother, moulds the man.* Mothers are more constantly with their children when they are young. They have their attention when their affections are first developing, and their intellects are beginning to expand. They have it then in their power to sow the precious seed, which it is almost impossible wholly to eradicate in after life. The whole world is an illustration of the influence of parental example, and yet the

tendency of our times to substitute the teaching of schools and the lessons of society for the teaching and lessons of the parents' lips and lives. Our public schools, and Sunday schools, are great blessings, if properly employed; but in just so far as they have caused parental oversight to be relaxed, and family government and family instruction to be diminished, in just so far they have done harm. The influence of parental example cannot be wholly destroyed; but there should be no substitute for it. *Our schools should be parental helps, not substitutes, and especially must the parent retain in his own hands the religious instruction of his children.* God has intended the parent to be the child's first instructor, and first priest. For months, after birth, the child gazes with an uncertain bewildered look on whatever objects are within its horizon. Its education has begun. And these surrounding objects, from which it takes lessons as fast as it can see, should be beautiful, well formed, and pure in all their associations and powers to produce suggestions as remembered in after life. The pictures, furniture and window views, landscapes, and all that comes within the child's vision, should be refined and in good taste. But the next stage of its education is imitation—catching and repeating the tones of voice, or the personal habits of those that surround it, or of the names of things it hears; and, in most cases, before the parents are aware of it, the child has adopted their principles of conduct, and imbibed the spirit that reigned in their hearts. Happy then if the child has detected no inconsistency between the teaching and the example of the parents! Happy is it if the principles adopted, and the disposition *absorbed* shall, I say, have been such as are according to truth and righteousness, for they are to be firm and enduring. They will grow with his growth, and when every thing else learned in after life shall fade away, and be forgotten, they will spring up in renewed power, and strengthen the soul for its last effort in leaving the body. It is in our earliest years the soul receives its coloring and shape for eternity.

2. In Mordecai's adherence to his religious principles we see that there are limits to the claims of social and official civility — bounds that duty does not allow us to pass in our respect for our superiors. True religion has much to do with our every day life, and its tendency is always to elevate and refine our social relations, and make us more conscientious and faithful in our duties to the State. An enlightened Scriptural fear of God always implies a proper regard for the rights and welfare of our fellow men. It is fanaticism, and not Christianity — it is bigotry, and not the Gospel, that persecutes men for their opinions. Our Constitution and laws guarantee, not toleration, but absolute, impartial, perfect religious freedom. And so does the Gospel.

Mordecai was bound to adhere to his principles, or be a traitor to his God. Accordingly, we find him taking heed to his conscience, and see, also, at the same time, that his conscience is an enlightened and educated one. He has carefully studied the laws of God. I do not, however, understand it to be a part of Christian politeness to flatter or lie, in paying compliments to the great. It cannot be a Christian's duty to violate his conscience for the sake of court etiquette. The Word of God is the standard of respectability and manners as well as of faith, and it forbids all lying and deceit, all flattery and all mean compliances with the wishes of others, however exalted. It does not allow us to do anything that is contrary to good breeding and the chivalry of right. It does not allow us to neglect our duties, waste our time or injure our health, merely to please a friend or a potentate. Let it be remembered, to the honor of one of the Presidents of the United States, (General Jackson, to whom I preached, as pastor of the Hermitage Church, for several years,) that he never allowed any visitors to keep him from the house of God on the Lord's day. He kept an open house, and was visited by many from all parts of America, and by not a few distinguished foreigners. The hospitality of his mansion was dispensed with a grace and dignity peculiar to one of the Almighty's true noblemen. It was his custom, when his house was full of visitors, when the hour for going to divine service arrived, to say, "Ladies and gentlemen, it is my habit to go to church. If you will accompany me, I shall be glad. Horses and the carriage are at your service. But if you prefer not to go, the library is open to you, where you will please entertain yourselves until I return." It is useless to say that his visitors generally went with him to worship God, and that, whether they believed in his religion or not, they respected him the more for his consistency and manliness of character. Nor does it require a single illustration to show that this was the way of true politeness. It was my happiness to know General Jackson intimately—to see him often in perplexing circumstances, and to know much of him as he was in his chamber and in his most unguarded and secluded moments—and I do not believe there ever lived a more pure-minded man, or a man of more ardent patriotism, or one that possessed greater attachment to high principles. He was the most incorruptible of men. And, in his last years, I have no doubt he was sincerely pious. The divinity of Christ, the inspiration of the Scriptures, and the realities of a future state, were, with him, always articles of faith that did not admit of debate. It was displeasing to him for a minister to condescend to argue such points.

CHAPTER X.

HAMAN'S REVENGEFUL PLOT.

"If weakness may excuse,
What murderer, what traitor, parricide,
Incestuous, sacriligious, but may plead it?
All wickedness is weakness."
Milton.

"Pish, fool! thou blunder'st through the book of guilt,
Spelling thy villany."
Coleridge.

WE are now introduced to Haman meditating revenge, not on Mordecai only, but on all of his race. *He was full of wrath, and he thought scorn to lay hands on Mordecai alone.* Customs and circumstances change; the occasions of the development of human depravity are varied; but, in all ages, the opposition of the human heart to God has always found ways to show itself. According to the Bible, and to experience, moral evil belongs to us, in our present degenerate state, as truly as any one of our animal appetites, or intellectual powers. It is comparatively a minor point as to how it comes. It is a fact, that you can as easily find a man without the appetite of hunger, or without memory or understanding, as you can find an unregenerate man without an unvarying propensity to sin. The occasions for the development of Pharaoh's hardness of heart were altogether different from those that surrounded Solomon when his heart departed from the fear of the Lord. The point of trial with Joseph was altogether different from that of Daniel; but both were sorely tried, and both conquered. And if, in Nebuchadnezzar's court, it was a great crime not to worship a golden image, it was not a less offense, in the Persian court, to pray with open windows toward Jerusalem, or, in Ahasuerus' court, to refuse to render homage to his minister of State.

Haman's proposition, which please read in Esther iii: 8, 15, contained truth enough to make it plausible, and error enough to make it cruel, and enough personally agreeable to the king to make it popular with him. It was true that the Jews were dispersed among the people, in all the provinces of the Persian empire, and in this scattering abroad was fulfilled the divine threatening contained in their own holy books, from Moses to Jeremiah, that such a calamity should befal them, if they did not keep their covenant with JEHOVAH. And it was true that *their laws were diverse from* those of all other people. They were the only true *theists* on earth. All other nations were *polytheists* and *idolaters*. Nor was any other nation under the same kind of political rule, nor governed by the LORD in the same way.

But observe the cunning malice of his address to the king. He does not say, there is an old Jew that has offended me, and, through me, offered an affront to your sacred majesty; therefore, let me execute vengeance upon him. No, not a word of this sort. He feared to show his real character for rancour to the king, or courtiers. He professes to have no personal motives, but to be moved altogether by a desire for the public good. There is "a people scattered," says he, as if they were of no consequence to the king's empire. They have no fixed home. *Scattered abroad, and dispersed,* say you, you son of Amalek? It is true; but is their dispersion their fault, or their misfortune? Their fathers sinned, and for their sins their God had sent the Assyrians and Chaldeans to chastise them, by laying waste their country and cities, and carrying them away captives. Are the children to be responsible for the sins of their parents and ancestors? A *certain people*—as if he meant to say, nobody knows who they are—whence they came—a fugitive, vagabond, Gipsy race—a curse to the kingdom. It was thus, under false and malicious representations, by false pleas, that he obtained his murderous decree. But if he scrupled not to kill them, it is not strange that he considered it no sin to tell lies on them, though slander is the worst kind of murder.

But Haman's scorn is exceedingly haughty. His anger is so fierce and excessive that he says within himself, "It is not enough to take the blood of Mordecai. This were a mere vulgar, plebeian revenge for such a lord as I. My fury shall fly higher. His whole nation shall perish for this insult. The blood of all the Jews is not more than enough to blot it out." And as all the Hebrews then in the world were probably within the limits of the Persian empire, it seemed to be within his power to hold all their heads in one hand, while with the other he might, by one stroke, cut all their throats. He was of the Nero school, who is said to have wished that all the Christians had but one neck, that by a single blow he might make an end of them. In his rage, it was nothing to Haman that the punishment is to far outrun the offense—that thousands of the innocent were to be included in this sweeping execution—thousands upon thousands that knew neither him nor Mordecai were to be slaughtered before or without knowing the cause at all. He hesitated not to imbrue his hands in blood which he could not help knowing was altogether innocent.

Neither keep they the king's laws. But, Haman, where is the proof of this? When and where were the Jews seditious under their Persian rulers? In all these provinces, is there a single Hebrew that has failed in obedience to the king, unless it be this personal enemy of yours? Out of all the millions in his empire, has the king any subjects so true as these Hebrews? For all the rest obey through fear; they only obey from conscience, or from a religious principle, for their laws teach them to obey and pray for their sovereigns, and "adjudge to hell all that are rebellious." There is not a syllable in proof that the Israelites in Persia were unprofitable subjects or troublesome to the government. It is true, as *Tacitus* says, and as we know from other sources also, that the Jews, though scattered, yet as a people, hold their religious rites distinct from all the world besides. It was a part of their religion and polity, and the design of God, that they should keep themselves separate from the heathen. But there is not a syllable of proof that the Jews were disobedient to the laws of the king of Persia, nor that they were unprofitable subjects. The contrary is proven by Haman's proposition to pay ten thousand talents to the *king's treasuries.* It is as if he had said the government derives a revenue from these people, but if the king will allow me to destroy them all, I will make up that loss out of my own property.

And in the conduct of Mordecai, remember what service he has done, and the principle upon which he is constrained to refuse. Ahasuerus had not now been on his throne but for his loyalty. Nor is it really the intention of the Persian Court to require a Jew to violate his conscience in matters of religion. It is your own malice that excites to this fearful revenge.

"*It is not for the king's profit to suffer them.*" It is, then, a question of profit or loss, not of right and justice. Never was there a scheme of villainy that was not gilded over with the plausible pretense of public utility. Nothing under heaven has made so many fools and so many heartless villains as supposed profit. The greatest good to the greatest number is indeed desirable, but such an object was never yet reached by a disregard of justice and right. Expediency is a fallacy. It is never allowed us to try the experiment of doing evil that good may come. This is the Devil's "elaborate lie."

How did it turn out in the case before us? The king is to get ten thousand talents for this execution. But instead of that his only profit was the blood and mangled bodies of thousands of his faithful subjects. Ah, cruel Haman! Are these the tender mercies of the wicked? Are these the profits of sin? What "if thou couldst have swum in a whole sea of Jewish blood, if thou couldst have raised mountains of their carcasses. What if thou couldst have made all Persia thy shambles, who would have given thee one farthing for all those piles of flesh, for all those streams of blood?"—*Hall.* Thus we see that Haman's proposition for the destruction of the Jews is backed with three arguments: *First.* They are so scattered, that their entire destruction will not depopulate any part of the empire—killed everywhere, they will be missed nowhere. *Secondly.* By their destruction, the empire would be consolidated and become more homogeneous. They were a people not assimilated. *Thirdly.* The king's treasure should be enriched with ten thousand talents. Ahasuerus was to lock up all the Jews in his chest, and Haman's chemistry was to convert them all into silver. But has it not always been thus? In what age or country has any one sought to wound the state, who did not first kiss it, pretending that he was seeking above all the public good? He loves Cæsar not less, but Rome more, and himself most of all. "The dear sovereign people," how the demagogue loves them, and how he hugs them to death, all for mere love; or while kissing them, perchance, either betrays them, or steals all the loaves and fishes! Americans, you have only two creatures on earth to fear, *religious fanatics* and *political demagogues.* The people are right, and are honest and may be trusted; but fanatical priests, and clergymen and demagogues, you must watch with more than Argus' eyes, and with "eternal vigilance."

As we find Haman assisted in his plans for a speedy

execution of Mordecai by his wife, so I have no doubt, he was prompted in his scheme for the utter extermination of the Jews by the priests of Orismades. It were not possible to get up such a work of horror without the fury of races and of religious fanaticism. It were no doubt an easy thing for the priests of Zoroaster's religion, to persuade such a man as Haman, that the state was in danger from the neglect of the Holy Temple of the Sun, and to charge this neglect upon the Hebrews, who were corrupting the people. Well may we imagine the horror with which the Magii contemplated the turning of their temples into Hebrew fanes, and the removal of their priests to make room for the sons of Levi. And if they knew that the queen was a Jewess, they might fear with reason that the king might forsake the religion of their holy Zend Avesta for that of Moses and David, and the worship of the sun for the worship of Jehovah. And when they had fired Haman's mind with fanatical fury, he exclaimed, yes, let them die. "Dogs! Deeves! may Ahrimanes clutch every soul of them! The spawn of Judah shall never put out our sacred fire!" And rushing into the waiting room of the king's apartment, he cried out, "Woe! woe upon Susa! Woe upon Persia and Media! The head priest tells me the gods are angry. Orismades hides his head from us. The sacred fire burneth dim. The good priests have studied the planets, and they say there is fearful danger that Ahrimanes shall make Persia as Tyre and Babylon." Now the great king Ahasuerus was a superstitious man, and trembling with alarm, he says: "What is the cause of this threatened evil, good Haman, what shall we do?" "The Jews! the Jews, my lord. Let the king live forever; but the Jews are the accursed cause of all this evil. Their presence is a curse to our temple and to our people." "You are certain, then, that these Jews are the cause of the anger of our gods?" And by trickery, the Magii and Haman convince him, that it is owing to the Jews that the holy fire is going out, and that if it should die, then woe, woe to the kingdom of Ahasuerus. Then said the king, let them die. Destroy, kill, and cause to perish all Jews, men and women, and all their little ones. See the Gleaner.

There are some who cavil at the largeness of the amount—*ten thousand talents of silver*—which Haman offered to pay into the treasury. We do not know whether the talents were *Babylonish* or *Jewish*. Either would have been a large sum. Ten thousand talents *Babylonish* would amount to about ten millions six hundred thousand dollars; but if counted as *Jewish* talents they would make more than double that amount. And here it must not be forgotten that gold was plen tiful in those days. It was before this that Solomon's revenues by one voyage from Ophir were *four hundred and fifty talents* of gold; that is, sixteen millions two hundred thousand dollars; and that his annual income was six hundred and sixty-six talents of silver—nearly equal to twenty-four millions of dollars.

Heeren says that we cannot avoid being struck by the prodigious abundance of the precious metals in early times in Central Asia. From the days of Solomon, and probably at an earlier period, the thrones of their princes, and the furniture of their palaces and of their tables, were of massive gold; their weapons were decorated and dresses and carpets embroidered with gold. And it is worthy of remark that the descriptions given by *Xenophon* in ancient times, and by *Chardin* in recent times, of the riches and splendor of the Persian kings, are so much alike that they might have proceeded from the same pen. And, in fact, so closely do the regal usages of modern times in the East resemble those of ancient times, that I believe there is not a single fact in the history of the Book of Esther which might not occur at the present day, and which does indeed often happen in part, or in various combinations.

Nor are we without collateral proof that such sums were by no means uncommon in and near the times of Haman. *Crassus* owned a landed estate valued at more than one million and a half pounds sterling, and *Ridorus*, after having lost a great deal in the civil war, left an estate worth one million forty-seven hundred pounds. And *Lentulus*, the augur, died worth three millions, three hundred and thirty-three thousand, three hundred and thirty-three pounds sterling. *Apicius* was possessed of above nine hundred and sixteen thousand, six hundred and seventy-one pounds. His wealth, however, was by no means satisfactory or sufficient for him. For after having spent vast sums in his kitchen, he was so miserable that he put an end to his own life by poison. These rich old Romans were not bankers or mere merchants and traders. These amounts did not merely pass through their hands in the way of trade. They were worth so much in hard money. Nor were all the *millionaires* of ancient times Romans. *Herodotus* says that *Xerxes*, in going to Greece, the father of Ahasuerus—or as some say, Ahasuerus himself, found *Pythius*, the *Lydian*, possessed of two thousand talents of silver, and four millions of gold darics, that is, about twenty-seven and a half millions of dollars. Lib. vii. And *Plutarch* informs us, that after *Crassus*, the Roman general, had given the tenth of all he had to Hercules, that he entertained ten thousand people at tables, and gave to every citizen as much corn as would support him three months; and then had seven thousand one hundred Roman talents remaining, that is, about twenty-eight millions of dollars. Surely then, there is nothing incredible in our history, because it speaks of ten thousand talents of silver. The truth is, we have glorified ourselves, until one might fairly infer from our Fourth-of-July orations and School Readers, that there was nothing in the world, before the Declaration of Independence, but acorns, buckskin moccasins, human skull beer bowls—not only that no brave men lived before "the king of men," but that there was no Agamemnon before our Washington, and no Nestor, Ajax, Ulysses or Cato, before our heroes. But history seems to me to tell a very different story. Our fathers and great men need no detraction from the great many men of any age or country. They are heroes among all the heroic. Let us then do justice to other times and to other nations. The wealth and luxury of the old world, in many particulars, surpassed our own times. The enormous debts contracted in the days of Alexander and of the Cæsars, prove that the wealth of those times was great—although this is a way to prove one's wealth by, that is not at all to my mind, especially for a Church. *Anthony* owed, we are told, at the ides of March, £333,333,13.4., which, however, it is said he paid before the calends of April, every penny of it. He was a man after my own heart. An honest man is truly a noble work of God. I hear it often said, moreover, that the officials of Government always make money. Well, what if they do? Why should they not live off their employment as others do? They serve Cæsar, why should not Cæsar pay them for their service? Why should they serve the sovereign people for nothing, when everybody else is paid? Why should they not make money honestly as all others do, or ought to try to do? But in fact, we do not understand this business half so well as the old Romans and Persians did. It was an easy matter with them for a man sent off to be a Governor or consul, or collector, soon to amass a very large fortune.

And to take the spoil of them for a prey. The people and their silver were given to Haman to do with them as he pleased, and, in making out the decree of extermination, Haman arms every Persian against his Hebrew neighbor, and whets his national enmity by giving him permission to take the property of every Jew he can kill. It was bloody work, but the play was large.

And to make Haman's authority perfect, he was invested with the king's signet ring, or privy seal. The custom of having the seal set in a ring, though not confined altogether to the East, has and does still prevail there, more than among western nations. Among the Romans none but knights were allowed to wear rings. When Alexander was dying, he took his ring from off his finger, and gave it to Perdiccas, by which it was understood that he was appointed his successor. So here, when the king gave his ring to Haman, it was meant to be a token of his affection and confidence. It was a mark of the high honor in which he was held. He could now use the king's authority for any kind of a decree he might wish to issue. The extent of the commission was fearful—*to destroy, to kill, and to cause to perish, all Jews, both young and old, little children and women, in one day,* throughout all the provinces. No mercy, no quarter. In every place and by all possible means, the whole race was to be instantly exterminated. I know not that a more impolitic, unjust, disgraceful and cruel measure was ever adopted by any Government on earth. The destruction of the Janizaries, or of the Mamelukes, bears no comparison with it in point of atrocity. This wholesale destruction of an entire people is so foreign to our customs and ideas, that we are almost alarmed at it, and almost hesitate to believe the history; yet have we not reliable records of similar catastrophes in modern times? How often have the Jesuits been expelled from the countries where they were living and prosecuting their work of instruction and proselytism? How many edicts have been issued against the Hebrews in Spain and other countries of Europe? What was the fate of the Moors in Spain? What has become of Poland? Are there not many Hamans now in the Turkish empire, who would, at a single stroke, cut off the heads of all the Christians in the empire? What is the meaning of the massacre of the English and French at Jedda, and of the slaughter of Christians at Joppa and Antioch? In 1770 the Grand Seignior, in the war with Russia, determined to cut off all the Greeks, as a punishment for their defection from Turkey, and but for the great exertions of the Turkish Admiral, the celebrated *Hassan Pasha*, it is believed all the inhabitants of Greece and the Greek isles would have been massacred. But if it were not that tyranny and despotism harden the heart as well as blind the mind, it would be almost impossible to believe that any king could be either so idiotic or so awfully wicked as to sanction this wholesale murder of so many of his innocent subjects—delivering, without full investigation, and without any cause, a whole race into Haman's hands, as lambs to the lion. In examining the credibility of this statement in our chronicles, we must remember the age and the country—the light and careless manner of absolute monarchs—their disregard of life—the peculiar influence of Haman as a favorite—the large sum offered—that the king was blind or besotted, if not drunk with wine—that the prejudices of races and the fanaticism of religious fury, were all invoked—and that it was, also, on the plea, not of private vengeance, or for the gratification of any personal feeling, but for the Public Good that this murderous decree was issued.

As the decree issued from the palace of the royal city of Susa, the people were much *perplexed. The king and Haman sat down to drink; but the city Shushan was perplexed.* It is no wonder the city was in astonishment and terror at such a decree. It was, no doubt, seen at once that a great many lives would be lost. The Jews would not all die without killing many of their assailants, and when once such a slaughter should have been commenced, who could tell where it would end. Might not some Persians be murdered for their property, by their own countrymen, under pretext that they were Jews, or united to them by marriage, or sympathized with them, or with the belief that such murder could be done, and be charged upon resisting Jews. The temper of the court, and of the city, was not the same. If proud and malicious men are not concerned at the price of their revenge, or of their wars and pomp, the people are. The people were sad, but the court was merry. *The king and Haman sat down to drink.* Perhaps Haman was afraid to leave the king, or to give him a moment's quiet reflection, lest his conscience should smite him. He, therefore, engages him in a sack of wine. They drink in honor of the gods of Persia, and confusion to the Jews. A dark cloud, however, covers the city. Shushan, the *delightful*, is sad. The people, in crowds, show marks of distress. The merry laugh is not heard in the bazaars. No doubt many of the Jews were known to their Persian neighbors as industrious, peaceable, law-abiding people. It was fearful to think of them all, men, women and children, being butchered in cold blood. Many business or domestic relations had, no doubt, also grown up between them. It was so, with Lot's family, in Sodom, and also with the Jews who returned to the Holy Land. Nor is any crime charged against the Jews. It is not pretended they had done anything worthy of death, or that they were, in any way, justly obnoxious to public justice. There are no such counts in the indictment. They are devoted to death simply because Haman has demanded it. No wonder this bloody edict was revolting to the right-minded heathen. No wonder the city was troubled at the idea of such summary and indiscriminate slaughter. It was impossible but that Shushan should have been perplexed.

1. This history is an illustration of the danger of a one-man power—of *an absolute despotism*. When the great king was exceedingly enraged with Vashti, he called his seven wise men, and took their advice—when he was troubled about the decree against her, he also called his ministers, and followed their counsel in procuring another queen,—and when the conspiracy against his life was discovered, he did not proceed to condemn and execute the conspirators until a full investigation had been made, and their guilt established beyond doubt, and then by, and with the consent of his senate, a decree was made, that they should be put to death according to law. But here, so tremendous is the influence of the envious and enraged new court favorite over the old monarch, and so bitter are the prejudices of the court against the Jews, that, at the first suggestion of Haman, without time for reflection, without counsel from his wise men, a general decree which, by the usage and laws of the empire, cannot be altered or repealed, is at once issued, consigning a whole nation to destruction, and transfering all their property to Haman. It may be, as some commentators tell us, that it took the wily minister a long time to overcome the king's reluctance—that he was overreached by the flattery and the religious zeal of the favorite—and that he consented, at last, only under the impression that he owed everything to his zeal and fidelity. But all this is no excuse. Ahasuerus was as bad a king as

he was a cruel husband. Rage and passion, the marks of royal weakness, are seen in his cruelty to his queen, and to his subjects.

The decrees of Roman emperors against the Christians, and the revocation of the edict of Nantes, and the massacre of St. Bartholomew, may belong to the same chapter of horrors that chronicles this wholesale murdering edict; but I have not found anywhere a decree so steeped in infamy and blood as this. Never shall we be thankful enough for our civil liberty, and freedom to worship God. Daily thanksgiving should be made to the God of our fathers for our *Bill of Rights, Habeas Corpus, trial by jury,* and a written Constitution and laws made in conformity therewith. And if history teaches us to fear the tyranny of a despot, it also teaches us to fear

> "That worst of tyrants, an usurping crowd.
> Mad, furious power, whose unrelenting mind
> No God can govern, and no justice bind."

It is almost enough to make an enlightened Republican loathe the name *citizen,* and the very idea of free institutions, to see how the newspapers, and advocates of lynch law, have praised "the resumption of sovereignty by the people," and their holding in utter contempt the constitutional courts of the country. "The moment citizens become soldiers, to interfere when and where, and for what length of time it may please an irresponsible, self-constituted, unconstitutional power to direct them, then we may bid farewell to freedom."*

*1 Vol. Sheridan's Works. His Speech in British Parliament on the Westminster Riots.

If we are governed by the multitude, without such courts and laws as our Constitution requires, then we have all the evils of the worst despotism, without the discipline or the security of a tyrant's rule. The liberty that rests on the selfishness, or the *inclination of one man, or of a hundred men, is suspended despotism*, and if we must choose between the rule of one man, or of thirty, without a written Constitution and laws, we should greatly prefer the one. In either case, our property and personal liberty are at the will of human caprice, or passion. In neither case may the sword be actually drinking the blood out of our necks, but it is hung close over them by the small brittle thread of human will, which a thousand things may suddenly snap asunder. As, under a despotism and an oligarchy, the tendency is to a greater and greater usurpation of power—the centralizing of the whole government in one man, or in a few, who, in the end, are converted into one; so, on the other hand, there is a dangerous tendency, under free institutions, toward the usurpation of too much power by the people. Our history, brief as it is, shows that this is the rock on which we are in the greatest danger of total shipwreck. Of this danger all our wise and great men, from Washington to this hour, have earnestly warned us. It is confessedly plain to every one, that with us there is a rapid tendency, in the popular mind, to exalt the will of the people above all laws, human and divine—to make popular favor the supreme good—the standard of right and wrong. Already this disposition is so fully developed that every aspirant for place is found under the strongest temptations to offer incense to the people, as to a god. And, of all heathen gods that man's fears, lusts, passions, and direful superstitions have ever formed, there is not one so inexorable, so many-headed, so bloody-minded, so insatiable, and so cruel a monster, as the sovereign people, when freed from the moral obligations of the word of God, and let loose upon one another without the restraints of civil government. Witness the reign of terror in France. It is well known what Pilate did when his conscience constrained him to ask the Son of God, *What is truth?* He went out, without waiting for an answer, to consult with the people. It is when Babel is to be built; it is when a golden calf is to be set up; or a traitor, like Cataline, wishes to overthrow the city, or betray his country; or when the Son of God is to be crucified, that the *vox populi* is appealed to, and the multitude blasphemously respond, it is the *vox Dei*, while the voice of history, and of reason, and of common sense, and of the Bible, says that the vox populi is not the vox Dei, but the *vox infernal*. The whole world lieth in wickedness, and is at enmity with God and all righteousness.

2. We see how greatly we are blest, in having a government, not of men, but of *just, mild, enlightened and equitable written and published laws,* guaranteeing to us liberty in the worship of God, and in the pursuits of life and the enjoyment of our institutions. The king of Persia, in some instances, seems to have been surrounded by the restraints of precedents, yet, in other cases, he could do what he pleased with the lives and property of his subjects. There was no written constitution. There were no laws and courts, like ours,

for the protection of the rights of the people. And even if, as some do, we allow that Ahasuerus is the same king that granted a decree to Nehemiah, and that he did it the same year that he married Esther, for the rebuilding of Jerusalem, instead of thinking any the better of his character, we have only the more proof of his inconsistency and want of principle. The fear of God did not enter into his decree in favor of Nehemiah, nor of Haman. His purpose was to gratify a favorite in both cases, but the one was a man of God, and the other was an accursed Amalekite.

A weak, vacillating, spasmodic Government is a great calamity. Woe to the people whose king is a child. As Christians, we are taught to thank God for a wise and stable Government, and to pray for all that are in authority, that the Church universal may have peace, and that all its members may lead quiet and peaceable lives, in all godliness and honesty. One of our most commonly used and ablest and best commentaries, in summing up some practical remarks on the character of Ahasuerus, says: "Whatever mere professors may be, true Christians are the best subjects under every Government; not only because they are more peaceable, honest and industrious than their neighbors, and conscientiously pay tribute and render obedience in all things lawful, but because their examples and conversation edify many, and their prayers bring down a blessing on the land in which they live in peace. No acquisitions of wealth, therefore, could compensate the loss of them, even in a political view, and without bringing into the account the enormous load of national guilt which persecution rapidly accumulates."—*Dr. Thomas Scott.*

3. We are never to despair of the Ark, even when it falls into the hands of the Philistines. God will never forsake his people. It is no new thing for the godly to have to suffer persecution. The Jews were misrepresented. Even what Haman said of them that was true, was so said as to give a false coloring to the whole picture. There is no proof that the Jews were factious under the Persian rule. On the contrary, from the lives of Daniel, Ezra and Nehemiah, we should infer just the opposite. They do not seem to have shown, in Egypt, Babylon or Persia, any of the turbulence that marked their subjugation to the Romans. Their circumstances, in the cases cited, were very different—so that their factiousness, in New Testament times, is easily explained. Israelites are usually remarkable for their submission to law and civil government. Haman's persecutions, then, were groundless cruelties, practiced upon God's ancient people. The slaughter of "the Innocents," the St. Bartholomew massacre, are startling proofs of what men may be led to do by malice and rage, all under the plea of doing God's service, in protecting the State and the Church. Thousands of non-conforming ministers, the very salt of Great Britain, suffered under the Charles, and God's dear people, in all past ages, have, in some form or other, past to glory through many tribulations. We find them fined, imprisoned, banished, despoiled of their goods, and put to death, as enemies to the Church and State, but upon false charges. Persecution always follows any favoritism on the part of a Government to any one religion in preference to others. It should not then be thought a thing incredible that the Israelites were

slandered and consigned to destruction upon false charges.

It is an old aspersion of God's people, to charge them with singularity. Would to God there was more cause for the imputation than there is. Not of a rude perverseness, but of a singularity that marks a high degree of devotion to God, and zeal for his service. But it is not possible for the Church of God wholly to escape persecution. The seed of the bondwoman loveth not the seed of the freewoman. The carnal mind is at enmity with God. Here we find the adherence of the Hebrews to their laws made the subject of a charge against them, for which they were to be put to death; and yet these very laws were their greatest glory, and the best on earth. They were the laws of the Lord their God, and it was their duty to die for them, sooner than disobey them, and to die for such a cause was a glorious martyrdom. The very thing, therefore, that constituted their glory, was made their offense. But it is better always to fall into the hands of God than of men. This was David's choice, and observation approves of it. The very reasons Haman gave for destroying the Hebrews, are among the very reasons why God will not let them perish out of the earth. That which whets the sword of men, moves the pity of the Almighty. And never was there a more deeply laid plot than this; and to human view, there seemed to be no possible way to escape. It was just so at the Red Sea, and yet it was there His power was manifested to save; and so it will be here. God sometimes leaves his people to come into the greatest peril, that his power may be the more easily seen in their deliverance. Pharaoh was raised up to show his power, and so was Haman. "God taketh the wise in their own craftiness, and ensnares the wicked in the works of their own hands." In the darkest hour, it is our duty and our highest happiness, still to trust in God. Behind a frowning cloud, His face beams with ineffable love. And if a day of fiery trials come, when for the testimony of Jesus, we must endure cruel torturings, even unto death, then martyr-grace will be given unto us. I believe there are thousands of men and women, in our own times, who would make as brave confessors and martyrs, as any that have ever honored Christ at the stake, or on the Roman arena. And why should we fear to die for Jesus, or at his bidding? Death is but departing to be forever with the Lord and with his saints in glory.

"The grave itself is but a covered bridge,
Leading from light to light through a brief darkness.
Death is but the lifting of a latch;
Only a step into the open air,
Out of a tent already luminous
With light that shines through its transparent walls."

Longfellow.

CHAPTER XI.

MORDECAI IN SACKCLOTH.

"——— Conscience, good my lord,
Is but the pulse of reason."
Coleridge.

"A man on earth may have too much love to weep. His highest duty is thought and then action."
Peter Bayne.

BATTLES and conquests, the rise of conquerors and the reign of kings and their fall—the treachery and flattery of courtiers and the toils of statesmen, chiefly make up the history of the world. Here and there, but, "like angel's visits, few and far between," we have an episode for harmonizing hostile nations into concord, and for the advancement of the glorious arts of peace. Such was the international jubilation for the *ocean telegraph*, which is, by no means, a failure, even if the lips of this cable should never utter another syllable. It cannot be pronounced a failure, because the laying of the cable was really and truly accomplished. It is a fact, therefore, added to the chronicled deeds of the human race. And again, communication by telegraph across the Atlantic is now certain. Enough has been done to prove that it is practicable. And, besides, the interchange of good feeling between the Old and the New World, on that occasion, was worth all the expense, and a great deal more than all the expense of the cable and the jubilee. It is seen to be a part of God's plan, in the government of the world, that a Howard shall appear, now and then, to remind mankind of the sublime benevolence of which they are capable. The internal history of the world is, however, a very different one from its external. The internal lies deeper. It is a history of hearts—the hearts of rulers as well as of subjects. For it is not true that the great and the mighty of the earth have no hearts. It may be that, sometimes, they try to hide their hearts, or to smother up, or enfeeble their higher and better natures. But kings and queens have human hearts. In the history before us, we have both external and internal conflicts pictured out. Our chronicle here is according to Esther, iv chapter.

If we could convict Mordecai of selfishness, pride, or wicked ambition, in his conduct toward the king or the prime minister; or of any unhallowed purpose in his presenting Hadassah, his angelic cousin, to the chief of the officers of the king's household, as a candidate for the crown royal, then we should now begin to fear for him, and say, with Job's friends, that it was for his iniquities this calamity had come upon him. But we have not found anything against him. We have, thus far, found him a well educated, refined gentleman, of high principles, tried integrity, and unwavering loyalty and piety. He may have felt a just satisfaction with himself in what he had done in bringing up Hadassah, and advancing her to the king's favor. This would not have been sinful. There was nothing dishonorable nor sinful in his conduct, nor in his cousin's relations with the king. But, doubtless, Mordecai's motives were higher than mere personal gratification or honor. His character is proof that he was an attentive observer of the unfolding providences of the God of his fathers. Indeed, throughout the history, we see the use of means in subordination to an overruling purpose. Esther's rare beauty, exquisite form, faultless features and radiant eyes were all given to her by Him who opened the heart of the chief officer to show her favor. And He whose Spirit moved Mordecai to use such means as were proper for the education and success of Esther, caused the pious Jewess, when she came before the king, to appear to him as a vision of perfect beauty and loveliness. Her personal charms were a part of the means to be used for the deliverance of the scattered Hebrews. There is no let or hindrance in the accomplishment of the Divine purposes, nor is there any confusion or cross-purposes between Divine efficiency and human effort. Man is free and God is sovereign, and salvation is always of grace—*free grace.*

When Mordecai perceived all that was done, he rent his clothes, and put on sackcloth. The promulgation of this decree must have been sad news throughout the empire. The king's posts flew with the royal command almost as swift as the winds, and throughout all the provinces, *withersoever the decree came, there was great mourning among the Jews, and fasting and weeping, and wailing; and many lay in sackcloth and ashes.*

Great was the wailing that filled the Hebrew quarters of the royal city and every synagogue. And, no doubt, Mordecai's former monitors, his fellow servants of the palace, added insult to grief. "Did we not tell you so? Did we not admonish you that such would be the end of your stupid obstinacy? It is strange you will run your head against a stone wall. You have come to a pretty pass. You would have none of our advice, therefore we will now leave you to your sackcloth, and may it be very soft to you! But tell us, old stiff knees, what is to be the end of a contest between a Jew, like you, and Haman, the favorite of the great king of Persia? Which will be the hardest, when your earthen pitcher knocks against his of brass?" And so, wagging their heads and greatly delighted with their own wit, they left Mordecai to his grief and to his pious meditations, the reading of the Psalms of David, the Book of Job, the prophecies of Isaiah and Jeremiah and the writings of Moses, and to find relief in prayer.

And Mordecai, in sackcloth, went out into the midst of the city, *and came even before the king's gate, for none might enter into the king's gate clothed with sackcloth.* It was and is still the law in the East, that no one in sackcloth can be admitted to the presence of royalty, nor in any habiliments of mourning, unless by special favor. Perhaps the reason of this prohibition was that the sight of such things would put the king in mind of sickness and death, and so disturb his pleasures. As Mordecai could not, therefore, enter the king's gate or palace, with such marks of oppressive grief, he *went out into the midst of the city.* His cry must have been peculiarly loud and bitter, because he had been made the occasion of this murderous decree. His enemy seemed about to triumph, not only over him, but also in cutting off his whole race—scorning to let his vengeance fall on him alone. As it was with Moses, so it was with him—what he had done for the deliverance of his people, was at first turned to their disadvantage. I fancy, as indeed the second Targum expressly says, I hear him crying aloud through the streets, saying: "A people is going to be destroyed, who have done no evil. What a heavy decree is this which the king and Haman have passed, not against a part of us, but against us all; to root us out of the earth." And the Jews hearing him uttering such a complaint, gathered about him, and he having caused the book of the law to be brought to the gate of the city, and being covered with sackcloth, read Deut. iv: 30, 31. "When thou art in tribulation and all these things are come upon thee in the latter days, if thou turn to the Lord thy God, and shalt be obedient to his voice, for the Lord thy God is a merciful God, he will not forsake thee, nor destroy thee, nor forget the covenant of thy fathers, which he swore unto them." And then he exhorted them to fasting, humiliation, prayer and repentance, after the example of the Ninevites. In the apocryphal Esther, we have a copy of the prayer which Mordecai is said to have used on this occasion, and at the time of the general fast. It is in the words following:

O Lord, Lord, the King Almighty, for the whole world is in thy power, and if thou hast appointed to save Israel, there is no man that can gainsay thee; for thou hast made heaven and earth and all the wondrous things under the heaven. Thou art Lord of all things, and there is no man that can resist thee, which art the

LORD. Thou knowest all things, and thou knowest, LORD, that it was neither in contempt nor pride, nor for any desire of glory, that I did not bow down to proud Haman. For I could have been content, with good will, for the salvation of Israel to kiss the soles of his feet. But I did this that I might not prefer the glory of man to the glory of GOD; neither will I worship any but thee, O GOD. Neither will I do it in pride. And now, O LORD GOD, and King, spare thy people, for their eyes are upon us to bring us to nought; yea, they desire to destroy the inheritance that hath been thine from the beginning. Despise not the portion which thou hast delivered out of Egypt for thine own self. Hear my prayer and be merciful unto thine inheritance; turn our sorrow into joy, that we may live, O LORD, and praise thy name, and destroy not the mouths of them that praise thee, O LORD. All Israel in like manner cried most earnestly unto the LORD, because their death was before their eyes.

But perhaps you are indignant at his useless wailing in the streets, and praying in the synagogue, and say, why does he not go at once and tell the queen? But can every porter rush into Buckingham palace and speak to her Majesty? Is every one that comes, admitted to the presence of the Empress Eugenie? In Persia it was a crime even to inquire what was done in the harem. And except on some very important business, even the guard never speak to any one outside, or convey any intelligence, either out or in. Mordecai, then, did not go to the queen for the very best of reasons. He could not. You must remember that the inmates of an oriental harem have their apartments altogether separate, and that they are guarded by a body of black eunuchs, who are as fierce, sullen, and silent, as so many black dragons. No one, upon pain of death, from without, is allowed to speak to any one within the harem. Though the queen was his cousin, Mordecai could have no communication with her, except through the guard. Even when he discovered the conspiracy, he was obliged to use one of the eunuchs as his agent of communication with her. Any one who has ever seen the guards of the seraglio of Constantinople, is ready, I am sure, to conclude that it were as easy to converse with so many dragons—and that one might as well undertake to tear out their hearts, as to get a syllable from them of the secrets that are within the walls and gates of the harem—regions so sacred and so secluded, that they seem to belong to another world. To understand this history, therefore, it is necessary for you to divest yourself of our republican ideas of freedom of access to high personages. And this explains why Mordecai walked, as in a preceding chapter, every day before the court of the women's house. This was the only way he had to gain any intelligence from within. So here, instead of going to the queen, he goes into the streets, and cries with a loud and bitter cry, and came even before the king's gate. His object, no doubt, was to arouse his people to an apprehension of their danger, and to attract the attention of some one from the queen's apartments of the palace, through whom a communication might be opened up with her. For a time, the queen knows nothing of the decree, nor of Mordecai's lamentations. But at last, "Esther's maids and her chamberlains came and told it her. Then was the queen exceedingly grieved; and she sent raiment to clothe Mordecai, and to take away his sackcloth from him: but he received it not. Then called Esther for

Hatach, one of the king's chamberlains, whom he had appointed to attend upon her, and gave him a commandment to Mordecai, to know what it was, and why it was. So Hatach went forth to Mordecai, unto the street of the city, which was before the king's gate." The queen's crown, though sparkling with jewels, was now as heavy as lead on her head, because of Mordecai's sackcloth and ashes. It is true friendship always to feel the condition of those whom we love. The queen seems at first to have supposed that Mordecai had been robbed of his clothing, and was in want. She therefore sent raiment to him, and was exceedingly grieved on his account; but he received it not. Then she sent again her most confidential servant, to know what was the matter. And now Mordecai tells him of the murderous decree of Haman, and commands him to *show it unto Esther, and to declare it unto her, and to charge her that she should go into the king, to make supplication unto him, and to make request before him for her people. And Hatach came and told Esther the words of Mordecai.* See verse 7, 8, 9. In the Greek, it is added, that in sending this message to the queen, Mordecai said also: "Remember your low estate, and how I carried you in my arms, and how I have nourished you; and that Haman who is next to the king, has gotten a decree for our destruction. Pray, therefore, to the Lord; and plead with the king, that we may be delivered from death." This is all good sense, and as far as we know, historically true, but there is not a word of it in the original text, nor in the Syriac or Vulgate.

The queen's reply to Mordecai through Hatach, was that, "All the king's servants, and the people of the king's provinces, do know, that whosoever, whether man or woman, shall come unto the king into the inner court, who is not called, there is one law of his to put him to death, except such to whom the king shall hold out the golden sceptre, that he may live: but I have not been called to come in unto the king these thirty days. And they told to Mordecai Esther's words."

The case seems exceedingly embarrassed. The difficulties were quite enough to discourage her woman's heart. She seems to say, I fear some rival has obtained the king's favor, or that his affection has cooled toward me; and if I were to peril my life by going into his presence, I fear my face, instead of recalling his love, would only excite his rage. But, says her foster-father, with a hero's heart, I command you, Hatach, to say to the queen: "Think not with thyself that thou shalt escape in the king's house, more than all the Jews. For if thou altogether holdest thy peace at this time, *then* shall there enlargement and deliverance arise to the Jews from another place; but thou, and thy father's house, shall be destroyed; and who knoweth whether thou art come to the kingdom for such a time as this?" Verse 13, 14. The queen's answer to Mordecai was a true account of the case, but to him it was the language of weakness—of unbelief. The fear, or imagination of a cruel death, did not make his heart fail. But if it is death that you fear, he says, what but death awaits you? The case is thus: Go and plead, and you may die, it is true; but if you go not, you are certain to die. Your blood is Jewish. No one is exempted from this decree. It were better then to act on the possibility of hope than to sit still and die. But I know there is salvation for Israel. The God of Jacob will not let tyrants root out and destroy His people. The Holy One of Israel will work miracles, as in days of old, sooner than that His promises to our fathers shall fail. And if you are not worthy of the post to which you are raised up, the honor of our deliverance will be given to some one else. It was to save His people, Jehovah has placed you on the throne, and He will not fail because of your weakness. Thus, in Mordecai's remonstrances with the queen, we see: *First,* That, for himself, though belonging to the king's household, and related to the queen, and for Her Majesty herself, there was no escape from Haman's decree. No Jew, high or low, was to be allowed to live. The case, therefore, was her own, as well as his, and of all their people.

Secondly, We see his faith and courage. He was not in despair; for, even if the queen would not do her duty, still he was confident the needful help would be obtained. Though one instrument, or agency, might fail, he did not doubt but God's people would be saved. The Divine covenant could not fail. He seems to argue thus: It may be God's rule to keep us in ignorance of our danger until it is necessary to arouse us to feel our dependence on Him, and to use the means which He has appointed for our deliverance. He may, in mercy, keep us ignorant also of our own strength and resources till we try ourselves what we can do. For it is only when we have done our utmost that we are authorized to commit our cause wholly to God, and rest alone upon Him for deliverance. It is when

Atrides sends his whole soul with his lance, that Jove carries it home to the heart of his enemy. Mordecai's faith was truly conquering. It was heroic. The clouds were thick and heavy. The decree is long, and broad, and deep, and it has gone forth to the utmost verge of the empire. And it is as irrevocable as it is cruel and bloody. The king is all-powerful. But still the Hebrew's faith failed not. He trusted in the promises of God—he thought them more powerful than the threatening decrees of a tyrant. "And this is the victory that overcometh the world, even our faith."

Thirdly, Though assured of deliverance, from some quarter, Mordecai was jealous that the queen should have the honor of it. *And who knoweth whether thou art come to the kingdom for such a time as this?* As if he had said, "Can you suppose Divine Providence has raised you up from so low a condition, in a strange land, to become the queen of the Persian Empire, merely for your own sake? Was there not some great public interest to be secured by this? It cannot be, O my lovely, and now royal cousin, that the God of our fathers has so highly favored you merely for your own sake, or for your personal ease, dignity and enjoyment. No. He has raised you to the throne that you may have the honor of doing some great service to the Hebrew race, and to the Church of the one living and true God, in the midst of a corrupt and idolatrous empire." To awaken her to a sense of her responsibility, and inspire her with faith in God, he is careful to urge her to recall to mind how Providence had taken care of her helpless orphanage, and had raised her to the throne, no doubt, for this very crisis. And that now, if she failed, it would show a great want of courage—great lack of love for her people, and a sad want of faith in God; and, for such a failure of duty, she must expect the wrath of God. For it was true then, as it is and has been ever since, that if, by sinful shifts, we seek to save our life, we shall loose it. That life is lost that is saved by sin, which is the highest dishonor.

It is enough. The queen now sees her responsibility. Her foster-father has, at last, touched the right cord—her duty, as a pious Israelite, to the faith of her fathers, and to her kindred. She, therefore, commanded Hatach to return this answer to Mordecai: "Go, gather together all the Jews that are present in Shushan, and fast ye for me, and neither eat nor drink three days, night or day: I also and my maidens will fast likewise: and so will I go in unto the king; which is not according to the law; and if I perish, I perish. So Mordecai went his way, and did according to all that Esther had commanded him."

CHAPTER XII.

THE QUEEN INTERCEDING.

"God's ear is open and there still is room."

THE last chapter opened with wailing and sackcloth in the streets of Shushan. The Sultana's crown of jewels was heavier than lead. Royal hearts were pierced with many sorrows. O, the living world of anxieties and apprehensions in which we now dwell, nor are thrones and palaces free from them. But the chapter closed with a great solemn religious convocation. Mordecai assembles the people for fasting and prayer. Every Israelite is now to go to his knees, not before idols, nor in the temples of the Sun, but before Jehovah, the God of his fathers. And the queen, perhaps the only worshipper of the true God in the palace, with her maidens, are to join Mordecai and the people in fasting and prayer; and, afterward, she says, "I will go in unto the king." Heroic resolve, worthy a Hebrew queen of the race of Miram, Deborah and Judith. Nor is life ever so well used as when to lose it is gain. Duty is more than life. Duty is ours, consequences are God's.

We have found a Hebrew maid, an orphan and a captive, on the banks of the Choaspes—a lovely damsel, a beautiful odalisque, a graceful, charming wife, a most fascinating Sultana; but now we find her the Heroine. Never till now has her mission fully appeared. The process of her preparation for her work has been long and varied and most wonderful, but her work came to her at last, and nobly does she perform it. It is in the noble resolve that she will offer her life a sacrifice, if necessary, to save her countrymen, that her real strength of character begins to develop itself. Here, at once, she rises to the dignity of a martyr. The proud, heroic blood of Mordecai speaks out in her when she says: *I will go in unto the king, and if I perish I perish.* She seems to say: My mind is now clearly made up. It is my duty to try to save my people, and I am resolved to do so, and if I lose my life in the attempt, I shall yield it cheerfully, because I am in the way of duty.

Though it is strange that there is no mention of God in their fasting and ceremonies, nor of praying to Him, yet it is certainly implied. I do not know why *prayer* is not mentioned, nor why the name of God is omitted. But, surely, it was not supposed by Esther or Mordecai that there was any *charm* in their fasting or rending of clothes. They must have thought that, in and by such acts of penitence, and such marks of grief, they could awaken the people to a sense of their danger and arouse them to call upon the God of their fathers, in this time of their extremity. The Queen's resolve implied her profound regard for God, submission to His will, and a great regard for the lives of her people. She had become satisfied that if she was to lose her life it was in a good cause, and that she could, therefore, safely commit herself to her heavenly Father. "Now it came to pass on the third day, that Esther put on her royal apparel, and stood in the inner court of the king's house, over against the king's house: and the king sat upon his royal throne in the royal house, over against the gate of the house. And it was so, when the king saw Esther the queen standing in the court, that she obtained favor in his sight: and the king held out to Esther the golden sceptre that was in his hand. So Esther drew near, and touched the top of the sceptre. Then said the king unto her, What wilt thou, queen Esther? and what is thy request? it shall be even given thee to the half of the kingdom. And Esther answered, If it seem good unto the king, let the king and Haman come this day unto the banquet that I have prepared for him."

There is a passage in the Cyropedia of Xenophon which proves that the kings of Persia used a golden sceptre, such as is alluded to in the text. It is in the sixth book. "It is not," said Cyrus to his son Cambyses, "the golden sceptre that saves the kingdom; faithful friends are the truest and safest sceptre of the empire." Other proof is not wanting, but not needed. The condition of the king and the queen, as they now come before us, is very different, and that of the queen very much changed. The last time we saw her was at her coronation. Now the king and Haman are drinking in the banqueting hall of the palace, but Esther is very differently employed. If you look into her apartments, they are gorgeously furnished. Light steals into them through the richly decorated windows by day, and golden lamps from marble columns pour their light upon golden divans—*pulvinaria*—worthy of a goddess by night. Her chambers are filled, every day, with the most costly perfumes. Fruits and flowers and wines, from Shiraz and the Happy Isles, cover the tables. But the queen is not under the spell of such enchantments. For two days and nights she has neither tasted food nor drink. It is now the third day since she and her maidens begun their fasting. Hunger and thirst, and mental agony still more, are making deep inroads upon her physical strength, if not upon her beauty. Pale and almost haggard, her lustrous eyes begin to grow dim with weeping, and her lips, though almost parched with thirst, are still moving in prayer. Her knees ache from long prostration on the tesselated floor. But, as hour after hour passes, and her heart pours forth its sorrow, she feels her courage growing stronger, until she has gained strength for the terrible interview. But, before she rises from her knees to make her toilet, let us hear one of her prayers. We take it from her apocryphal life, where it is said: "Being in fear of death, queen Esther resorted unto the LORD, and laid away her glorious apparel, and put on the garments of anguish and mourning; and instead of precious ointments, she covered her head with ashes and dung, and she humbled her body greatly, and all the places of her joy she filled with her torn hair. And she prayed unto the Lord God of Israel, saying, O my LORD, thou only art our king, help me, a desolate woman, which have no helper but Thee: For my danger is in mine hand.

From my youth up I have heard in the tribe of my family, that thou, O LORD, tookest Israel from among all people, and our fathers from all their predecessors for a perpetual inheritance, and thou hast performed whatsoever thou didst promise them. And now we have sinned before thee; therefore hast thou given us into the hands of our enemies, because we worshipped their gods. O LORD, thou art righteous. Nevertheless it satisfieth them not that we are in bitter captivity, but they have stricken hands with their idols, that they will abolish the thing that thou with thy mouth hast ordained, and destroy thine inheritance and stop the mouth of them that praise thee, and quench the glory of thy house and of thine altar. And open the mouths of the heathen to set forth the praises of the idols, and to magnify a fleshly king forever. O LORD, give not thy sceptre unto them that be nothing, and let them not laugh at our fall, but turn their device upon themselves, and make him an example that hath begun this against us. Remember, O LORD, make thyself known in time of our affliction, and give me boldness, O King of the nations and Lord of all power. Give me eloquent speech in my mouth before the lion, turn his heart to hate him that fighteth against us, that there may be an end of him and of all that are like minded to him. But deliver us with thine hand and help me that am desolate, and which have no other helper but Thee. Thou knowest all things, O Lord; thou knowest that I hate the glory of the unrighteous, and abhor the bed of the uncircumcised, and of all the heathen. Thou knowest my necessity, for I abhor the sign of my high estate, which is upon mine head in the days wherein I shew myself, and that I abhor it, and that I wear it not when I am private by myself. And that thine handmaid hath not eaten at Aman's table, and that I have not greatly esteemed the king's feast, nor drunk the wine of the drink-offerings. Neither had thine handmaid any joy since the day that I was brought hither to this present, but in thee, O LORD GOD of Abraham. O thou Mighty GOD above all, hear the voice of the forlorn, and deliver us out of the hands of the mischievous, and deliver me out of my fear.

The queen and her maidens have been fasting and engaged in solemn devotions in their apartments, and Mordecai and all the Jews, fasting and praying in all the synagogues, while the king and Haman have been quite otherwise employed. But their revelry is over. It is court day and audience hours. And as no sovereigns ever assumed more haughty airs, or claimed higher royal honors than the Persians, it will be interesting to get a view of the Palace, the throne, and the king. The history of these monarchs informs us that no one could approach them unveiled and uncalled, without peril of life, and that into *the inner court* of the harem, no person ever entered but the king and the woman he had called. No one of his court, neither the prime minister, nor the queen herself, ever dared to go into this chamber, unless ordered to do so, or led by the king himself into it. And in this case, the queen's difficulty was increased by the fact that, the king had not called her for *thirty days.* And according to Herodotus, after the time of Deioces, king of Media, in order that the person of the king might be more secure, it was a law that no one should be admitted into his presence, when on the throne, until special leave had been obtained. The ordinary rule was that all business with the king was to be transacted through the medium of his ministers.

But the hour has come when Esther must either find favor for herself and her people, or forfeit her life and leave her crown to another. She has been grieved, alarmed, and deeply agitated; but she feels that she is in the way of duty, and now on the third day of the fast, she suspends her prayers to adorn herself for the presence of the king. With the courage and resolution of a queen, and the piety of a Hebrew, she begins her preparation for the great trial. Her face now assumes its wonted cheerful and beauteous expression. Her abstinence and devotions have made her more beautiful than ever. The same God that was with Joseph in Egypt, and with Moses in the wilderness, and with Daniel and his companions in Babylon, has been with her in Susa. The pulse and water, with God's blessing, was a better diet for the Hebrews than the king's meat and wine, so that at the end of the ten days, *their countenances appeared fairer and fatter in flesh, than all the children which did eat the portion of the king's meat.* Dan. i: 15. And it was just so here, God whom she worshipped, made her the more beautiful, because of her humiliation before Him, and because she had put her trust in Him, and was now offering her life as a sacrifice to him, for the sake of his people.

There is something worthy of special notice in the difference of her preparation, this time, for going before the king, and her preparation for meeting him the first time. Under the tuition of the chief officer of the harem, she was prepared with myrrh and sweet odors, and kept twelve months in a state of purification, that she might be reckoned fit to be presented to the king. But here she has not the assistance of Hege, and has only three days, and they are spent, not in the sweet baths and in the vigorous use of oils and odors, but in fasting and prayer. As far as her personal appearance could avail in her behalf, it was chiefly her face that was to win the king, and this she makes thin and pale by abstinence and mental agony. Would not the wisdom of this world have pampered the flesh, that the wanton eyes of a Pagan king might be the more easily inflamed? It was the queen's faith that taught her *to languish to please*—to trust in prayer rather than in carnal beauty—to rely on God to touch the king's heart, rather than anything she could do herself, and yet she was assiduously using all and the very best means within her power to make her effort successful. All things being done by herself, and her people and Mordecai—being at peace with God, and having her cause right in His sight, the queen now prepares to go to the king. Never did she take so much pains with her toilet. Never before did she direct her long black tresses to be so carefully braided over her polished forehead—never before did she use so much skill in trying to enhance her every personal charm, and make her beauty irresistible to the king. She was arrayed with the snow-white woolen stuffs of Damascus and the roseate silks of Persia; the royal tiara of twisted silk and gold sparkling with most precious jewels, and proclaiming her rank and relation to the king, while, at the same time, it set off her figure to great advantage—over her shoulders flowed the purple velvet mantle, embroidered on the edge with heavy pearls. And never did royal robes become her so well. She looked more like a goddess, dropped from the clouds, than a being of clay. Her maidens were also very beautiful, and most elegantly arrayed. When she came to the threshhold of the palace, she stopped a moment to breathe a fervent prayer, and swallow down the choking sensation that almost suffocated her, and to gather up her failing strength, and then she passed into the throne-room, where sat the king, with his golden sceptre in his hand, and surrounded with his nobles, and the crown upon his head. The king was an aged man—his locks were long and white as snow, and his beard soft and glossy as a Turk's of three-score years, flowing down upon his breast, after the manner of Mehemet Ali. His robe was of Persian purple and strips of silver; his diadem was massive with priceless gems—the richest crown then on earth. His tunic was a brilliant mass of gold and jewels. The throne was of ivory, all glittering with gold and precious stones. Though his arms were long, he was considered a very handsome man. And, under such circumstances, thus arrayed, in a magnificent saloon of marble, inlaid with ivory and the most costly sweet woods, and hung with cloth of gold tissue, and an immense plane-tree, wrought in gold, overhanging his throne, his appearance must have been splendid, and well calculated to fill a spectator with awe. As the queen entered, the king, hearing a slight ruffling, as of female robes, turned to see who it was, and, behold! before him stands Esther, speechless. The paleness of her cheeks, from mental agony and fasting, made her face more transparent; and, as she stood, shrinking from fear, the king must have detected a shadow of melancholy, if not of great suffering. Her penciled brow was slightly contracted by the intensity of her feelings, and her long lashes were dripping with tears, and her lips trembling with agitation. More beautiful than ever, and though silent, her eloquence was enough to have moved a heart of stone. The apocryphal chapters of this history are more full and minute than our text, but in no way contradictory to it. According to them, when Esther saw the king, surrounded with his nobles, and recollecting the fate of Vashti, and knowing that she was setting at defiance a law of the palace, and that the king was a man of violent passions, and exceedingly fierce in his jealousy for his personal honor and the dignity of his throne, her heart failed her, and, fainting, she fell into the arms of her maids. And when the king first saw her, he was greatly enraged, but, as he gazed upon her lovely form, his heart began to soften. The nobles and princes, also, were moved with silent sympathy, for they all loved Esther; and though they dared not open their lips to plead her cause, yet their eyes and countenances spoke as plainly as if every line of their faces were a fiery tongue. In breathless awe the whole court watched the king's face, for it shone with terrible fierceness, waiting for the issue. By her very appearance, the queen says, Nothing but an affair of life or death could have brought me into this awful presence. Her marble lips, as she lies in the arms of her maidens, say: "Oh, dread sire, my lord and my husband, the sovereign of all the provinces from India to Ethiopia, it is dire necessity, not any wish to disobey your laws, that has constrained me to appear before you, uncalled. And, now, I am ready, live or die, as it shall seem good to your imperial majesty. I remember my predecessor lost her crown for not coming when sent for, and I know I put my life into your hands by coming, unbidden, into your presence. But may I not hope for your pardon?" But, as yet, no sign is given. The haughty king has not yet spoken. His thoughts of dignity, power and fame—of his vast empire of one hundred and twenty-seven provinces—are in conflict with his feelings. And, oh, king Ahasuerus! must this lovely creature die? No. God changed the king's spirit into mildness, and, unable any longer to dissemble his feelings, he leaped from his throne, and took her up in his arms, laid the golden sceptre on her neck, and spoke to her in the most endearing manner, saying, Thou shalt not die; I am thy brother. *What wilt thou, queen Esther?*

And no wonder that a king was overcome with such transcendent beauty and loveliness, when, like a snow-wreath, she sunk at his feet in the consciousness of a painful duty well done. No wonder the whole court was a sobbing gallery, when they saw the queen was saved. Tears of joy—of relief, rolled from every eye, as they saw the crisis past. And now, the queen reviving, touched the golden sceptre in token of perfect submission; and then she said to the king, "When I saw thee, thy terrible majesty made me afraid, and I thought you would be to me as an avenging angel, and my heart troubled me, and my strength went from me." Think no more of it, my lovely queen, said the king. *What is thy request and it shall be given thee, to the half of the kingdom.* "Only this, my lord, if it seem good unto the king, let the king and my lord, prince Haman, come this day unto the banquet that I have prepared for him." Womanlike, no sooner has she conquered than she is prepared to make the most of the victory, nor will she risk her influence now by telling him all she really wants, but only asks the king, and his favorite, to a banquet with her the next day.

1. *Observe the queen's modesty*—her extraordinary prudence at the very moment that she is most successful. Her request was a simple invitation to have the king come to a banquet of wine the next day, and as a mark of regard for his preferences, she wishes him to bring Haman. I do not say, however, that she may not also have thought this a good way to prevent his suspicions from being awakened, and to keep him from adopting any hasty measures against the Jews. It was wise to show this much respect for the king's partiality, and then it served to secure his presence when his plot was to be unmasked to the king. The queen put her life in danger, and she not only lives, but obtains favor besides pardon. The king promises her half of his kingdom. He had, at Haman's demand, given him the lives and the goods of all the Jewish race; but here, before she has asked for anything, the king offers the queen half his kingdom. This must have astonished her as much as she had been in fear of his imperious temper. But recovering herself as she remembered that "the king's heart is in the hands of the Lord; as the rivers of water, He turneth it withersoever He will,"

she did not prefer her great request at once. She wished to have the king more fully prepared for so important a matter. It is not good breeding, nor wise policy, "to swallow favors too greedily, lest they either choke us in the passage, or prove hard of digestion."

2. In Esther's fasting and prayer, and pious courage, we see that faith and piety are not always shorn of their fruits under unfavorable influences; they may flourish in a palace. The atmosphere of the court of Susa, and the power of a Persian husband, have not crushed out all Mordecai's catechism from her soul. In every condition of life, if we are faithful to ourselves, the grace of God is sufficient for us. A slave in the field, or in the mines, or in the galleys; or a member of Nero's court, or near Belshazzar's throne; in Egypt or Persia, at home or abroad, the grace of God is promised to us according to our day. As the sun makes the laughing waves to glisten, and the high mountains to shine with light, and yet makes glad the weary captive in his dungeon, or in the dark recesses of the noisy mill, so the Gospel dignifies a throne, and makes glad a hovel. In a chaotic state of society, a pious man may have greater difficulties to overcome in maintaining a goldy walk, but then, in overcoming these difficulties, he will gain a greater degree of spiritual strength. Where there are trials to develop the strength of one's character, there the good will be like Jeremiah's figs, very good, and the bad will be very bad.

3. *Queen Esther was a true representative woman.* Every one is raised up as she was, not to be a Sultana,

and do just the work she did, but to do his or her own work. Every one has a duty to perform—a post to maintain—a lot to fulfill. Every one of us is brought to the kingdom, at such a time, and under such circumstances as God sees best to order, and it is our first and highest duty to improve them all for His glory. Mordecai's great argument with the queen was, that God had raised her up at that very time to the throne of Persia, that she might do this service for His church. It is a great blessing that we have been made to do something, and happy is he who finds his work, and does it with a hearty good will. There is a work for every one of us. Let us be diligent and careful in performing it, lest we let our opportunities slip for serving our generation. The providence of God may not design us to sit on thrones like that of Persia, but we have our duty to do just as much as Esther had. We are all God's stewards, and will have to render a strict account of all the gifts, graces and opportunities bestowed upon us. We must watch for opportunities to do good, and to arrest evil. We must ever be ready to follow the leadings of Providence.

4. It may sometimes be our duty to ourselves, our country, our fellow-men and our God, to put our *lives in jeopardy for the truth, or for the church, and for the sake of Jesus.* This Samson did when his hair grew and his strength returned, and he prayed and pulled down the heathen temple.* This is just what David did when he went to meet the giant of Gath. The prophets and apostles did not think of saving their lives, but only of serving God faithfully. So, in our history,

* See my volume, "The Giant Judge," pp. 303–5.

Esther's duty was plain. True piety ought to make men brave. It is not for a Christian to shrink from duty for fear of death, or persecution. We ought, says an apostle, to lay down our lives for the brethren, for Christ gave his life a ransom for us. Our lives are His—we ought to surrender them then at His call.

5. *We should never fear to do our duty.* The God whom we serve is able either to sustain us under our trials, or to deliver us out of them. He will always do one or the other. His compassion cannot fail. Like as a father pitieth his children, so the Lord pitieth them that fear Him. Why, then, should we shrink from any degree of suffering or of persecution? Why should we ever fear to avow our principles, or ever turn aside from the performance of a trying duty? Why should we yield to the fear of man, that bringeth a snare, seeing we are in the hands of Him who holdeth the hearts of all men and of devils in his hand? Satan could not sift Peter, nor touch an article of Job's estate, nor a hair of his head, till express leave was granted him. And so it is now. All our foes are chained; and the extent of their reach is determined by the pleasure of Him who loved us so much as to die for us. It is His purpose to destroy the works of the Devil. If he careth for us, it is enough. Let us commit our cares to Him, and go on our way rejoicing. It is sinful to pass our time on earth in bondage to the fear of death—or in slavish apprehensions of any evil. Sufficient for the day is the evil, and sufficient also is the grace of our Lord Jesus Christ. Why should we indulge tormenting fear about health or comfort? All

things are in our Heavenly Father's hands, and He knoweth what we have need of. If he says, let Providence prosper that man, it is done. He succeeds. For the blessing of the Lord maketh rich. If He says, let floods and fires, plague and pestilence, be abroad on the earth—it is done. And men are poor, and sick, and dying. But if He says to sickness, touch not my servants; then the pestilence may walk in darkness, and the destruction rage at noon-day; and a thousand may fall at his side, and ten thousand at his right hand, and it shall not come nigh him. We are immortal till our change comes. While God has work for us to do, He will uphold us, and when His will is fulfilled with us in this world, then we should go cheerfully to another.

6. *The privilege and efficacy of prayer.* The murderous plot for the extermination of all the Hebrews in the world, to human eyes, seems perfect. But God's thoughts are not as our thoughts. By the breath of the God of their fathers, all this grand contrivance, stretching through so vast an empire, and employing so many agencies, shall become as desert sand before the wind, and be blown back in an overwhelming mass upon its author. But Mordecai, the queen and the people, all work together. They have all committed their cause to God, by fasting and prayer; and while the people and Mordecai continue pleading with the King of kings, the queen put her life in peril, and went to plead for favor from the great king of Persia. The queen's example is worthy of imitation, in two particulars, namely: *First,* as Henry remarks, here is an example of a mistress praying with her maids, that is worthy of

being followed by all house-keepers and heads of families. And, *secondly*, we are here encouraged to ask the sympathy and prayers of others, when we undertake any great or perilous enterprise. And especially are those who are called, in the providence of God, to stand forth boldly in perilous aervices, in the high places of the Church and of the State, entitled to the united prayers of their brethren. When Peter was put in prison, the Church made prayer unceasingly for him, and God sent his angel to deliver him. How often and earnestly does the great apostle ask for the prayers of believers? And how instructive the fact, that, while the Jewish High Priest was within the Holy of Holies, making intercession for the people, the people were all praying without. And while Joshua leads on God's hosts amidst the Amalekites, Moses stands praying, and Aaron and Hurr hold up his hands; and the battle waxes or wanes as the praying prevails or grows slack. Wonderful is the efficacy of prayer. It was in answer to prayer the God of Esther's pious fathers moved the heart of the king to hold out the golden sceptre. And her bold approach to the king is a fit illustration of prayer. Our Lord, from the Parable of the Unjust Judge, has taught us that men ought always to pray, and not to faint. Esther came to a proud, imperious, sinful man; we come to the God of love and grace. She came uncalled—nay, not only not called, but forbidden, by law, to come, upon pain of death—we are invited. The Spirit and the Bride say come. She came with a law against her, in her face; we come, pleading the invitations and promises of the Gospel. God invites the broken-hearted and the contrite in spirit into His presence. Queen Esther had no friend near the throne who dared to open his lips to plead her cause. The king's favorite was her greatest enemy. But, brethren, if any man sin, we have an Advocate with the Father, even his own Son, Jesus Christ, our Lord. He ever liveth, to make intercession for us. The golden sceptre in His hands is always stretched out. He is touched with a fellow-feeling for our infirmities.

7. One of the gracious designs of affliction is to make us feel our dependence upon God. A gracious result of trials to the people of God, is that it drives them to prayer. But the court of heaven is not like that of Persia, into which there was no entrance for those that were in mourning, or clothed with sackcloth. Such could not come near the palace of Ahasuerus. But it is the weary, the heavy laden and the sorrowing, that are especially invited to the throne of grace, and invited to come boldly. Is any among you afflicted, saith the apostle James, let him pray. Call upon me, saith the Lord, in the day of trouble, and I will deliver thee. Doubtless the iminent peril into which the Jews were brought, was to remind them of their dependence on the God of their fathers. They were, as we are, ready to forget him, and especially so, when far from home. But now that there seems to be no other ear to hear, no other hand that can save, they are brought to their knees—and with fasting, and humility, and fervency of spirit—they call upon God, that peradventure He will be gracious to them. It was so also with Manasseh. And it was when the prodigal began to be in want, he thought of returning home. Afflictions sanc-

tified are blessings. And how exceedingly appropriate for you, poor sinner, is the queen's resolve. As a sinner, you are condemned, and under sentence of death. There is no escape for you but to believe in the Lord Jesus Christ. Nor is there a moment to lose. To-morrow, even to-morrow, may be too late. Remember, then, that Jesus Christ came to seek and save that which is lost. He casts out none that come unto Him. He is the sinner's friend. Try his love this one time, by casting yourself as a guilty sinner upon his mercy. Say with the hymn:

I'll go to Jesus though my sin
  High as a mountain rose,
I know his court, I'll enter in
  Whatever may oppose.

Perhaps he will admit my plea,
  Perhaps will hear my prayer;
But if I perish, I will pray,
  And perish only there.

I can but perish if I go,
  I am resolved to try;
For if I stay away, I know
  I must forever die.

CHAPTER XIII.

THE BANQUET AND THE SLEEPLESS KING.

"No action, whether foul or fair,
Is ever done, but it leaves somewhere
A record, written by fingers ghostly,
As a blessing or a curse.——"

Longfellow.

WE have seen that the king promised to attend the queen's banquet, and ordered Haman to make haste, that he might do as Esther had said. *So the king and Haman came to the banquet that Esther had prepared.* See verses 6, 7 and 8 of the *fifth* chapter of Esther.

At the banquet the king is delighted, and demands of the queen what she desired, and declares that her request, even to the half of the kingdom, shall be granted. This seems to have been a common form of court promises, meaning that nothing would be denied. Herod made a similar proposition, but instead of giving half of his kingdom, in compliance with a wicked woman's request, he gave her the head of John the Baptist, which was of more value than the whole of his kingdom.

Among the Persians and Orientals, generally, wine banquets were common, they seem to have been designed chiefly for pleasure, rather than for eating—delightful social intercourse, and as tokens or occasions of showing honor, rather than for the gratification of the appetites—"the feast of reason and flow of soul" —"a dejuner sans fourchette." Our authors are not agreed, however, whether the wine banquet was before or after the principal meal, or whether it was a feast above and independent of all other kinds of fare. It is clear, however, that some of their wine banquets comprised fruits, and mutton, rice, fowls, game, as well as Shiraz wines.

And the queen answered, "My petition, and my request is, if I have found favor with the king, let him and Haman come to the banquet that I shall prepare for them to-morrow." Now why did not the queen at once acquaint the king with the matter so much in her heart? We answer, by delaying her petition she showed that it was one of no ordinary importance—proved her modesty and self-command—and perhaps she was a little daunted by the king's august presence—her heart may have been ready to fail her—and perhaps she thought it best to try how far she had gained on the king's affections, and to test the influence she had over him—and perhaps she thought to-morrow the king will be more amiable and ready to grant my petition; or, in the meantime, Haman may show some signs of insolence, or make himself less agreeable to the king, or God may, in some way, display his power, and open up some other door of hope—whether any or all of these thoughts passed through her mind, we do not know; but it is recorded that the queen deemed it most becoming—that it was wisest to engage the king's affection by a second entertainment before she made him acquainted with the great matters that were on her heart. And, above all, I see no inconsistency in supposing that she was influenced to this delay by a kind Providence, to make way for the events of the coming night, that were to prepare the king for the success of her enterprise. It was a wise policy, on her part, to repeat the banquet, for thereby she was gaining the confidence of the king, and strengthening her forces for the great demand; but God's hand was in it also, for, speaking, after the manner of men, Providence wished to gain time for the developments of the following night, and succeeding day, of which we have an account in the sixth chapter of Esther. It is not heresy to say that Providence usually helps the bravest and best disciplined troops. On the contrary, it is genuine orthodox Calvinism to trust in God and keep the gunpowder dry. It is an interesting theological and historico-philosophical fact, that the very men who have believed most thoroughly in the Divine Sovereignty, are the very men that have been distinguished as the hard workers of the race. Witness Paul, Calvin, Knox, Cromwell, Napoleon and Edwards. The belief that God works in us to will and to do of his good pleasure, is the strongest possible motive to put forth our own efforts in the same direction.

From this first banquet "Haman went forth *joyful and with a glad heart;* but when he saw Mordecai in the king's gate, that he stood not up, nor moved for him, he was full of indignation against Mordecai." Nevertheless he refrained himself from taking sudden and summary vengeance upon him, but goes home full of pride and rage—of pride because of the honor he had received in being called to the queen's banquet with the king alone, and full of rage because Mordecai would not do him homage. But when he reaches his palace, he calls his friends, and his wife Zeresh, and tells them, in true oriental style, of "the glory of his riches, and the multitude of his children, and how the king had advanced him above the princes, all his servants, and even the queen did let no man come in with the king unto the banquet but himself; and to-morrow am I invited unto her also with the king."

Observe here: 1. How God restrained the heart of a wicked man. Haman could easily have had Mordecai put to death. He had the king's signet ring to take measures to kill, root up, and destroy every member of the hated Hebrew race. By his own hand, or that of his servants, therefore, he could have destroyed Mordecai at once. But an unseen power controlled him. Divine Providence disposed of the case until the plot should ripen.

2. Haman's *glorying* preceded his fall. Pride cometh before destruction. Even the wisdom of Ahithophel is perfect folly when the Lord curses a man. It is by no means an uncommon thing for us to make fatal mistakes in our ignorance, and to rejoice when we should fear, and to sorrow for things that either never happen, or if they do, turn to our joy and comfort. In Haman's boasting while he gratified his own vanity, he designed, no doubt, to aggravate Mordecai's impudence in the mind of his friends. Favors are sometimes done by men to their fellow-men for the

purpose of ensnaring them. And even in the providence of God, we find men allowed to wax fat, or to grow rich and great, in order that they may make a full trial of themselves, and prove to themselves, and to the world, what is in their hearts. So here, Haman is honored with the king. The queen does not invite the king without Haman. Nor can he read the queen's heart. He sees not, on her face, the petition which she is preparing to lay before the king, which is to cover him with shame, and send him to hang on his own gallows.

3. Haman's riches and glory, and children, however, were not enough. *Yet all this availeth me nothing, so long as I see Mordecai the Jew, sitting at the king's gate.* His malice is equal only to his envy, and his envy is equalled only by his bitter prejudice against the Jews. No honor, no privilege, did he allow to a Jew, much less to one who, like Mordecai, would not worship him. What a cloudy epilogue is this, after so much royal sunshine! How impatient his malice—how unrelenting his hate! Already he has fixed on the month Adar for the slaughter of all the Jews, as well as of Mordecai, but he is not willing to wait.

4. Observe *the wife's advice.* "Then said Zeresh, his wife, and all his friends unto him, let a gallows be made fifty cubits high, and to-morrow speak thou unto the king that Mordecai may be hanged thereon; then go thou in merrily with the king unto the banquet. And the thing pleased Haman; and he caused the gallows to be made." *Fifty cubits high*—say seventy-five feet. *The highth* was intended to deepen the disgrace of

Mordecai, and strike terror into the hearts of Haman's enemies—as if Mordecai's ignominy was to be measured by the hight of the gallows. From the ninth verse of the seventh chapter of Esther, we learn that this gallows was *in the house of Haman;* that is within the square court yard which was the centre of his palace buildings. The Hebrew word for gallows, *ets,* signifies simply wood, tree or pole, without designating the form. It was probably similar in its construction to the gallows of modern days, or in the shape of a cross, such as was afterward used by the Romans, with an extension beam for the rope. It appears from the edicts of the Emperors Justinian and Theodosius, abolishing the custom, that the Jews, in the early ages of Christianity, were in the habit of burning Haman in effigy, (as is now sometimes done with Judas Iscariot by Christians,) and with him a wooden cross, in imitation as they said, of the gallows which he had prepared for Mordecai, but which the early Christians thought was intended to show them contempt. In the earlier ages of the church, there was unfortunately great prejudice and much bitterness between Christians and Jews. We see it in the Acts of the Apostles, and in the Epistles, and even in modern times, we know that Christians have persecuted the Jews, and perhaps there is no Government in the world but our own that is wholly free from the charge of some intolerance, illiberality or persecution toward the Israelites. Thank God, the Government of the United States has never shed a drop of blood in persecuting men for their religious opinions. May this be true of it forever!

But we have now to go from Haman's council chamber to the palace, and find a monarch that cannot sleep. Though the throne of Persia was then the most glorious on earth, its master could not sleep. Every luxury, every anodyne that wealth could buy was his, but the king could not sleep that night. If too much fruit and wine made him restless, it was only a controlling providence that brought out the result. The king's sleep fled away, and neither Persian scimitar nor courier could bring it back. See Esther vi: 1, 3, inclusive.

And he commanded to bring the book of records of the Chronicles. When and by whom writing was invented is not known. But the expression of thoughts and the recording of events, by characters or signs, is as old, or nearly so, as the race of man. Writing-tables were in use before the age of *Homer*, for he speaks of writing pernicious things on a two-leaved table. These tables were made of wood, consisting of two, three or five leaves, and were covered with wax, and, on these, impressions were made which were quite durable and easily read. It was a Roman custom for the *pontifex maximus* to commit to writing the public affairs of each year, and publish them on a table, so that the public could become acquainted with them. It was, also, their custom to hang up the laws that had been regularly made and approved, and recorded on tables of brass, in the market-places and in their temples and places of public resort, that they might be seen and read. It was thus the edicts of the Emperors against the Christians were published. Even in the life of so great a man as Cicero, we find him making a strenuous effort, on a certain occasion, to carry off the brazen tablets, on which the law of the Senate that had sent him into exile was engraved, for the purpose of destroying them. Expunging resolutions are not, therefore, original in the American Congress. It were well, however, if there was no occasion for them.

It is plain, from the Bible, that the Hebrew prophets were used to writing and making public, by recording on tables, in the temple or in their own houses, so much of their own prophesyings as concerned the people, or as it might be enjoined upon them thus to publish. Thus Habbakuk ii: 2: "And the LORD answered me, and said, Write the vision, and make it plain upon tables, that he may run that readeth it." And Jeremiah was repeatedly commanded to write down his visions. And we know that the Almighty wrote, with his own finger, the Ten Commandments on tables of stone. If the art of writing was not known before, it could surely have been learned from the tables of the law. But if the Mosaic Decalogue is not the original of all writing, (and I do not say it is,) it is, nevertheless, an instance of the knowledge of letters in a remote age. Moreover, all the world is now acquainted with the fact, that the history of cities and empires, and of great conquerors, especially of their battles, prisoners, victories, honors and offerings to their gods, was written, in olden times, on clay tablets, bricks, stones and cylinders—on the walls of temples, tombs and palaces—and that this kind of writing goes back far beyond the reign of king Ahasuerus ; and that we have the key which enables us to read these monumental records. There is nothing, then, contrary to history in the statement that the sleepless monarch commanded to bring *the book of records of the Chronicles to be read* before him. These chronicles are called, by Ctesias, *diptherai basilikai*. They seem to have been written on leather or parchment. The custom of the Persian kings, in keeping a corps of scribes or royal historiographers about them, whose duty it was to write down what they said and did, has already been referred to and illustrated from cotemporary history. Similar chronicles, or registers of State, are referred to several times in the history of the Hebrew kings. The same custom prevails, to this day, in the Ottoman empire. "The king," says Bruce, "has near his person an officer, who is meant to be his historiographer; he is, also, keeper of his seal, and is obliged to make a journal of the king's actions, good or bad, without any comment of his own upon them. When the king dies, or soon after, this journal is delivered to the council, who read it over, and erase everything false in it, while they supply every material fact that may have been omitted, whether purposely or not."

Nor were *the records of the Chronicles* of the Persian empire so dry and stupid an affair as many suppose. There was not within his reach any composition better suited to his perturbed state of mind than these records. They were instructive and usually well written, and in verse. The records of Persia are still kept in this way. *Ferdusi*, who is regarded as the *Homer* of India, spent thirty years in writing his great poem, which contains one hundred and twenty thousand lines. And as the *Sultan* had promised him a dinar, perhaps two dollars and a half, for every line, we are not surprised at its length. This poem is nothing but a collection of the chronicles of former poets, brought down from the creation to the reign of *Mohammed Ghezny*, in the beginning of the tenth century. This famous epic poem is said to be written " in all the harmony, strength and elegance of the most beautiful and harmonious language in the universe. It flows deep and strong, like a river of oil over every kind of channel."

Nor was the custom wholly confined to the East. The " Chronicles of the Cid," William of Malmesbury's "Chronicles of the kings of England," the six old English Chronicles, viz : Asser's Life of Alfred, and Chronicles of Eldred, Ethelred, Nennius, Geoffrey of Monmouth, and of Richard, and " the Chronicles of the Crusaders," of Robert of Gloucester, and Ossian, and the famous Spanish and English ballads, are a part and parcel of the history and literature of our own day. " The poet laureate" of her Majesty, is the modern successor of these royal scribes—the crown paid register of eulogies. Such I conceive to have been the records read to Ahasuerus. In explaining the king's wakefulness, the *Targum* tells us that the king first had a dream that night, to the effect that he saw a man, who wished to speak to him, saying, " Haman desireth to slay thee and to make himself king in thy stead. Behold he will come unto thee early in the morning, to ask from thee the man who rescued thee from death, that he may slay him; but say thou unto Haman, What shall be done for the man whose honor the king studieth ? And thou wilt find that he will ask nothing less from thee than the royal vestments, the regal crown, and the horse on which the king is wont to ride." This looks very much like telling where a thing is lost after it is found. It is well known, however, that the Ancients and the Orientals still are much given to dreams. Homer makes Rhesus die in a dream, from the sword of Diomed. That is, just as he was agonized with such a dream, it literally came to pass.

The king did not know why he could not sleep, but thought the reading of the Chronicles might amuse his mind. There were many other sources of pleasure or amusement at hand. His wives and concubines, and singers and musicians—why did he not turn to some of them for relief? The answer is, Providence designed to bring before his mind another matter. In Haman's house, his friends and his wife are arranging to have Mordecai hanged, but in the king's palace, God is disposing of matters for a very different result. The plots are to ripen, but the victim is not to gratify Haman's cruel prejudice.

It were a great gain to the intelligence and morals of our day, if more of the sleepless hours of young people were spent in reading standard histories, rather than in corrupting their minds and polluting their imaginations with the flash literature or the sensation poetry and essays of the day. It is not easy to overstate the pleasure and profit of history. Perhaps the king hoped by having the records read, to deceive the tediousness of the night, or that the pleasant passages would either invite slumber, or enable him to endure his wakefulness with greater ease. Zaccheus, says the quaint old Thomas Fuller, and may his shadow never be less, was low and little in stature; but when he had borrowed some hight from the fig tree, the dwarf became a giant—but last minute beneath the arms, now grown on a sudden above the heads of other men. Thus our experimental knowledge is, in itself, both short and narrow. It cannot exceed the span of our own life. But when we are mounted on the tree of history, we can not only reach the year of Christ's incarnation, but even touch the top of the world's beginning, and at one view, oversee all the remarkable accidents of former ages.

CHAPTER XIV.

THE ROYAL HONORING.

"Array him in the robe of honor,
And place a chain of gold around his neck,
And bind around his brow the diadem,
And mount him on my steed of state,
And lead him through the camp,
And let the Heralds go before and cry
'Thus shall the Sultan reward
The man who serves him well!'
Then in the purple robe
They vested Thalaba,
And hung around his neck the golden chain,
And bound his forehead with the diadem,
And on the royal steed
They led him through the camp,
And Heralds went before and cried,
'Thus shall the Sultan reward
The man who serves him well!'"

Southey's Thalaba.

It was found, on reading the Chronicles, which the sleepless king had called for, that the portion read told how Mordecai had saved the king's life, but as there was no record of any reward or honor having been shown to him for such distinguished service, the king inquired whether there was an omission in the record, or whether this man had been neglected. And his servants that ministered unto him, said: "There is nothing done for him." And the king said, who is in the court? Now Haman was come into the outward court of the king's house, to speak unto the king to hang Mordecai on the gallows that he had prepared for him. And the king's servants said unto him, "behold, Haman standeth in the court." Esth. vi: 4, 5. Though Haman was a great favorite, he could not enter till called. There was a waiting room where the servants and visitors were to remain in readiness to come in whenever called. Herod. lib. iii: c. 120.

It is plain enough why Haman is so early this morning in the waiting room of the king. Although he knew nothing of the king's dream nor want of sleep, he is early in the outer court, just as the Targum already cited says the king's early night vision had revealed to him. Haman's pride and revenge would not let him sleep. As soon as the king is informed that Haman is in the waiting room, he says, *let him come in,* and then, without giving him time to make any request, puts the question direct to him: "What shall be done unto the man whom the king delighteth to honor?" At first blush, Haman thought this promises everything I can ask. For the thought in his heart was, "To whom would the king delight to do honor more than to myself?" See also vi: 7, 11, inclusive.

Here let us observe, *first,* the discovery of neglect toward Mordecai prepared the way for his honor. Being a Jew, no reward had been given him for his fidelity to the king; or, through the envy of courtiers or forgetfulness of the king, nothing had been done for such signal service. But a record had been made of it. This was all ordered by Divine Providence, that the developments might all be made at the proper time. And so, also, *secondly*, Haman's spleen and malice brings him early to the court of the king. Impatient to have his revenge, he intends, this morning, at the very first moment, to ask the king to have Mordecai hanged, and has everything in readiness. So politic was he, that, though he had the power in his own hand, he preferred the king should, personally, order the execution. Neither Haman nor the king could sleep. The cause of their wakefulness was different, but both are working together, without knowing it, for the same result. And, *thirdly*, although Haman was exceedingly impatient and burning with rage, he could not enter the royal presence until called to come, and although the king knows nothing of the high gallows which he has had built for Mordecai, nor anything of his designs against him, yet he does not give him time to open his mouth, before he demands from him, *What shall be done unto the man whom the king delighteth to honor?* And Haman, believing no man was so high in the royal favor as himself, and that, in giving advice, he was only issuing a decree to heap glory on himself, said: "For the man whom the king delighteth to honor, let the royal apparel be brought which the king useth to wear, and the horse that the king rideth upon, and the crown royal which is set upon his head: And let this apparel and horse be delivered into the hand of one of the king's most noble princes, that they may array the man withal whom the king delighteth to honor, and bring him on horseback through the street of the city, and proclaim before him, Thus shall it be done to the man whom the king delighteth to honor. Then the king said to Haman, Make haste, and take the apparel and the horse, as thou hast said, and do even so to Mordecai, the Jew, that sitteth at the king's gate: let nothing fail of all that thou hast spoken. Then took Haman the apparel and the horse, and arrayed Mordecai, and brought him on horseback through the street of the city, and proclaimed before him, Thus shall it be done unto the man whom the king delighteth to honor."

Royal honoring, in this style, was common in those days. Kings had horses kept especially for their own use, and robes and apparel, of all sorts, that no one else was allowed to wear, or, if bestowed on any one else, they were not used again by the sovereign. In 1 Kings i: 33, we find David making Solomon ride upon his mule, as a token of the great honor he would have put upon him. Ancient authors, as Justin, Curtius and others, bear testimony to the use of such robes of purple, interwoven with gold. Scarlet and purple are royal colors. Commentators do not agree as to the crown; whether it is the meaning of the text, that the crown royal itself was placed on the horse's head, or a mere effigy of the crown; or a make-belief of placing it on the horse's head, but really setting it only on the king's head. It seems to me the meaning of the passage is, that the king's crown was set upon the horse's head. 1. The original Hebrew, as well as our translation, favors this construction. 2. This is, also, the Chaldee and the Jewish interpretation. 3. No mention is made of the crown in the verses, after the eighth verse; but only the horse and apparel, which seems fairly to imply that the crown was identified with the horse, as one of his ornaments, from the moment of his decoration to the end of the triumphal procession. And, 4. It is known, from history, that such a custom did prevail among the ancient Persians and Ethiopians, and, at a later period, in Italy. The crown royal was put on the head of the horse that was led in state, and the horses attached to the triumphal chariots were adorned with crowns, just as in our gala days our horses are adorned with flowers, ribbons and flags. It is written that a Roman consul, once, put the insignia of his office on his horse's head, and then told the people, so fickle and corrupt had they become at their elections, that his crowned horse was the best consul the Romans had ever had. Let Americans profit by the lesson. When Alexander entered Babylon, the way was covered with flowers and branches of trees, and his horse was made to walk on roses, sugar and cloth of gold. And you all recollect the history of our Lord's entrance into Jerusalem, not long before his crucifixion. The proclamation made before Mordecai was according to oriental custom. The same was done for Joseph in Egypt. (Gen. xli: 43.) When a Pasha rides through the streets of an Eastern city, it is the custom, to this day, for a man to run before, flourishing a long whip, to clear the way for the great man who cometh—sometimes calling out his name and titles, that all may get out of the way, or fall down in humble prostration before him. And observe, *fourthly*, how terribly bitter was this pill to Haman—to fail to receive the honor himself, and to be compelled to bestow it, by his own hand and with his own lips, upon the man whom, of all others, he hated with the most hearty good will. It is no wonder the Targum should say, that, when he received the king's command thus to honor Mordecai, he begged the king to kill him, rather than degrade him by compelling him to render such service to a despised Jew. No wonder he went home, that night, *to his house, mourning and having his head covered*—verse 12. It was an ancient custom, among the Jews and Persians, and, perhaps, other nations, also, to cover the head in times of great sorrow and mourning, and, also, as a token of reverence and submission. On the days of mourning for the dead, or showing affection for them, one may see multitudes in the grave-yards of Scutari, and other Asiatic cities, with their heads covered, engaged, on theis knees, at their devotions. Elijah wrapped his head in his mantle at the mouth of the cave, as we read in 1 Kings xix, in token of his reverence and readiness to hear and obey the voice of the Lord. And so, when David fled from Absalom, he "went by the ascent of Mount Olives, and wept, as he went up, and had his head covered, and he went barefoot; and all the people that was with him covered every man his head, and they went up, weeping as they went up. (2 Sam. xv: 30.) And so, also, the nobles in the time of famine, in Jeremiah xiv: 3, 4, were confounded and ashamed, and "covered their heads."

Here we have a foreshadowing of the future. The feet of the gods, as the proverb says, may be shod with wool, and they may be slow as well as soft in their coming; but their coming is certain and terrible. Mordecai is at last honored. Justice seemed tardy, but came at last, and with a reward all the greater, on account of her tardiness. But he wears his honors meekly. He is not puffed up with vanity to-day, because yesterday the streets of Shushan were ringing with the honors the king had bestowed on him. *And Mordecai came again to the king's gate*—as prompt and diligent at his humble post, as if no honors had been granted him. But Haman, poor miserable man, ready to plant

> "Hensbane and aconite on his mother's grave,"

if he could only satiate his revenge on Mordecai, hastens home, boiling over with rage. Rapidly, however, is his cup filling up. If the gods in Persia have been traveling with leaden feet, now they will strike with iron hands. If their mills grind slowly, they will grind to powder at last. Haman had the gallows built—rushes to court to have Mordecai hanged on it, is called in, considers himself flattered, prescribes for his own exaltation, as he supposed. But alas! how bitter his disappointment! How unexpected the turn of events that day! The great honor he had plotted for himself, he has himself been compelled to bestow upon his most abhorred adversary, and then to go home under public disgrace. And worse still, the very first to reproach him, are those that advised him to pursue this malicious course toward Mordecai. Ah! this was the bitterest part of his cup. "And Haman told Zeresh, his wife, and all his friends, everything that had befallen him. Then said his wise men and Zeresh, his wife, unto him, If Mordecai be of the seed of the Jews, before whom thou hast begun to fall, thou shalt not prevail against him, but shalt surely fall before him." Sage counsellors! Fools! why did you not think of this sooner? Are you now afraid that Mordecai is indeed of Abraham's seed? He has been much talked about of late, how is it that you are not certain whether he is a Jew or not? And now that you find Haman in trouble for following your advice, how is it that you are so ready to overwhelm him with reproach? But on what ground do you conclude that if Mordecai is of Abraham's seed, and if Haman had once begun to fall before him, that he must ultimately be crushed by him? Is it merely from views of general policy and the custom of courts, that when once a new favorite appears, old ones are sacrificed?—that in politics the rising, and not the setting sun is worshipped? Or is it because you are somewhat familiar with Hebrew history? Are you acquainted with the predictions of the old Hebrew prophets, and are you afraid of the great and all-powerful God whom these Jews worship? Have you read of the miracles of Moses and of the overthrow of Pharaoh, of the exploits of Joshua, and the conquest of Canaan? Are you afraid of the slaying of your first born, or of another miracle like that of the Red Sea? And are you searching the chronicles of the reign of David, and of the overthrow of Sennacherib's mighty host? The history of Daniel was recent and must have been known to them.

The septuagint asserts here, that Haman's wife said, Thou shalt surely fall before him, *for the living God is with him.* This was true in every particular. The living God was with Mordecai, and, on this account, Haman was sure to fall before him; but how did such a wicked heathen woman come to utter such a sentiment? Were the surrounding heathen under an abiding, indefinite, but deep impression that the Jews were a peculiar people, and that extraordinary Providences attended them? Or were they under an *instinctive* knowledge that Mordecai was a protege of Divine Providence? Or rather, did not the spirit of God give them some intimations of the glory that certainly awaited the seed of the Jews,—such as Balaam and Caiphas had?

1. In Haman honoring Mordecai, we have a remarkable verification of the fable of the dog and the shadow. He gaped after the shadow and lost the substance. Folly generally rides after pride. Haman grew more and more insolent, and arrogant, as he advanced in wealth and power, until he reached the highest point allowed to him by Providence. He did not consider that he who does not climb gets no fall, and that he that climbs too high is sure, at last, to come down with a terrible crash. His temerity is remarkable. Thinking, however, that he was ordered to cut out his own honor, it is natural he should have made the measure large. So vaulting was his envy that he must have Mordecai swing on a gallows *fifty cubits* high, when five cubits would have answered just as well, but then the ignominy would only have been five cubits high, whereas he was resolved it should be fifty. And so sharp set was he for Jewish blood, that he cannot wait for the general massacre, but must break his fast on Mordecai. But there is an unseen Divinity shaping his destiny, whose plans never miscarry. The king calls for the Chronicles, and God's hand, on the margin, points the reader to the place

where Mordecai's services are recorded, but not rewarded, and this leads at once to Mordecai's honor and Haman's severe mortification.

2. How completely wretched are the envious and the proud. Pride is the canker-worm of the soul. It always renders us unhappy. As soon as the angels let it enter their hearts, if it be correct that their sin began in pride, they became wicked and wretched. Adam sought the forbidden fruit to satisfy his inordinate desires. Solomon's proud heart ceased not to pursue his pleasures and ambition till he was obliged to confess all was vanity and vexation. Ahab had enough, but his covetousness did not let him rest till he had Naboth's vineyard, and, with it, Jehovah's curse. Haman was prime minister of the greatest empire then in the world, but how wretched, because this contemptible Jew would not render him such homage as his proud heart exacted. It is ever so with those who have not a new heart. The most wealthy and highly honored are not content. There is something still wanting. There is something they still complain about. They make themselves miserable when they ought to be happy. Oh, how little a thing is earthly grandeur! How little a thing may embitter all human honor and affluence! An Eastern proverb says, a gnat may run an elephant mad. A dead fly spoils the pot of ointment, says the Bible. So it was with Haman. The pride of his heart deceived him. The fear of God was not before his eyes. Always feeding his vanity, and his selfishness, his envy grew to such a size that it allowed him no rest. Day and night it tyrannized over

him, filling his soul with the most envenomed resentments and tormenting passions. There can be no happiness on earth till there is self-denial and trust. There is no happiness till we begin to crucify selfishness, and to trust in God as the portion of our souls. Even if Haman had been wronged, which was not the case, how much more Godlike would it have been to forgive? There can be no happiness without God's favor. For it is life, and His loving kindness is better than life; but we cannot love God, nor enjoy His favor without loving our fellow-men. Our Lord's rule is, that with what measure we mete to others, it shall be measured to us again. If we do not forgive one another our trespasses, our Heavenly Father will not forgive us our trespasses against Him. And even now, in this life, in the course of Providence, every man's observation for a few years is sufficient to show him, that men generally meet with those evils which they have been the means of inflicting on others. There is more justice in the world than is generally admitted. The world is very apt to treat a man as he treats it. At least, in the long run, he is sure to reap what he has sown.

3. We see here how great a misfortune it is to have friends and counsellors who are ignorant, wicked, or evil disposed. There is a great deal of truth in the proverb, Save me from my friends, and I will take care of my enemies. It is sad, when a man's bosom counsellor is not true and faithful. And there is always danger to be apprehended when the advice of a professed friend is pleasing to our own angry or revengeful feelings. There are no enemies so bad as those of our

own household; but a man's worst enemy is himself. As long as he is true to himself, neither men, nor devils, nor women can hurt him. How much of Haman's wickedness is justly to be charged upon his wife, we have no moral chemistry by which, at present, to ascertain. But, as in many other cases, so here, if not at the bottom of the business, a woman is in it. Lord Bollingbroke is reckoned among philosophers and great men, but one of the most sensible things he ever said was this: "When I am making up a plan of consequence," said he, "I always wish to consult with a sensible woman." Women are noted for their wit on emergencies, but in this history it was more than Greek with Greek—it was woman against woman—and, at one time, it looked as if the wife of the Amalekite would outwit the Queen of Shushan. Both have been at work, and, to-morrow, both are to make their final demonstration. But she has the victory who trusteth in Him that keepeth Israel, for He neither slumbereth nor sleepeth. If Haman's wife had been a meek, quiet, prudent, intelligent, God-fearing woman, her advice, at first, had been altogether of a different sort, and her bearing toward her husband, when he hastened home from court, almost heartbroken with disappointment and rage, would have been altogether different from what it was. Instead of adding fuel to his malignant passions, she should have endeavored to moderate and restrain them. And, instead of bruising a heart already broken, by adding taunt and reproach to grief, she should have sought to calm him, and make him feel that, with her, in his own home, he was still with friends, respected and beloved, however much he had suffered at court. It may be true of young men, as Schiller says, that they carry the stars of their destiny in their own bosoms, but it is not true of married men. *Wives carry the stars of their husbands' destinies in their bosoms.* The husband's fortune is more fully in the hands of his wife than anywhere else. It is for her to conform to his circumstances. This is both her respectability and happiness. I know not where to find sublimer exhibitions of fortitude and virtue than have been made by women who have been precipitated suddenly from affluence to absolute want. Then, again, a husband's fortune is in his wife's hands, for she, more than anybody else, can help him to make it, and to take care of it. I do not mean that she is to write his brief for the Supreme Court, or that she is to ride in his gig to see his patients for him, or that she is to manage his office; but I do mean, that his health, his vigor, both of body and mind, and his *moral strength*, depend upon her, and that it is only with these we have a right to expect him to succeed. It is her's to make his home happy, and to gird him with strength by sympathy and counsel. When his spirits are almost overwhelmed, she alone, of all human beings, is the one to minister to him. Her nursing is as sovereign to his sick soul as it is for his ailing body. It is her gentle tones only that can steal over his morbid senses with more power than David's harp. And when his courage is almost gone, her patience and fortitude will rekindle his heart again to dare and do, and meet anew the toils and troubles of life. When I think of Haman's wife, and her bitter reproach when he came home, I am not so much astonished at his wickedness, as that he did not go further. I wonder, when she chided him, he did not go and hang himself on the gallows she had caused him to have built for Mordecai.

What a misfortune it was that Haman had not a sweet CHRISTIAN HOME to retire to after the terrible disappointments and bitter experiences of that day! Yes, a sweet quiet Home. But you tell me I forget that he was a man of large estates, great honors, and the owner of a princely palace. True, but a palace is not always a Home. What is a home? It is something for which many of earth's babbling tongues have no term. A home is not a mere residence for the body, but a place where the heart rests and the affections nestle and dwell and multiply. *A Home* is the place where children romp and play, and learn to love, and where the husband and wife toil smilingly together, as they trudge up the hill on their way to a better world. If men are not happy anywhere else, O let them be happy at home. Have you not stood before the picture, "the soldier's dream," until you could hear your own breathing? But why so much enraptured with that picture? Is it not because you see the soldier by his bivouac fire fast asleep?—but to-morrow's drum is to awake him to battle and to death. Sleep on, then, happy dreamer. See in the visions of that heart of hearts, that can meet death at the cannon's mouth, your sweet "wee ones" and loving wife, with streaming hair and outstretched arms, welcoming you back from the wars. Yes, it is of Home the tented or the dying soldier thinks. And it is of Home the sailor thinks, on his lonely watch, far away on stormy seas. And the traveler, amid the feathery palm trees, and while gazing on the birds of bright plumage and gorgeous flowers, why does he seem to be staring on vacancy? "His heart is far away." Seas and lands and mountains, are all past in a moment, and he hears not the birds on starry wings that warble their Asiatic notes for him, but the lark that used to sing above his father's fields; and again he sees his fair-haired brother with a light foot chasing the butterfly by the spring branch, or the sweet sister that left them all to go and sing in the choir of the angels. Home! none but the weary and the worn, the traveled and the soiled of earth can know what it is. And our Home in heaven, the new Jerusalem—shall we not long for it, as birds about to migrate to those sunny lands where there is no more winter, "nor any more sorrow, nor any pain, nor any dying?" Just in the proportion that a good woman is a blessing, in the same proportion is a bad woman a curse. Woman's mission is a high and grand one. She is connected with everything that belongs to our race that is noble, refining and hopeful.

Great is the calamity, then, for a community to be under the influence of such opinions or sentiments as are degrading to its women. One bad woman can do more harm in society than a dozen of bad men. An ambitious, ungodly woman as a wife, or a mother, or a member of society, is a poisonous Upas, whose deadly influences are continually exuding and permeating the surrounding atmosphere. As she is man's best helper in meeting the cares of life, and making his way upward to God and heaven, so when she is herself without the fear of God, she is his most dangerous companion, and will utterly destroy his soul and body, and cast him down to perdition sooner, I had almost said, than the devil himself could do it. It is difficult—indeed I do not know that it is possible—to overstate the importance of female influence in our country. As long as our sisters, mothers and wives are pure, patriotic and pious, so long our Institutions are imperishable. As long as a husband has a wife, or a son has a mother to pray for him, so long there is hope of him. The husband or the son may be engrossed in the pursuit of wealth, or of pleasure, or of fame, but as long as his name is daily breathed up to the ear of God by a pious wife or mother, so long is there a golden chain still holding his soul to the anchor of hope. It may often seem to be ready to break, yet the chances are that at last he will be saved. "They that rock the cradle, govern the world."

CHAPTER XV.

HAMAN'S FALL AND DEATH.

"Then the king said, Hang him thereon."
Esther vii. 9.

"The vengeance-hour is come,
He tarried not—he past
The threshold, over which was no return."
Southey's Thalaba.

It appears that Haman was not in so great a haste to go to the second banquet as he had been to attend the first. For while he was yet talking with his wife and friends, about the mortification he had received, and his probable downfall before Mordecai, *the king's chamberlains came and hastened to bring him unto the banquet that Esther had prepared.* It is not hard to divine the reason of his tardiness. He had prepared himself for another feast, of a very different kind. He had more appetite for Jewish blood than for the queen's wine. Perhaps, indeed, he had some forebodings of his doom. Wicked men, even professed skeptics, are exceedingly prone to omens, and all kinds of superstition. The Orientals are great believers in the evil eye, and in signs and lucky days, and lucky faces, and lucky persons. Among them an individual, thought to be an unlucky person, is shunned. They do not wish him to travel with them, nor to do any business for them. We have seen Haman "with fuller reach and stronger swell, wave after wave advancing," until he seemed to have secured his purpose, the utter destruction of the Hebrew race. But he has gone the full length of his tether. He is now brought to his last feast. Here his life is to pay the reckoning. To him this wine banquet is to be like Mohammed Ali's to the Mamelukes—"The feast of death."

But let us go with the king and Haman to the second wine banquet of the peerless queen of Shushan. At the banquet the king said to Esther, "What is thy petition queen Esther? and it shall be granted thee, even to the half of the kingdom. Then Esther, the queen, answered and said, If I have found favor in thy sight, O king, and if it please the king, let my life be given me at my petition, and my people at my request." Esther vii: 3. As if she had said, save me, and the lives of my people, from the malice of our enemy. We are sold to destruction. We are delivered to be destroyed, and to be killed, and to utterly perish, by the very man that offered so large a sum for the destruction of the Jews. And had it been a calamity in anywise short of the extinction of the people from whom I am descended, I would have kept silent. But it is their utter annihilation that is decreed. And the ten thousand talents promised, if paid into the king's treasury, *will not countervail the king's damage*—will not repair his loss of tribute from the Jews within his dominions.

"Then the king answered, and said unto the queen,

Who is he, and where is he, that durst presume in his heart—that is, whose heart hath filled him *to do so*—to do such a cruel thing, and by it deprive me also of my revenue, and of my queen?

And Esther said, The adversary and enemy of the king, and of me, *is this wicked Haman.* "Then Haman was afraid before the king and the queen. And the king, arising from the banquet of wine in his wrath, went into the palace garden: and Haman stood up to make request for his life to Esther the queen; for he saw that there was evil determined against him by the king." It was a well-known custom, that if the king left a feast displeased with any one, and retired to the women's apartment, that there was no hope, and that when the king ordered an execution no one was permitted even to ask for mercy.* By rising in anger, therefore, it was the same as if sentence of death had been pronounced. Rosenmuller gives an instance from *Olearius* to this effect. *Shah Sefi*, of Persia, once felt himself offended by some unseasonable jokes that one of his favorites allowed himself to indulge in, accordingly he at once arose and left the apartment, by which the favorite knew his life was forfeited. He went home in alarm, and in a few hours the king sent for his head. Another instance is given in the books of a high officer having displeased the Sultan, who immediately ordered his head to be placed on the top of a pyramid of fruit that had just been brought into his court. Persian

* En Perse, lorsque le roi a condamné quelqu'un, on ne peut plus lui en parlet ni demander grace. S'il etait ivre on hors de sens, il faudrait que l'arret s'executal tout de meme; sans cela il se contredirait, el la loi ne peut se contredire.—Montesquieu L'Esprit. Des Lois Liv. iii: C. 8.

and Egyptian kings affected so much majesty that they did not allow a malefactor, or any one sentenced to death, to look at them. Hence they covered Haman's face when the king's displeasure was manifested—"putting him in a winding sheet that was dead in the king's favor." When a criminal was condemned by a Roman judge, he was delivered to the executioner in these words: "I, Victor, caput obnubito arbori infelici suspendito." *Go, Seargent, cover his head, and hang him on the unlucky tree.* Perhaps, indeed, they covered his face partly also because the king was in such a rage that they wished to hide from him an object that was so displeasing to him. In addition to the places cited in the previous chapter, where the covering of the head was significant of reverence, distress and submission, we find other Scriptures that speak of the covering of the head as expressive of the hatefulness of the person—as of one condemned, and his fate unchangeably fixed. See Job ix : 24; Isa. xxii : 17.

The original for "who is he, and where is he," is peculiarly emphatic. *Who?—He—This one? And where? This one?—He?* Modes of expression that show the great excitement of the king—as if his mind was at once filled with the idea of a terrible conspiracy, and as if he expected armed men to leap out of the divans and hanging curtains, and from the silk festoons, and take his life. Under the circumstances, and considering that he was an Oriental despot, he shows considerable forbearance in leaving the banquet, and going into the *palace garden*—out of sight of the infamous wretch—to cool his anger, and consider the extent and bearing of the mischief intended. He may have felt that he was in danger of doing something rash, if he did not leave Haman and reflect. We can hardly suppose him lost to all shame. He was still jealous of his reputation as king of so great an empire.

The bed, of the eighth verse, was not such as was used to sleep in, but the divan used at banquets. The king, no doubt, in his rage, either misconceives, or affects to misconceive, the action of Haman, as if he desired to have some more palpable cause for his immediate death. He seems to say, for the information of others, "This wretched man has not only attempted to take the queen's life, but now, behold, he will force the queen also before me in the house." Whether he really believed this or not, he was quite willing to have the worst possible construction put upon his conduct. The moment the king went out into the garden, Haman knew there was no hope, unless he could prevail upon the queen to intercede for him; and as he knew she had already, at the peril of her life, approached the king, he may have had a faint hope that he could convince her that he did not know that she was a Jewess, and that he was able, and would prevent the execution of the decree for her sake. But it was in vain. The king has determined evil against him, and nothing but evil.

In the queen's address to the king there is great tact and power. She begins by saying: *Let my life be given me at my petition.* As if, at once, she sought to arouse the king's feelings, and awaken in his mind the inquiry, Is *her* life in danger?—a life so dear to me! And, if so, is not my own life in danger, also? And then she adds—*and the life of my people at my request.*

It is after the king is bound by the threefold cord of a promise thrice made, that the queen astonishes him with her request. It was not for half of his kingdom, nor for wealth nor honor for herself nor for her friends, but for life—her own life. When the moment came for her petition, she says: If, indeed, oh king, thou hast any affection for your adoring queen, now is the time to show it, for my life is now at stake, and a whole nation, dear to me, also. Her address is well-timed. Perhaps there is no superior piece of natural eloquence, unless it may be Judah's address to Joseph for Benjamin. In referring to the price for which she and her people were sold, she touches the tender part of the king—if there is any such spot in the heart of the master of an oriental harem. She intimates he has been deceived and overreached. Haman had obtained the decree, under false pretences, for his own advantage and personal revenge, and to the manifest detriment of the public treasury. It were easy to see that such an address would have a powerful effect on the king's mind. What he imagined was a great deal worse than what she really said. Amazed, he cries out, Is it possible there are conspirators in the harem? —that my adored queen is to be murdered? "Who is he and where is he?" And then the queen, nothing daunted, fixing her eyes, flashing with fire, on the Amalekite, she says: "The adversary and enemy, my Lord, oh king, is this wicked Haman. I would not make the charge behind his back, but here before his face. For this purpose, I invited him to come with you to my banquet. Let him speak. Let him deny it, if he can. I am prepared with all the proof. He has thus sought to have me and all the people put to death, and to make the king himself a partaker in his awful deeds." The queen's petition was somewhat slow in coming, but her words struck home with a killing effect when they did come. The king's servants and his own had often lied to Haman, calling him great, noble, magnanimous, virtuous and sublime; but the queen makes him hear, perhaps for the first time in his life, his true title—*this wicked Haman.* No wonder he stood confounded—without sense or motion—his limbs refusing to do their office—his lips trembling with fear and his tongue faltering, and only sufficiently recovered to be able to begin to speak, as the king comes back from the garden. His condition is now, in every point of view, most alarming. The queen is his accuser—the king is his judge—the murderous decree is in evidence against him. His own hands—the much-coveted signet ring—his deeds and words—the details of his interviews with the king—the quarrel with Mordecai, and his hot haste to have him *hanged,* and his own conscience, are all in evidence against him. Nor did the king's retirement into the garden lessen his resentment. He is ashamed to ask advice of his wise men, the seven great counsellors of State, about undoing what he had so rashly, so thoughtlessly done. He is sorely vexed at himself for having been so rash—for allowing himself to have been overreached by Haman—and vexed at Haman for his avarice, pride, ingratitude and treason; yet he would not trust himself to say a word till he had had time for sober second thoughts. A woman's first thoughts are generally the best, but it is not usually so with men—never is it so with men hot in anger. And, now, as the last link in the chain, Harbonah, one of the chamberlains, and, possibly, one of Haman's creatures, says to the king: "Behold, also, the gallows, fifty cubits high, which Haman had made for Mordecai, who had spoken good for the king, standeth in the house of Haman." It is enough. "Then said the king, Hang him thereon."

1. Oh, how great are the vicissitudes of life! When Haman thought himself secure, then he was nearest to his ruin. In the fullness of his fancied strength, he was cast into the net by his own feet. What a variety of feelings, emotions, fears and hopes possess the bosoms of men and women, at the same time and in the same place! At the wine banquets Esther is anxious and hopeful. She has a great matter on hand. Haman is agitated and feverish, and, at the second banquet, particularly out of humor, but he must go with the king. The king goes to the banquet in high glee, but flies from the feast, in a rage, to the gardens, whither he usually went for pleasure; but, now, to recover some self-command. The end of this feast was very different from the beginning. It began with wine and ended in a bloody tragedy, as many other feasts have done since.

2. How sudden and astonishing the change that takes place in the feelings of those about the court. Yesterday, everybody envied Haman for his prosperity, but hated him for his insolence. Yesterday, they bowed the knee, and did him homage, but now that they see he has fallen, they are just as hearty in their rejoicings at his downfall. As soon as they see that

evil is determined against him, they all vie in readiness to act as agents of his destruction.

> ——— "In the hour
> Of man's adversity, all things grow daring
> Against the falling. ——"

Turba odit damnatos is a true proverb. If Haman be going down, they all cry, "down with him." And as Mordecai is now the favorite, all are ready to exalt him. The old Louis dead in Versailles, may rot or bury himself, while the courtiers and countesses are making fair weather with the rising sun. Haman's sentence is severe, but speedily executed, which was according to Persian custom, as Xenophon tells us.

3. Haman pleading at Esther's feet, is a proof that "the heathen are sent down in the pit that they made: in the net which they hid is their own foot taken. The Lord is known by the judgment which he executeth: the wicked is snared in the work of his own hand. The wicked shall be turned into hell, and all the nations that forget God." See Ps. ix: 15, 17; vii: 15. Prov. xi: 8; xxi: 18. And while Haman receives the reward of his own doings, the faithfulness of God is seen in his mercies to his people. As the Lord had been with Joseph in Egypt, with Daniel in Babylon, so was He with Mordecai and Esther in Persia. The remnant of Jacob shall be as the dew. The Jews' enemy, and the adversary of the Hebrew orphan, a suppliant at the queen's feet, illustrates how God regarded the low estate of his handmaiden, and scattered the proud in their imagination.

4. Another lesson learned from Haman's gallows,

perhaps, better than from any other stand-point of this history, is to beware of the first risings of evil passions.

> "For there is nothing in the earth so small that it may not
> produce great things,
> And no swerving from a right line, that may not lead eternally
> astray."

The personal slight as he considered it, from which we date the rising of Haman's envy, was only the key that opened the gate of a sweeping flood of old hatred, the prejudice of race and an animosity descended from the sires of many generations. But it was the spark that set on fire his treasured up vengeance, a vengeance that had been so long treasured up and added to, that in the explosion it overshot itself. For in trying to wreak it on all the Jews, he lost his revenge on Mordecai, and paid the forfeit with his own neck.

5. We see again that human prosperity is wholly unavailing in the hour of calamity. The glory of Haman yesterday only enhances his disgrace to-day. As mere wordly prosperity does not contain, in itself, the true principles of human happiness, so it does not produce in the human heart the means of enduring adversity. It enfeebles rather than strengthens the mind. It foments desires and raises expectations not proper, and then fails to satisfy them. It fosters a false delicacy that sickens in the midst of indulgence, and by gratifying our sickly-appetites, blunts our desires for what is healthful. And thus the story of the sybarite, whose rest was disturbed by the rose leaf doubled on his couch, is realized. The real cause of Haman's wretchedness was not in the stiffness of Mordecai's knees, but

in his own heart and mind, that were distempered by his prosperity and alienation from the truth. And should not this reflection make us moderate in our desires for wealth, and in our pursuit of earthly pleasures? They are not soul satisfying while we have them, and besides corrupting the mind when abused, they enfeeble it, and engender internal misery. They that will be rich pierce themselves through with many sorrows. Riches lead us among precipices. At the very moment Haman thought himself nearest the accomplishment of his fell designs, that moment a righteous providence was digging the pit for his fall. It was his own hand that plucked the thunderbolt on his own head. His prosperity ruined him—it wove around his head the web of destruction. It is true

"He had been ill brought up and was born bilious;"

He was sprung from an accursed family, but there was no fatality that doomed him personally to so terrible a destiny. It was his bad or neglected education, and the influence of his wicked wife, that brought out his own depravity and crowned it with so fearful a catastrophe. His success, for a long time, but inflamed his pride, and his pride increased his envy, and his envy swelled his revenge, until he was resolved to have the blood of the whole race to which Mordecai belonged. But his plans all miscarried. He failed and lost his own life.

6. It is then an unfair, limited, and partial view of Providence to say that GOD's favors are not wisely and equitably distributed among men. Jacob's complainings on the supposed death of Joseph, and the hard neces-

sity that required Benjamin to go down to Egypt, were all wrong. The very things that he said, in the agony of his heart, were all "against him," on the contrary, were all working together for his good. As in the raging tempest, every drop of the waves is as obedient to the laws of nature, as are the water drops of the spring branch, that babbled away its sparkling streamlets in the sun the long summer day at the foot of the hill, or by the door of the home of our early youth; so all things in earth and in hell in their wildest excesses, as well as in their calmest flows, are subservient to God's will. There is no event beyond his Almighty power. All times, and all the passages of life are full of melody, if we only believe; if we would only hear of them with love in our hearts to God, and with filial trust in Him, and with good will toward our fellow men. "The Lord God is a sun and a shield; He giveth grace and glory, and no good thing doth He withhold from them that love Him."

The purposes of God are not to be judged of by the events of a moment, nor by the occurrences that are near together. The chain of Providence has many links, some are so high, and some are so far away, that at present we cannot see them, nor can we judge correctly of it till we see the whole chain together. Sometimes God seems to look one way and work another, and to bring about his own ends by unlikely means. Thus we may say, with reverence, it was his purpose to raise up the needful deliverer for his people, at the time of their great extremity. To accomplish this, and yet leave his agents free, He casts around and fetches instruments together, that in the ordinary course of things would never have met. Vashti is to be dethroned. The seraglio is to be filled with Persia's fairest damsels. Esther is only to please the king. Mordecai is to displease Haman, and Haman is to be disgraced, and Mordecai is to become Grand Vizier in his place, and the Hebrews are to be saved. And all this is done without a single failure. Every thing comes out just right at the right time, and every agent works all the time as if the gratification of his or her own purpose was the only, and the ultimate end in view. The external appearances of Mordecai and Haman, at the opening of the history, are by no means equal, nor were they a true index to the happiness of the one, or the misery of the other, even the very day before Haman's fall. All Persia was envious of Haman, when he was the most thoroughly wretched man in the empire. His honors and riches availed him nothing, so long as Mordecai sat at the king's gate. I know not where to find a confession more humiliating and expressive of deeper wretchedness than this. It was an internal fury that consumed him. Opulence and pleasure could not tame his envy into submission. The sad tale of grief or bereavement, or of losses and persecution, may grow light by being poured into the listening ear of sympathy or of friendship, but where is a man to find relief from a bad disposition? It must have been an astonishing decree of torment that made Haman break through all reserve, and confess that the envy of his own heart made him completely wretched, amid such honors and wealth as should have made him perfectly happy. His domestic council to whom he laid open the cause of his misery must have been greatly astonished, and by such a confession he must have sunk very low in their estimation. Ah, it were better to have all the evils of poverty or distress heaped upon us, than to have the heart stung forever by the darts of envy. When suffering from affliction in our own person, or in our families, or from the loss of friends or property, the mind can exert itself and suggest relief, and the mind properly speaking is the man himself. But when the cause of our suffering is the disorder of the mind itself—the outbreak of passion, or the gnawing and ever consuming worm of envy, within the very heart—then the last resource is attacked, and the very powers of thought which are for our relief are converted into instruments of torture. The envious man is a candle burning out at both ends; melting away from the heated stick at the lower end, and consuming by the flaming wick at the other. Envy, as the Roman said, has no feast days. It enjoys nothing; even its own advantages are tormented with what others possess. "Invidia festos dies non agit."

7. You must learn, my young friends, to discriminate between real and apparent happiness. Human nature is a poor weak thing, and is the same in all ages and countries. All Persia supposed Haman happy, and envied his honors; but you see how miserable he was—"Even all this availeth me nothing, so long as I see Mordecai the Jew, sitting at the king's gate." The wicked are not so happy after all in their boasted prosperity. "To the wicked there is no peace. They are like the troubled sea when it cannot rest. They travel with pain all their days. Trouble and anguish prevail against him. Terrors make them afraid on

every side. A dreadful sound is in their ears; and they are in great fear when no fear is. I have seen the wicked in great power, and spreading himself like a green-bay tree. Yet he passed away, and lo, he was not: yea, I sought him, and he could not be found. Mark the perfect man, and behold the upright, for the end of that man is peace. But the transgressors shall be destroyed together; the end of the wicked shall be cut off. But the salvation of the righteous is of the LORD: He is their strength in the time of trouble. And the LORD shall help them, and deliver them: He shall deliver them from the wicked, and save them, because they trust in Him."

In your setting out in life, or in your beginning business, and establishing a character in a new place, commit your ways to the Lord, and He will guide you. With dependence upon Him, and trust in His fatherly goodness, you carry your fortune in your own hands, and your happiness in your own heart. The destruction of your purity of character is the destruction of your peace. *Keep your heart, with all diligence*—govern your thoughts and desires—*for out of it are the issues of life.* And in all your sorrows and disappointments—in the city full, or desert waste; on the wild rolling waves, or lonely mountain hights, remember that, "Like as a father pitieth his children, so the Lord pitieth them that fear Him. For He knoweth our frame: He remembereth that we are dust. Call upon me," saith God, "in the day of trouble, and I will deliver you."

CHAPTER XVI.

THE LAW OF RETRIBUTION.

"So they hanged Haman on the gallows that he had prepared for Mordecai."—*Esther* vii: 10.

——— "Retribution!
Haunted and dogged him, through the shadows dim,
Outran his heavy step, awaited him,
As through his spacious halls he passed and sought
His private chamber."—*Two Millions.*

A proverb says: "Harm watch, harm catch," and it is a true saying. The Sacred writings teach, by direct precept, and by narratives, that there is a Providence that makes the way of transgressors hard, so that the sinners own wickedness reproves him, and his own backslidings correct him. A gallows is not a pleasant pulpit, nor an agreeable place for a sermon, yet we cannot leave one so high as Haman's without some further moralizings. *Fifty cubits high,* the highest, I presume, ever built since the foundation of the world. The cubit, among the ancients, was of a different length among different nations. The Roman cubit is generally estimated at seventeen inches and four-tenths;

and the Hebrew cubit, at a little less than twenty-two inches; and the English cubit, at eighteen inches. Haman's gallows was, therefore, some seventy-five to ninety feet high.

In Haman's history, as in that of Samson, we have a most remarkable illustration of the terrible law of retribution, which the Supreme Ruler of the universe has ordained, the presence of which runs like a flame of fire through all history, and through all the dispensations of Providence. In selecting foxes as instruments of his vengeance, Samson selected the animals which, of all others, were the most appropriate to the nature of the insult. Foxes are cunning, and it was through their wit the Philistines had prevailed against him. They won the garments from him, at his wedding, by stratagem, and their cornfields were burnt by foxes—animals proverbial for their cunning.

But the judgments of God that begin on a man's property, if not arrested by penitence and forgiveness, soon take hold on his person. This was the process with Job, and with the Egyptians, though, in them, the attributes illustrated are different. From the murrain among their cattle, the Lord proceeded until their first-born were slain. And if judgments begin at the house of God, what will be the end of the ungodly, who obey not the Gospel?

When the Philistines saw their cornfields, vineyards and olives destroyed, they at once understood how, and for what it was done; they, therefore, came and burnt Samson's wife and her father, inflicting upon her the very death threatened, and to escape which she had betrayed her newly married husband. And because

Samson had burnt their fields of corn, the Philistines burnt the Timnites. They must have felt that Samson had been unjustly treated, and hoped, by this means, to appease him. The retribution upon Samson's wife and father was most inhuman and barbarous, and, in every way, out of all proportion in its severity. For it does not appear that either of them had anything to do with the burning of the cornfields, yet their own countrymen burnt them for what the Hebrew Samson had done. Samson's wife, in trying to avoid Scylla, fell into Charybdis. She betrayed her husband, because she feared her Philistine brethren would *burn her, and her father's house, with fire*, and yet, by their hands, she was burned with fire, and her father also. She leaped into the flames she meant to avoid. And so the Jews, who crucified our Lord, did the same thing. The Pharisees and priests did violence to their conscience—and were determined not to receive Jesus as the Messiah. According to their ideas of the character of the Messiah, if they received Jesus as such, the Romans would come down on them with fire and sword. Their convictions were on the side of Jesus' miracles, but their fears were against His claims to be the Messiah. Their rejection of Him, therefore, was not on the ground that he did not perform miracles, but because of what they supposed would be the consequences; and here they made a great mistake. They did not act from principle, but from expediency. They consulted not what was right, but their prejudices and their fears. Their unbelief arose not from a defect in the Gospel evidences, but from their low views of religion, and their supreme selfishness. They thought their self-interests required them to reject Jesus, and, therefore, they would not receive Him as the Messiah. They professed to proceed against Him, and to put Him to death, as Cæsar's friends, lest the Romans should come and destroy them. And they succeeded in crucifying Him, but the Romans came, and burnt their temple and city with fire.

These cases, as also the case of Pharaoh, show most conclusively that it is foolish and vain for men to attempt to stifle conviction by their supposed self-interests. It is a great mistake to sacrifice truth for fear of any temporal calamity. The history of Divine Providence demonstrates that it is the rule of His retributive justice to bring on men the very evil they try to escape by doing violence to their convictions, or even to what should have been their convictions, for the stupidity, obtuseness, or indistinct conceptions of truth, or duty, do not in anywise invalidate their paramount claims. It requires no argument to prove that it is common for men to pursue what they suppose, at the time, to be for their own interest, in spite of their convictions, and it is scarcely necessary to present illustrations of God's punishing such men for their disregard of right principle, by bringing on them the very calamities which they hoped to escape by wrong doing. The forms under which the principles that are stated and illustrated in the cases just cited—of the Pharisees and priests—may have been various at different times, and with different persons, but the lapse of centuries has not changed the Divine Rule. It has never been repealed. There has been no dying out of the principle. Our streets and prisons are full of illustrations of a retributive Providence.

Let it, then, be repeated, the history of the world, in the light of Divine Providence, is but an illuminated volume of Retributive Justice. The punishment which God inflicts, seen from a Bible stand-point, takes the shape of the very calamity which men sacrificed *principle* to escape, or hoped to avert by continuing in sin. This was, literally, the case with the Jews. They thought to propitiate the Romans by crucifying Jesus; but, because of their rejection of Christ, God stirred up the Romans to come and destroy them. And so, always, the resort to unlawful means to avert an impending evil, or to prevent evil, is only to make the matter worse. And the Divine judgments frequently, if not always, carry in them the stamp and print of the sin for which they are inflicted. There is a conformity between the crime and the punishment. Nor is there any view of sin, or of the Divine Justice, more awful than this. The Romans did come and take away the place and nation of the very men who sinned in trying to propitiate them. The Jews acted on the principle of doing evil that good might come, but the good did not come, and the evil increased to sevenfold vengeance. This is a striking case, but by no means the only one in the Bible. In the conquest of Canaan, we find that a certain king seems to have been treated in a barbarous manner. His thumbs and great toes were cut off. But even the heathen and savage Adoni-bezek recognized the principle that he was treated as he had treated others. "Three score and ten kings," said he, "having their thumbs and great toes cut off, gathered their meat under my table: *as I have done, so hath the Lord God requited me.*" Pharaoh decreed that all the Hebrew male children should be drowned, and he was himself and his host drowned in the Red Sea. Eli's great sin was in not restraining his sons, and he was punished in their death. Hezekiah's weakness was in showing his treasure to the servants of the king of Babylon, and he was punished in having it taken from him, and his own eyes put out.

Now, as we are not endowed with omnipresence and with omniscience, so it is not fair to require us to support this rule by an appeal to individual histories in our day. And yet I am perfectly sure that, in every community, intelligent observers will be at no loss to find illustrations in point. The rule of God's retributive justice is, that when conscience is set at nought and principle sacrificed, for the sake of some imagined advantage, then the result is a reaction, that brings upon the sinner a punishment, in kind and sort, appropriate to the nature of his sin. To support the truth of this rule, it is not necessary to prove that it is applied, in the present world, in every individual case; but only, that we have sufficient proof that it is the general rule. And this, we think, can hardly be denied. How is it with the tradesman or mechanic, who, against the principles of his education and his conviction of right, continues his business on the Lord's Day, for the sake of some supposed necessity or temporary advantage? In the long run, is he prosperous? Is any Sabbath-breaking community, in the long run, a truly happy one? And the merchant, or banker, who, for the sake of preventing apprehended bankruptcy, sacrifices principle—does he come out well in the end? Does not all experience prove that *honesty is the best policy?* Take any given period of twenty-five years, or even half of that number, in any of our commercial emporiums. Give us the full and faithful history of all the young traders, merchants and clerks who have figured, during that time, in Boston, New York or New Orleans, and say, who are the happiest and best to do in the world? With whom would you prefer your lot to be cast? With those who have maintained a conscience void of offense toward God and man, or with those who have sacrificed principle for the sake of some temporary benefit? On which side of the divine rule does your observation of every day life place those who are blighted in name, bankrupt in estate, and broken in heart? Is not the preponderance of such vastly on the side of those who are palpable violators of right principle? And do you not believe, from the lessons of our streets, that if faithful biographies were written of its moving masses, that it would be seen that their wrongdoing is the fruit of *wrong principles,* either avowed, or allowed to enter into their calculations, and that the turning point of their moral delinquency was just where *right* and *expediency* battled for the supremacy—the point just where conscience rose in arms, and made a stand against corrupt principle, marking out clearly the pathway of duty, and where, on the contrary, imagined interest said, stoutly and defiantly, *No;* but this line of conduct must be pursued, at least, for the present—and they yielded, and are lost. Every one has witnessed such cases—perhaps numerous instances of singular vicissitude. One misfortune after another falls upon a man; and, like a camel in the slime-pits of the Dead Sea, his flounderings only sink him the deeper. All his efforts to recover himself prove unavailing. The Romans are upon him, and, to escape them, he sacrifices principle; but, instead of being appeased by his sacrifice, they come upon him with tenfold vengeance, and, now, of all men, he is the most miserable. The bitterness of present degradation is enhanced by the recollections of former prosperity, and by the consciousness that he sold his convictions of right for the purpose of some imagined benefit. The sting of the never-dying worm, that gnaws in his vitals, is, that he feels that he is reaping what he sowed. His punishment has an awful and mysterious conformity to his sin. The avenging eye and drawn sword of Nemesis are ever and always upon him. *He himself is hell.* A monument of the justice of God upon one that swerves from right for the sake of what appeared to be profitable. And even if it be possible for some individual, or for several, who have adopted expediency rather than principle, as their rule of conduct, to go on, unvisited by the Romans, to the end of life; it only proves that there is a future state where the account must be settled; and, unless repented of and forgiven, the delay only enhances the terribleness of the retribution. Nor is there any fact or principle revealed in science or religion that annuls this fearful connection of sin and punishment; and, if the same character is preserved to retributive justice in a future state, then will the sins of the finally impenitent and unforgiven eternally reproduce themselves in their self-procured tormentings. We have only to suppose a remorseful and agitated conscience, pursuing the incorrigibly wicked, and we have an agent of torment as endless as their own existence, fixing the precise kind and degree of punishment adjudicated. Suppose a man, now, sacrifice right for the sake of gratifying any of his wicked passions, and that he is adjudged to have those passions ever raging and never gratified—the vulture to gnaw and the liver to grow, and the vulture still to gnaw. And is not this the fire that is unquenchable? Or, that a man who sold his conscience and bartered his principles for wealth or political station, is sentenced to hankering eternally for gold, or is doomed eternally to climb for eminent stations, and yet be as eternally sliding down and clasping his hands in the most excruciating poverty; and then say, have we not here the worm that dieth not? In God's reckoning, nothing is gained by doing violence to a sense of right. *True principle is the only expediency known in the annals of eternity.* The conciliation offered to evil, to avert it, is the agent for bringing down its fearful results on our heads. The man that will be rich by fraud, is heaping up riches for the Romans to dissipate—building a gallows to hang himself upon. When a man surrenders his principles of right to gain a name or a position in the world, he is building a gallows for himself. It is an unrepealed law of Heaven, that, as we measure to others, so it shall be measured to us again. What God commands we must do. His will is always right and always supreme. Our duty is obedience.

Again, it is a singular and significant proof of an overruling providence in regard to this rule of retributive justice, that so many of the inventors of the means and instruments for taking the life of their fellow men, have perished by their own inventions.* Thalaris was consumed in his own brazen bull. The regent Morton, who first introduced the "Maiden," a Scotch instrument of decapitation, like the inventor of the *Guillotine,* perished by his own instrument. The same is true of Brodie, who induced the Edinburgh magistrates to use the "new drop," the same still in use. Marat, the bloody minded, died from the assassin's dagger. Danton and Robespierre conspired the death of Vergniaud, and of his Republican confreres, the noble Girondist, and then Robespierre lived only long enough to see the death of Danton, before perishing himself on the same guillotine. The Duke of Orleans, the infamous Egalite, voted for the death of Louis XVI, and not long afterward was guillotined himself. The wicked are taken in their own net. They fall into the ditch their own hands have digged. "Bloody minded and deceitful men shall not live out half their days." Sinning is a sure paymaster, and if delayed, the interest compounds rapidly. It is not necessary to adjourn to the court of futurity to know that sin is an evil thing and bitter. It is in vain that unbelievers reason against the presence of a divine government in the world. The facts of every day life—the painful lessons of our streets, display before our eyes the most convincing evidence that the way of transgressors is hard. Who has not seen the Almighty pursuing the sinner with evil? What else is this condemning voice of conscience within?

* ——— "Nec lex est justior ulla
Quam necis artifices arte perire sua."

Nor is there a more just law than this, that the fabricators of death should perish by their own invention. This subject is more briefly presented in my "Giant Judge," and partly in the same language. See the latter part of chapter xi.

What meaneth this anguish of the heart? What are these wounds, inflicted by the terrible disorders of the passions? There is enough now to prove that the sinner is his own destroyer. God need not come forth from the secret place of his majesty to punish the poor sinner. He has only to let Ephraim, who is joined to his idols, alone, and they will turn and devour him. The infernal fire is kindled by his own hand. The worm that never dies, he has nursed in his own heart until it has grown so venomous as to seize it for undying torture. The way of transgressors against both natural and moral laws is NOW HARD. The day of reckoning follows close after sinful indulgence. Nature is inexorable. Her outraged laws must be avenged. The libertine and the drunkard find it to be so. Their bodies and minds soon bear the marks of guilt and punishment. Passions and appetites abused, soon change the body into a prison for the soul. No fugitive escapes the police of God and Nature. The penalties annexed by the Creator to the violation of the laws of our physical constitution are as awful as they are inevitable. Sooner or later, at home or abroad, on land or sea, conscience will awake and seize the guilty, and abused nature will cry out, and fearful retributions will fall upon them; or if not in this life, they will be all the more fearful because they fall upon them beyond the grave, where no repentance nor acts of pardon are known. Is there then no escape for the impenitent? No—none for the impenitent, but there is forgiveness for the penitent. This is the day of grace. This is the hour of pardon. There is a great Redeemer, the Lamb of God, who taketh away the sin of the world.

And if we confess our sins to God, He is faithful and just to forgive us our sins, and to cleanse us from all unrighteousness. THE BLOOD OF JESUS CHRIST HIS SON CLEANSETH US FROM ALL SIN.

CHAPTER XVII.

THE COUNTER-DECREE ISSUED.

"Write ye also for the Jews ——. And he wrote in the king's name, and sealed it with the king's ring, and sent letters by posts on horseback, and riders on mules, camels and young dromedaries. So the posts that rode upon mules and camels went out, being hastened and pressed by the king's commandment. And the decree was given at Shushan the palace."
Esther viii.

"——So many are
The sufferings which no human aid can reach,
It needs must be a duty doubly sweet
To heal the few we can ——."
Coleridge.

In the previous chapters we have witnessed the plotting of Haman and his fall. We have seen him hanging on his own high gallows in shame greater than his honor had ever been. And so palpable are the lessons of retributive justice in his doom, that I suppose every Jew and Gentile, to this day, who may stop a moment to contemplate his gallows, is ready to say, "O Lord, so let the malice of the wicked come to an end, but establish thou the just."

Now that the enemy of the Jews had met his fate, Mordecai is advanced in the king's favor, for the queen told the king how nearly he was related to her, and he was made a prince of the empire. Probably up to this moment, although others were aware of it, the king did not know that Mordecai was her foster cousin, and most likely, till the queen told him in her petition for her life, the king did not know that she herself belonged to the seed of the Jews. *The house of Haman* was given by the king to the queen; that is, his estates. These he had justly forfeited, so that the king could rightly bestow them on the queen as a sort of compensation for the danger she had been in. And Esther made Mordecai her steward over Haman's estates, and the king gave him the signet ring which he had formerly given to Haman. And as to both the queen and Mordecai, we should observe how respectful and modest they were. It is some four or five years since she was crowned, and yet she has not troubled the king to provide for her relations. And Mordecai, too, was as modest and diffident in presenting his claims as he had been brave and faithful in deserving honor and rewards. He has been diligent in educating and protecting the queen in her helpless orphanage, and he saved the king's life when his chamberlains had conspired against him; but, up to this time, where is his reward? Why he has had the best of all rewards, an approving conscience and the approbation of his God; and now both the king and queen conspire to heap honors upon him. Ahasuerus makes him lord keeper of the Privy seal, or Lord High Chancellor, in the place of Haman, removed, and the queen makes him Lord High Steward in the management of Haman's estates. How happy a change for the Jews! Instead of the wicked Haman, they have now near the throne a bosom friend in whom they may repose, without fear of confusion, and on the throne a queen all powerful, acknowledged to be of their own blood. How true the Bible proverb, *he that heapeth up riches, knoweth not who shall gather them;* and that other saying, also, "Promotion cometh neither from the east nor from the west, nor from the south. But God is the judge: he putteth down one and setteth up another. All the horns of the wicked also will I cut off; but the horns of the righteous shall be exalted, saith the LORD." Ps. lxxv and xxxix.

Haman has fallen—Mordecai has risen, and God's people are saved. Haman inherits the gibbet he had prepared for Mordecai, and Mordecai falls heir to the house and place and honors of Haman. It is the Lord's doings, and is truly marvellous in our eyes. And yet both reaped as they had sown, and gathered the ripened fruits of their own doings. Evil doing and honest innocence have now paid their debts to both their clients. There was no injustice nor overreaching, nor double-dealing in all this. No unlawful nor violent proceedings had in the case, for Haman having justly forfeited his life and his estates, and Mordecai being fully entitled to reward for his services, and morally fitted to enjoy the royal favors, why shall he not have them? But how terrible are the reverses of princes, and how sudden the fall of statesmen. Wolsey, Raleigh, Essex and Louis Phillippe, are only a few out of many, that illustrate how slippery are the steps of thrones and the standings around them. One hour changed the whole face of the Persian empire. In the morning every knee but that of Mordecai bows to Haman, but in the evening, he hangs "like a despised vermin, for a prey to the ravens;" and he who in the morning was designed for the gallows, is now prime minister, and rules over the princes and captains of the empire. He who was faithful to his God and loyal to his king at the gate, is now called from the gate to sit up next to the throne. How wonderful are the retributive providences of God? And on that very day *did the king give the house of Haman, the Jew's enemy, unto Esther.* If the proud and wicked courtier had place and wealth to do mischief with, but has forfeited them, why shall they not now be given to the queen to do good with, and why may not Mordecai take care of them? If the arch-plotter is hanging on his own gallows, and Mordecai is possessed of his estates, is it not as the good Book saith: "A good man leaveth an inheritance to his children's children; and the wealth of the sinner is laid up for the just?" Prov. xiii: 22. And again: "This is the portion of a wicked man with God, and the heritage of oppressors, which they shall receive of the Almighty. If his children be multiplied, it is for the sword: and his offspring shall not be satisfied with bread. Those that remain of him shall be buried in death: and his widows shall not weep. Though he heap up silver as the dust, and prepare raiment as the clay. He may prepare it, but the just shall put it on, and the innocent shall divide the silver. He buildeth his house as a moth, and as a booth that the keeper maketh. The rich man shall lie down, but he shall not be gathered: he openeth his eyes and he is not. Terrors take hold on him as waters, a tempest stealeth him away in the night. The east wind carrieth him away, and he departeth: and as a storm hurleth him out of his place. For God shall cast upon him, and not spare: he would fain flee out of his hand. Men shall clap their hands at him, and shall hiss him out of his place." Job xxvii: 13, 23.

But we must not forget that, though the queen and Mordecai are now saved, and their great adversary is out of the way, still the cruel decree is in force against the Jews, throughout the Persian empire. We are not, then, surprised that the queen wept, and besought the king to arrest the mischief designed her people by Haman. And it pleased the king to accept her supplication. So he *held out the golden sceptre.* And when the queen arose and stood before the king, she made a most beautiful and eloquent plea. By various well-timed expressions, she insinuates her purpose into the king's mind, and shows her profound respect for him, and submission to his good pleasure. She is careful to ascribe all the mischief devised against the Jews to Haman. She relieves the king from any suspicion of envy and hatred toward them, and repeats, again and again, that Haman was wicked and deceitful and selfish and treacherous. She shows the king that Haman had imposed upon him—that, in this whole business, he had contrived to gratify his own malice, fill his own chests, and despoil the kingdom. The decree was obtained by craft and on false pretences, and should, therefore, be repealed. And then, mildly, she closes by an appeal to the king's regard for her: "I cannot see the destruction of my kindred. My heart will sink under it. It will kill me to see such a catastrophe come unto my people. And she fell at the king's feet, and besought him, with tears, to put away the evil of Haman and his device against the Jews." (Esth. viii: 1—6.) Her pleading is remarkable for its respectful tone—its earnestness and feeling. She does not seem to have any tears for herself, when her own life was chiefly at stake; but the fountain of tears was unsealed, when she came to plead for her kindred. David had tears to shed over the wickedness of men, though he had slain a bear as a lion rends a kid, and Goliath of Gath with a smooth stone from the brook. And Jeremiah's head was a fountain of tears, because of the desolations of Zion, and the calamities of his countrymen. And so of Paul; we read not of his tears when he was stoned and left for dead, or shipwrecked, or beaten with stripes, or contending with wild beasts. Neither the lions nor the axe could bring tears from his eyes; but anxiety for the salvation of his countrymen, the Jews, overwhelmed him with many tears. His heart's desire and prayer to God for Israel, was that they might be saved. It is proper to feel an earnest desire for the salvation of our fellow men, and to do all we can for them. *John Knox* was known to spend much of his time in prayer, and was often heard pleading with God alone in his chamber, as a man talketh earnestly with his friend, saying: "Give me Scotland or I die." And God heard him, and he gave Scotland an open Bible, and education to her people, and a preached Gospel, and Scotland has nobly honored him, and there she is, to-day, a monument of Knox's prayer and faith. What heroism is greater than to live for the Church of the living God and die for her interests?

"I love thy Church, O God!
Her walls before Thee stand,
Dear as the apple of thine eye,
And graven on thy hand!

"For her my tears shall fall;
For her my prayers ascend;
To her my cares and toils be given,
'Till toils and cares shall end!"

In replying, the king reminds the queen that he had shown the greatest readiness to comply with previous requests, and that he was now desirous of equal promptness for arresting Haman's decree, as far as it could be done consistent with the unchangeable laws ot the empire. "For the writing which is written in the king's name, and sealed with the king's ring, may no man—not even the king himself—reverse." What, then, can be done? The case is an urgent one. The queen is importunate—a whole race of people are in danger—the whole empire is to be bathed in blood—the king had legal authority to do his will upon Haman, but he cannot revoke the cruel decree of Haman against the Jews. This fundamental law of the Medes and Persians, that their laws could not be changed or repealed, was unwise and preposterous. It was, in fact, blasphemous—the assuming of infallibility. They had no right to put such a law into their "Magna Carta," or such a clause into their "Bill of Rights." The proverb is true which says, that "a wise man changes his opinions, a fool never." As it is human to err, so it is wise to reform.

But so thought not Herod. He sinned in keeping an oath which he sinned in making, whereas such an oath was not binding, and should have been disregarded, A man is not bound to keep an unlawful or sinful oath. But Ahasuerus thinks it better to run the risk of deluging his kingdom with blood, by issuing a counter-decree, rather than to violate the laws of the empire by revoking the former one. It may have been that such was the temper of the times—so numerous and desperate the partisans of Haman—that this counter-decree was, under the circumstances, the best course for the king to take. It was not, certainly, his desire to have his subjects slay each other. He must have hoped that the second decree would nullify the first, and be tantamount to its revocation. Accordingly, the second decree is equal, in every respect, to the first. It is as broad, and as long, and as terrible, and as irrevocable. The powers granted to destroy the Jews are not recalled—they cannot be—but it is made lawful for the Jews to stand and defend themselves. Here read Esther viii: 7, 12, inclusive.

But the empire is vast. Is it possible to send this counter-decree through all the provinces? Yes, for there is yet nine months to come before the day appointed for the massacre. There is then time enough to reach the most distant provinces. But, to make sure of conveying this new decree to the Jews everywhere, from *India to Ethiopia*—that is, from Hindustan to the heart of Africa, more care and speed were used than in sending the former one. It was sent *by posts on horseback, and riders on mules, camels and young dromedaries.*

It is interesting to observe how historical researches corroborate the facts, and even the correctness of the proper names of the Bible. The name *India*, for example, which we find in this history, and which designates a portion of the globe that is much talked of in our day, and is, no doubt, to be the scene of great events in the church of the future, is from the Hebrew, *Hoddo*, in Syriac, *Hendoo*, and, in Arabic, *Hind*, from which, doubtless, *Hindustan*. In all the versions, I believe, the Hebrew is rendered as in our text, *India*. And the country thus designated in the days of Ahasuerus was, probably, all that part of Asia that was east of the *Indus;* but, subsequently, it came to mean that portion that lies between the Indus on the west, Birmah and Thibet on the east, and between Caucasus on the north, and the Indian Ocean on the south. The means and modes of traveling in Persia are very different from what we are generally accustomed to. Not much change has taken place there since the days of the great king Ahasuerus. There are erected, at convenient intervals, along the routes of travel, khans, or post houses, for the purpose of defense against the Bedouins, and of affording provision for caravans of traveling merchants, or of pilgrims. A khan is usually a square building of stone or unburnt brick, resembling, as seen at a distance, a fortress. It is surrounded with a lofty wall, and flanked by round towers. A main gateway conducts into an open court, around which are stalls for goods and animals. In the centre of the area is a platform used for prayer and sleeping. Some of the better class of khans have an arcade, terrace, and towers. They are generally ankle deep in chopped straw and filth. The fleas, and such like insects, may be measured by the bushel. The well, or tank of water, usually smells very strong of leather. The pilgrim caravans often carry felt covered coffins, which contain dead bodies to be interred in the sacred cemeteries. And when the pilgrims, their coffins and animals, in great crowds, are shut up in one of these khans in hot weather, for several days, the whole atmosphere becomes charged with noxious gases, that produce sickness and death. "It is estimated," says Mr. Loftus, in his Susiana and Chaldea, "that, in healthy seasons, a fifth of the travelers, overcome with fever and other diseases, find their graves in the desert; while, in times of cholera and epidemics, the average is much larger of those who fail to return to their distant homes." The same author states that, in 1831, out of a population of 70,000 in the city of Bagdad, 12,000 died of fever. (pp. 8 and 14.)

Though there may be some difficulty, as we observe in the writings of learned men on the subject, in defining the meaning of the names given to the animals mentioned in the text as having been used for carrying the royal decree, it is very certain that the swiftest and the hardiest, or most enduring the empire could furnish, were employed. Horses were in use before the Trojan war, and mules, and camels, and dromedaries belong to a very ancient period of Asiatic history. The camel is common to the whole East, from Africa to China. This animal can live on a little paste, or a few beans and dry sticks, and can do, comfortably, seven or eight, or even ten or twelve days without water, and when made to trot and gallop, will go a great distance in a day. Authors vary in their statements on this point, from one hundred and fifty, to four hundred miles in twenty-four hours. The couriers of the Incas and of the ancient Mexicans, like the couriers and runners of South America at the present day, performed wonderful feats in conveying news great distances in short time. Such official messengers as were employed by Mordecai and Esther, have been in use from very early times. In the days of Job, certainly prior to the time of Esther, the swiftness of the post was well known. In the book of Job, the rapidity with which the life of man passes away, is compared to the post, the swift ship, and the eagle hastening to his prey, (ix Job.) The *administration of the post* can hardly be said, however, to have been regularly established before the reign of Cyrus the Great. Couriers mounted on swift dromedaries, had been often employed to convey news, and carry expresses between distant places, but a regular system of post, by relays of horses, and other animals, is believed to have been first established by Cyrus, in Persia. Cyrus ascertained, by experiment, how far a horse could travel with ease, and there caused stables to be built, and thus established lines of posts in many directions throughout his dominions. He appointed a postmaster, and kept horses and camels, and dromedaries, and men at each of their stations.

The posts traveled day and night, without intermission, fresh riders and animals being supplied at the stations. And Xenophon declares that these posts of Cyrus, thus traveling, day and night, went "faster than the cranes can fly." The same system is established in Persia at the present day, and substantially the same in Turkey and throughout all Western and Central Asia, except that it is usual for the same rider to perform the whole journey, but with frequent change of horses. The first rider is empowered to "impress," or seize, for the public service, whatever animals he needs on the way, and the head man or chief of every village, is bound to have a horse in readiness for him the very moment he arrives. And, as the *king's business requires haste,* it is wonderful in how short a time these couriers will perform long journeys. It should be remembered that animals, pressed into the public service by post-riders, are to be paid for by the Government, or commuted for taxes, but such settlements generally inure to the benefit of a man's heirs. The adjustment requires about as much time as a suit in English chancery. The history of posts, as illustrative of Bible allusions, is worthy of a brief notice. Diodorus Siculus (book xix) tells us that the Persians, before the time of Cyrus, that they might have intelligence of what was passing in all the provinces, placed sentinels on high places at convenient distances, where towers were built; and that these sentinels gave notice of public occurrences to one another, with a very loud and shrill voice, and that, by such means, news was transmitted from one extremity of the kingdom to another. The same means are employed by the savage tribes of this continent, with the addition of runners, where the sentinels are so remote as not to be able to communicate. It is wonderful, also, how far the Indian sentinels can throw their voices, so as to make their shrill notes intelligible to their friends. The transmission of intelligence in the wilderness, in the night, by the shrill notes of the savage, from his mountain tower, to his fellow on the opposite peak, in sounds which even a backwoodsman or mountain trapper can scarcely distinguish from the hooting and screaming of wild animals, is no very agreeable discovery to the white man who may be encamped in the neighborhood, as I can testify, from my own experience, in more cases than one. But to go back again to the Persian posts. According to Xenophon (book viii) and Herodotus (book viii) Cyrus was not satisfied with what had been done to transmit news, and established the posts as we have just said. Xerxes, according to the same authorities, planted posts, from Shushan, the city of Esther, to the Ægean Sea, on his famous expedition against the Greeks, in order that he might send notice to his capital of whatever might happen in his army. The Greeks borrowed posts from the Persians, and the Romans from the Greeks. It was Augustus who first run post-chariots and horses. Adrian improved the posts, until the post-horses and chariots of the Roman empire were nearly equal to those of Troy or Concord. Charlemagne and Francis XI are distinguished for their efforts to improve the posts of modern Europe. The first postmaster general that I have been able to find any account of, was Taxis, in Germany, in 1616, whose name was quite a good one for his office; nor was it in vain, for he obtained a well-lined patent of the office for his heirs for ever.

It is easily seen, therefore, that this part of our story is credible. Posts were established. The rapid transmission of intelligence, from one part of the empire to another, was as easily done in those days as it is now, and even more so. Accordingly, the king's commandment went forth from the palace, with the royal signature, and was published unto all people, that the Jews, everywhere, should be ready, upon one and the same day, in which it had before been decreed they should be put to death, "that they should gather themselves together, in every city, to stand for their life, to destroy, to slay, and to cause to perish all the power of the people and province that would assault them, both little ones and women, and to take the spoil of them for a prey." This decree is as broad and as long and as deep as the former one. It was intended to meet the former one. And as the former could not be repealed, the king, no doubt, hoped to render it unavailing, by making a new one, just its counterpart, and when once the fatal day named in the decree should be past, then both would fall to the ground. There is no record of the women and children having been killed. Nor is there any probability that such was the fact. The counter decree was intended to make it lawful for the Jews to fight fire with fire; and with the hope, no doubt, that they would save themselves, and prevent any slaughter.

There is nothing uttered here as to the right or the wrong of killing the women and the little ones. If there is any body here to be blamed, it is not Mordecai, nor the queen; nor is it to be charged against our holy books and their authority from this passage, that they are cruel and blood-thirsty. Whatever cruelty attaches to this history is to be laid to the account of the Persian king and court. All our narrative is responsible for is the correctness of the record. And as this second decree was designed to meet the first, so it is its exact counterpart. It is as broad and as long, as bloody and as irrevocable; but not more so. It was intended to give to the Jews the same lawful power to defend themselves that had been given to their enemies to destroy them. It was and is common in the East to make a man's family, his children, and even his cattle, suffer for his offenses. In the Iliad, we find Ulysses and Diomed killing Dolon in the night excursion, on account of his father, and everywhere, Homer and cotemporary writers, recognize the same law of revenge. And even in the Bible we find such a law carried out in Achan's* history, and in the punishment of the Canaanites. And in our own day we see children suffering on account of the sins of their parents. This is a fact of the streets. How will the rejector of the Bible explain it?

"And Mordecai went out from the presence of the king in royal apparel of blue and white, and with a great crown of gold, and with a garment of fine linen and purple." Esth. viii: 15. There is nothing in this account contrary to reliable history. These are the colors and such the usages that prevailed at the time, and were common with the Persian kings and grandees. Daniel (v. 29) was honored in a similar way by Belshazzar. He was invested with the insignia of his office—with scarlet and a chain of gold about his neck. In the East, if a person has been called into the presence of a prince, and comes out in a garment different from the one with which he went in, it is always understood that he has been promoted, and is entitled to great honor. Jewels and gaudy colors and fine apparel, are much more highly valued in the East than they used to be in the West. The wealth and distinctions of the Orientals have always consisted

* See my "Wedge of Gold." Page 86, 90.

in a great degree of such things. Mordecai being now prime minister, or Grand Vizier, was invested with the robes of his office. The same custom prevailed in ancient Egypt, as we learn both from the Bible (Exo. xxv) and from the ancient monuments; and the same custom is still found there. When a new *Sheikh bellet* is made, the Pasha invests him with the robes of his office, and this is as good as a proclamation announcing his authority, and commanding all the village to obey and honor him.

Nor is *the great crown of gold* any difficulty in our way, for it is admitted that the Persian Princes were sometimes crowned—not, perhaps, allowed to wear the very same crown the sovereign used, but crowns like unto it. *And the city of Shushan rejoiced and was glad,* is so natural a state of things that, if it had not been recorded, we should certainly have been authorized to have added such a statement to our narrative. A majority of the people of the royal city could never have desired to see their streets running in blood; and as the city was perplexed at the promulgation of the former decree against the Jews, so it was glad when the counter-decree was made known. When the wicked perish, there is shouting; when the righteous are in authority, the people rejoice. They that sow in tears, reap in joy; and the more joy, the greater the danger threatened, but escaped. Surprise has been expressed —indeed it has been urged as an objection to our history—that, in view of the exposition of the nature of this plot, any Persian was found willing to attempt the execution of the countermanded decree. Doubtless it was known—at least it might have been known—to all who desired correct information on the subject, that the grounds of this edict were false and malicious—that its author had died in ignominy on the gallows—that a great change had taken place in the palace in regard to the Jews; and that it was now with peril that any one should lift his hand against one of the seed of Abraham; still he must be blind to all history, who does not know that, in all countries, and in all ages, there are those, and their name is legion, who are always waiting for a time of tumult and carnage, to gratify their own evil passions. It is of no consequence to them whether the war, or the slaughter, is for a good cause or in a bad one—whether the innocent and helpless perish or not. All they want is an opportunity for pillage and revenge. Excitement and sensual pleasure are more to them than justice and mercy. Such are found in all our cities in times of conflagrations and civil commotions. And again, he must be a very careless observer of mankind, who does not see that all who live godly in Christ Jesus do suffer persecution. The seed of the bondwoman loves not the seed of the freewoman. The carnal mind is at enmity with God, and, of course, loves not God's children. The church of God would cease to be itself, if it were free, in this world, from all persecution. True Christians are the sect everywhere spoken against by the self-righteous, the vain and the ungodly. It was a saying of the good Bishop Hall, that God's people have but three suits of apparel; two of them they wear on earth, and the other in heaven. The two they wear on earth are the black robes of mourning, or the red robe of persecution; and the apparel reserved for them in their heavenly wardrobe, is white—the glorious robe of triumph. Let us then be contented to make our way to heaven as Jonathan and his armor-bearer passed betwixt two sharp rocks—and even if the way is so thorny and sharp that we have to pass along on our hands and knees, still we are sure to come out at last in victory and triumph.

It is difficult to conceive of a greater calamity to a good man than to be rendered useless—to be paralyzed in the midst of his days, either by being hindered or opposed by his enemies, or by affliction; yet this is sometimes, and no doubt for good and sufficient reasons, a part of God's plan of governing the world at present. To persecute a really able and good man, is to do him great service; and to kill him outright, is to make him a martyr, and give him horses and chariots to ascend the skies to a throne of glory.

CHAPTER XVIII.

THE PICTURES TO BE STUDIED.

" Few, but full of understanding, are the books of the library
of God,
And fitting for all seasons are the gain and the gladness they
bestow:
The volume of mystery and GRACE, for the hour of deep com-
munings,
When the soul considereth intensely the startling marvel of
itself;
The book of Destiny and Providence for the time of sober study,
When the mind gleaneth wisdom from the olive grove of history."—*Tupper.*

" And the two dragons are I and Haman. And the nations were there assembled to destroy the Jews; and my nation is this Israel, which cried to God and were saved—therefore hath He made two lots, one for the people of God, and the other for all the Gentiles. And these two lots came at the hour, and time, and day of judgment, before God among all nations."—
Mardocheus' Dream.

"Cursed be Haman! Blessed be Mordecai! Cursed be Zeresh! Blessed be Esther! Cursed be all idolaters! Blessed be all the Israelites!"—*Purim service.*

It was by studying the laws of nature that Newton and La Place made such great discoveries in astronomy. The study of the heavenly bodies revealed to them the great laws of the planets. In the works of God, even in the smallest plant, there is perfect symmetry; so in the Words of God, there is the most systematic perfection, and not only all, but each part of the sacred writings should be studied most carefully. The diction of the sacred writers is not like the language of any other writings; it is a language of its own, but still it has a precise meaning, and that meaning is within our reach. It was a saying, and a true one, of Origen, confessedly one of the most learned men of his age, or of any age, that there was no word nor phrase in the Holy Scriptures without its meaning, if they were carefully studied. A modern writer says: "We need not scruple to affirm, that in precision of expression, in pure and native simplicity, in delicacy of handling, in the grouping of words and phrases, in dignified and majestic simplicity, it has no rival in the world. As it is in the Book of Nature, so is it in the pages of Holy writ. Both are from the same Divine Hand. And if we apply to the language of Holy Scripture, the same microscopic process, which we use in scrutinizing the beauties of the natural world, and which reveals to us exquisite colors, and the most graceful texture in the petals of a flower, the fibres of a plant, the plumage of a bird, or the wings of an insect, we shall discover new sources of delight and admiration in the least portions of Holy Writ."—*Dr. Wordsworth.*

There is as much system, plan, design and symmetry, in the Word of God, as there is in his works—as much perfection in the moral as in the physical world. It is for us, then, to study the great picture gallery of Shushan, into which we have been introduced by the Divine Spirit, the descriptive catalogue of which is the Book of Esther. We have feasts and wine banquets, princes of the empire, queens, conspirators and servants, and officers—a murderous plot almost consummated, but its author exposed and hanged, and the Jew, Mordecai, made Grand Vizier in Haman's place, and the Hebrew race so nearly cut off by a wholesale simultaneous murdering are saved. I wonder there is not in the Dresden, Berlin, Dusseldorf, Paris or London galleries, a whole series of historic paintings, by the first masters, illustrating the life of the Hebrew-Persian Queen. I know not where, whether in fable, romance or sober history, to find subjects more appropriate, and more suitable for displaying artistic skill. There are a few pictures of Esther, but her history is yet to be illustrated. The whole series of pictures as described by the sacred historian are in bold relief and wonderfully lifelike. The king of Persia, an aged man, of strong passions and an imperious will—absolute monarch of the wealth and power of the greatest portion of the globe; and Haman an ambitious, wicked man, prospering for a while, but then his end was dreadful; and the Hebrew maid that was made queen, as modest and pious as she was beautiful; and Mordecai the Jew, the man of genuine principles and living faith. These are pictures to be studied, in the light of Divine Providence; and, it seems to me, the lessons which we are here taught are more effective—ought to make a deeper and more lasting impression upon us, than if they had been announced in dogmatic terms, or embodied in phrases like the Decalogue. As we see men and women of like passions with ourselves—as we stand around the Persian's throne, or walk in his gardens, or visit his feasts, or wonder at Haman's gallows, and Mordecai's honors—so we behold in the concurrence of such ordinary agencies—in their contrivance and in their suitableness for, and in their bringing out the desired results—more that teaches us to fear to sin, and to trust in God, and to rely cheerfully on Him for support or deliverance in the time of distress, than if the same result had been effected by a miracle like that of the Red Sea.

1. Although, then, as has been already said, the grand design of this whole Book of Esther is an illustration of a retributive Providence in working out the deliverance of the chosen people; still it is better for us to note the proofs of such a Providence, as they occur, in detail—even if, in so doing, we fall into some repetitions. For it is a lesson we need to have often sounded in our ears, that there is neither wisdom nor counsel nor might that can prevail against JEHOVAH. It is His rule that he who digs a pit for his neighbor is to fall into it himself. The steps of Providence, in the chapters now under review, are as plainly to be traced out as they are wonderful to behold. *We see Mordecai advanced*, and we see the steps that have led to his advancement. The king could not sleep. His Magi could not close his eyes in sweet slumbers. The marginal reading here is very strong and proper—*The king's sleep fled away*. It fled away as something frightened off, and he could not woo it back, for He who "giveth His beloved sleep," did not give it to the great king Ahasuerus. Then the calling for the records, and the reading, from the huge rolls of the Chronicles of the Persian Empire, the account of Mordecai's unrewarded services in saving the king's life. And then Haman's burning impatience to get Mordecai hanged, brings

him early to court to be commanded to honor him. And then we have been led on until we were almost in despair at Haman's plotting; but, at last, we have seen him hanged, and the Jews saved. "Verily, there is a reward for the righteous; verily He is a God that judgeth in the earth." Ps. lviii: 11.

2. We see here, as well, indeed, as also in other portions of sacred history, and as the lessons of all history and of every day life also demonstrate, *that God, in the exercise of His sovereignty, uses men of very different characters as instruments for fulfilling His supreme purpose.* Both Esther and Ahasuerus—both Mordecai and Haman, were divine agents for bringing about the Hebrew deliverance. God used Mordecai to work out the divine glory, and yet promote Mordecai's own honor and happiness. And he used Haman to work out the divine glory, and, at the same time, bring upon himself dishonor and wo. But both Mordecai and Haman were free agents, and both were dealt with according to the strictest justice, and in regard to both, and in every other case, God is sovereign. Peter, in speaking of the crucifixion of Christ, boldly asserts the same things. It is a part of God's plan, in governing the world, to employ agents, and to teach principles and laws by examples. Every one that knows the history of Joseph, or of Moses, thinks of Pharoah. Daniel reminds us of Nebuchadnezzar; Paul of Nero; and these names are but the concrete expositions of whole systems of faith and Providence. Moses and Pharaoh illustrate the same principle that we find in Haman and Mordecai. But observe how the great difference between

their characters and their destinies is respectively made the cause or agent in appropriately bringing out the final result. They both worked out their own destinies. Haman's blood was bad. His wife was wicked. His own heart was a festering sore, that sent corruption through his whole frame; so that, knowing his character, we might foretell his fate. But look at Mordecai, standing, like a marble statue, when his principles were involved, although every one else was bowing to the royal favorite. He was distinguished for the grandeur of his intellect, the nobility of his heart, the integrity of his purpose, and for his unwavering attachment to his religious faith, and for his abiding piety. Nor were these high attributes inconsistent with his care for and attachment to the lovely and gentle creature that had ripened into womanhood in his home—who had been, for many a day, the one bright bird that cheered the house of his exile. No doubt it was a trial to give her up. No wonder that he lingered around the palace gates, hoping that, now and then, he might get a glimpse of her, or hear something from her in whom his life and his hopes for Israel were bound up. Nor is it at all probable that all was sunshine in his own heart. Haman was younger in years, and, in everything, the very reverse of himself. It is possible, therefore, that, at times, he had fears of his influence as prime minister and court favorite over the young queen. He was a man of like passions with ourselves, and had his fears and trials, his joys and sorrows; but he suffered and toiled, believed and hoped, and prevailed. So, by God's help, let us all try to do. Mordecai was a man precisely such as you are, and if he was a greater and a better man, it was by God's help, whose grace is as truly and as freely offered to you as it was to him.

3. These pictures show us that we are to construct men's reputation for character out of their whole life and principles, and not from any one moment, nor from any word or act Our laws do not, indeed, allow us to condemn a man unheard, because he may be everywhere spoken against. No amount of public clamor can be received as evidence on which to convict a man. The crime must be distinctly stated, the counts of the indictment and the witnesses named, and the specific charges must be sustained, and all this must be done according to law and in a constitutional court. All this is true, but, on the other hand, it is a hard rule to make a man an offender for a word. A man's general character ought certainly to be taken into the account in forming a judgment upon his actions. Cicero has well said, that "in every case, oh judges, we must judge a good deal as to what every one has wished, or intended, or done, not from the counts of the indictment, but from the habits of the person who is accused. For no one of us can have our character modelled in a moment, nor can any one's course of life be altered, or his natural disposition changed on a sudden." And, from this position, he argued that Cataline, in the judgment of all good men, was born for civil war, and died at the hands of justice, fighting against his country, just as his whole life had given evidence of his bad character. Whose ears, asks he, could have believed anything else of him, since he had spent his whole life,

from his boyhood upwards, not only in intemperance and debauchery, but had devoted all his energies and all his zeal to every sort of enormity, lust and bloodshed? And I am fully persuaded, also, that the records of our police and criminal courts will show, as the Roman orator said, that their subjects are, generally, men convicted by their manner of life, before they were condemned by legal trial. Audacious, violent, licentious, intemperate, profligate, and fond of bad company, and, by such a course, they have come, at last, to exposure, public shame, and, it may be, to the gallows.* In the pictures of our tableau, then, we have not the result of a mere momentary daub of an artist. We have just what the artists have themselves been making all their lives long, up to this moment. Influences, unconscious as well as designed, known and unknown, have been unceasingly at work, and here we have the result. This is true of the king on the throne, of the sultana with the crown royal on her head, and of Haman, the prime minister, and of Mordecai, the inflexible Hebrew.

4. We are here taught *to feel the deepest interest in the welfare of our fellow men*, especially of those who may be associated with us, or be bound to us by social ties, or by blood and nationality. The Romans had a good saying, to this effect: " *Omnibus bene velle, et quam plurimis possit benefacere*—There is nothing more divine in man than to wish well to all men, and to do good to as many as we possibly can."

It was not enough—it should not—it did not satisfy

* For the original, which is exceedingly strong and beautiful, see Oratio pro P. Sulla. Cap. xxv, passim.

Esther that "the Jews' enemy," "the wicked Haman," was dead, and her kinsman advanced next to the king, and she herself safe and more honored and beloved than ever. This is all well, but still, while the bloody decree of Haman was unrepealed, and the fatal day hastening on, she could not rest. The murderous decree was, indeed, surreptitiously obtained—gotten under false pretences and rashly given; but still, according to law and usage, it cannot be repealed. The only relief, then, was to issue another of such a nature as to countermand the first one—such as will, probably, prevent all attempts to execute the first one on the day fixed, and thus render it null and void. If a Persian law cannot be reversed, it may be counterchecked; that is, if Mordecai, with the king's ring and seal, cannot write in the king's name, "Let no Jew be killed," he can, however, write in the king's name, "Let all Jews arm themselves and meet, in battle array, at the appointed time, and stand, for their lives, against those that would slay them." And this decree, as broad and as long and as emphatic as the former, flies after the first so fast that it overtakes it, or reaches the most distant provinces, in time for the defense of the Jews. There was a wonderfully wise and gracious Providence in this counter-decree. For there are some who are held in subjection to the right only by their own conscience; and some are awed more by the example and countenance of those that are high in authority; and others are restrained from evil-doing only by the terrors of the law. It is an advantage to society and to the individuals themselves to be restrained from vice by any or all of these barriers; but it is better still to keep from evil, out of an enlightened fear of God and with a regard for His will, and love for the right way. The fear of the Lord is the best guarantee a young man can possibly have against doing anything dishonorable and vicious. Sin is the only thing in the universe to be afraid of. Where there is no sin in the heart the devil himself is no more than a scarecrow.

5. I am perfectly sure that in the lives of the men and women as illustrated in the sacred writings, we are taught the mind of God himself, as to the precepts and principles which are agreeable to Him; and that it is in the teachings of the WORD OF GOD, and in it alone, that we can find the true principles of all proper reforms. It is in the Bible, and in the Bible alone, we have the principles of happiness—the only true principles of reformation. Human philosophy has attempted to be wiser than God in many ways; but the many inventions of mankind, by which they have sought to produce needful reforms, have failed; nor can they ever succeed. They do not begin at the right place. They do not put forth the right principles. They daub with untempered mortar. They cry *peace, peace,* when there is no peace. No reformation is deep enough or abiding, that does not comprehend a heart renewed and at peace with God. The Church of God is, therefore, the divinely constituted teacher and Reformer of the world. It is God's teaching Institute, and is perfect of itself for its work. It is the Church—the body of Christ's people as such, and not the State, that has received the commandment to preach the Gospel to every creature. And it is this glorious Gospel of the Blessed

God, and it alone, that can purify and save mankind. There is in it a power to transform the moral character —a power that belongs to no other code, system or book, on earth. Conventional rules, society regulations, like the laws of a mutual insurance company, and legislative enactments, are mere temporary remedies. They do not renew the heart; they do not take away the love of sinning; nor implant a hungering and thirsting after holiness. But the Gospel works from the depths of the heart outward. It leavens the whole lump. It operates as a dynamical spirit upon the whole mass of society, by sanctifying the individuals that compose it. It embraces everything; but is not anything else than itself. Its individuality is as immutable as its fruits. In all the faculties and functions of man, it operates as the air we breathe, and yet remains separate and pure and powerful, as if it had not exerted itself upon the body. It is the keen blade of the sword of the Spirit, that can reach the deep and dark recesses of the heart, and probe it to the core, and make a new affection expel the old, and thus purify the fountain, and make the stream sweet. The Gospel is the mighty power of God, not only unto salvation unto all that believe, but also, and in order to salvation, it changes the lion into the lamb—makes the drunkard sober—the profane pure, and the thief honest. The Gospel of Christ is the only true and radical reformer. Nor has any people greater interests at stake, or in any way more deeply involved in the correct understanding of this subject than we ourselves. For the more our commerce extends over the world, the wider our field of labor and trade; and the more complicated the machinery of society, the more are we in need of an enlightened conscience. No men are more interested in the conscience of a community than merchants. They live on confidence and credit. If man's confidence in man is destroyed, you take away the foundations of our warehouses, and may turn our banks into carpenters' shops. But what safeguard is there for the preservation of a good conscience, like the fear of God? Given young men for the command of your ships, or to act as supercargoes, or correspondents and agents, and confidential clerks, whose consciences are enlightened by the word and spirit of God, and who therefore fear to sin against him, and who cannot act dishonestly, because it is a sin against God, and you have the best possible guarantee that your business will be well and satisfactorily done.

Did you ever think, my friends, what it is that makes the rose or the violet so fragrant? The delicate scent, is it from the root? The root smells of nothing unless it is of earth. Nor from the stalk, that has no more fragrance than the root. Nor does this delicate scent belong to the ground, for out of the same ground may grow grass and weeds. Nor is it from the leaf, nor from the bud, for before the bud is opened there is none of this precious fragrance; but now, in the expanded flower it is here. Nor is this a miracle; for all violets and roses yield the same fragrance. It is true, the fragrance was potentially in the root and stem, in the ground and air, and that the Almighty has given the several virtues of plants to them, and draws them out at their season. And is it not just so with christians? It is out of the renewed soil of a heart turned to the Lord, watered with the dew of heaven, and warmed with the beams of the Eternal Spirit, that the sweet odors of grace are brought forth. And if the worm eats the flower, it is when it is wrapt up, when it is not sending out its fragrance. And does not this teach us that selfishness is the bane of our happiness? And does not this illustration teach us to give God the glory, even for our amiable instincts and commercial integrity? for every good and every perfect gift cometh from above; and especially to exalt his grace, which is above all, and which cometh only through his Son, Jesus Christ. To be happy, we must learn to know the luxury of doing good.

The sun gives ever; so the earth—
What it can give, so much 'tis worth;
The ocean gives in many ways—
Gives paths, gives fishes, rivers, bays;
So, too, the air, it gives us breath—
When it stops giving, comes in death.
Give, give, be always giving;
Who gives not, is not living.
The more you give
The more you live.

God's love hath in us wealth upheaped;
Only by giving is it reaped.
The body withers, and the mind,
If pent in by a selfish rind.
Give strength, give thought, give deeds, give pelf,
Give love, give tears, and give thyself.
Give, give, be always giving;
Who gives not, is not living.
The more we give,
The more we live.

6. We see here how great a blessing we enjoy in having *mild, equitable, salutary laws, and in having a written Constitution, that provides for its amendment, and*

points out the way for the repeal or alteration of any laws that may be made in haste, or in ignorance, or through party zeal, that are found to be unconstitutional and not for the good of the people. No people under heaven are under greater *moral obligations* to abide by their laws than the people of the United States, and, consequently, the guilt of lawlessness among us is very heavy. I see no possible excuse for disobeying our laws. And the sin of so doing is a sin not only against our country but against God, and is enhanced in enormity by the general mildness and excellence of our laws, and the fact that obnoxious laws may be repealed, or redress had without resorting to violence. The boasted perfection of Persian law was blasphemous; for it is a prerogative of God alone to be perfect and never to repent. It is human to err, and godlike to forgive. And it is also an evidence of God's goodness to us to open our eyes when we have erred, and enable us to correct our errors. Though the first decree of Ahasuerus was beyond repeal, the second decree implied the revocation of the first--though that revocation was only implied. It was not expressed in words. Our Government is, happily, altogether of a different kind from that of Persia. We are a free Representative Republic. And the more free we are from compulsory laws, the more necessary is it that we should be pious from choice. Whatever may be true of other nations, with us Liberty and a pure Christianity are inseparable. As De Tocqueville has well said: "Despotism may govern without religion, but liberty cannot." Religion is much more necessary in a Republic than in any other government. How is it possible for society to escape destruction, if the moral tie be not strengthened in proportion as the political tie is relaxed? The people who are sovereign are their own master; what will they not do, if they are not bound by religious obligations? "Not only in theory, but in fact a republican government must be administered by the people themselves. They, and they alone, must execute the laws. And hence the first principle in such governments, that on which all others depend, and without which no other can exist, is and must be, *obedience to the existing laws, at all times and under all circumstances.* This is the vital condition of the social compact. He who claims a dispensing power for himself, by which he suspends the operation of law in his own case, is worse than a usurper, for he not only tramples under foot the Constitution of his country, but violates the reciprocal pledge which he has given to his fellow citizens, and has received from them, that he will abide by the laws, constitutionally enacted; upon the strength of which pledge, his own personal rights and acquisitions are protected by the rest of the community."*

7. The difficulties of the Persian monarch, growing out of his rash decree, even after the author of it has been punished, are a warning to us to beware of the consequences of our words and actions. The only relief from the evils of his rash decree, that seemed to the king available, was to put the Jews on an equal footing with their enemies. The author—the base contriver of this murderous plot, has received his just desert, but

* This is from a note by the American editor of De Tocqueville's Democracy in America, p. 448.

the consequences of his wicked contriving have not been arrested. And it is so still, the evil as well as the good that men do live after them. Their wickedness survives when they have gone. The rich man in the parable feared to meet the consequences of his evil principles and bad example in the perdition of his brethren, and feared that their accusations against him for having led them to do wrong, would increase his own misery. And so it is with the writers of bad books. They publish thereby a law that works evil and nothing but mischief. They sow broadcast over the land evil seed, that grows and ripens, and reproduces itself, waning in successive harvests, it may be to the end of the world. And even if the author of a bad book should himself be saved as a brand plucked from the burning gulf—snatched by sovereign grace at the last moment from its flaming jaws—still his work survives; the poison he has injected into the mass of society spreads on and works death. It has past beyond his control. *Our influence is immortal.*

8. This history teaches us to trust in God for *the vindication of his own ways and the justification of his judgments* against the wicked, as well as in his faithfulness to his people, in remembering to keep and fulfill, at the right time, all his promises to them. There may be more love in what we think his frown, than there could be in his smile. As many as I love, says God, I rebuke and chasten. Let us remember, also, that He who "tempers the wind to the shorn lamb," tempers his chastisements to the infirmities of a weak and simple mind—while the transgressions of him whose na-

ture is strongly marked, are visited by severer tokens of divine displeasure. The mind and the heart are closely linked together, and the errors of genius bear with them their own chastisement, even upon earth. The man of a weak mind and imperfect education sees God dimly and through many shadows; but the sinner of genius and talent and moral education, sins in "the broad noonday of a clear and radiant mind, and when at length the delirium of sensual passion has subsided, and the cloud flits away from before the sun, he trembles beneath the searching eye of that accusing power which is strong in the strength of a godlike intellect." It is then a law of Providence, that where much is given, much is required; and also, that where much is given and abused, there the guilt is great, and the injury of evil doing is in proportion to the violence that it offers public sentiment, and to the violence that it does to one's own conscience. "Men," says De Tocqueville, "are not corrupted by the exercise of a power or debased by the habit of obedience; but by the exercise of power which they believe to be illegal, and by obedience to a rule which they consider to be usurped and oppressive." It is the violence then done to conscience, and to public sentiment, and to the law of God, that destroys self-respect, and leads to utter depravity. Sin is a fearful transgression of law.

9. *The delay of judgment against evil-doers,* instead, therefore, of encouraging them to boldness in sin, should melt them to penitential sorrow. Instead of lulling them into security, it ought the more to alarm them: For, *first,* the delay of Providence to punish the wicked

does not change the *nature of sin*. It remains intrinsically the abominable thing that God hates. It is impossible, in the nature of things, that sin should ever meet with His approbation. The patience of God, therefore, produces no mitigation of the enormity of wrong doing. It is no proof of Divine indifference to sin—or of its being a trifling offense in the sight of God, *that He does not instantly express His abhorrence of it*, and pour out His wrath upon the guilty. Men kindle immediately into a transport of passion, when provoked. But God is not a man. He punishes sin not from passion, but *from principle*—not to revenge Himself for any injury He sustains from sin, but in order to maintain a righteous government for the happiness of His creatures. And the punishment of sin will only be the more severe, because of the aggravations of abused mercy. Delay amongst men may lessen the certainty of punishment, leaving room for escape, or for the loss of opportunity, or of ability for inflicting the punishment; but it is never so with God. One day is, with the Lord, as a thousand years, and a thousand years as one day. Is there not then something fearful in treasuring up wrath against the day of wrath, by an abuse of Divine goodness?

But, *secondly, an evil work is itself a judgment.* It was so with Haman. He was allowed to go on his own way, until he fulfilled the Psalmist's words: "He made a pit, and digged it, and is fallen into the ditch which he made; his mischief shall return upon his own head; and his violent dealing shall come down upon his own pate." His whole history shows that pride goeth before destruction, and a haughty spirit before a fall—that God can easily so direct human affairs as to thwart the best laid schemes of wicked men. If, at Mordecai's refusal to bow before him as to a god, Haman swells with rage, and says to himself: "Well, he will not bow his knees—I will see if a halter cannot break his neck;" and if, as he plans for this, his malice, and envy, and rage, grow by what they feed on, until he will not stoop to be revenged on Mordecai alone; if he will not rest until, like the Egyptian kings portrayed on the old palace walls of the Nile, he can hold the hair of all Jewish heads in one hand, and by one stroke of the king's sword, cut them all off at once; if one lark is not enough for the stomach of this Amalekite, but, like a vulture, he would have the whole flock, why then we have only to wait for the sequel, and we shall see who prevails. For it was not against Mordecai alone, nor merely against Mordecai and the Jews that this heathen Agagite was raging. His heart was set against God's chosen people, and against Jehovah himself. It is no wonder then, that, contrary to all human appearances, his plans miscarried, and the Jews were saved. For who hath ever hardened himself against the Almighty and prospered? Is He not as wonderful in execution as in council? Let the potsherds of the earth strive with the potsherds of the earth; but wo to a man that striveth with his Maker! Who shall deliver us from His wrath?

The delay of the execution of the sentence against evil-doers, is not, in itself, a blessing, if it does not lead to repentance. It were a mercy to arrest them, and so prevent their increase of guilt. A thing is not good because it prospers, but because it is according to the will of God—because it is commanded by him. An act is not evil because it is punished at once, but because it is disobedience—because it is forbidden. The act—the sin itself—is a judgment upon the sinner. He that believeth not, is condemned already, and his continuance in unbelief and disobedience, against the offers of pardon and calls of grace, only enhances his condemnation. The tyranny of Haman's evil passions, instead of growing less by the opposition he met with, only became more and more violent. His revenge became a scorpion that could not rest. His heart was so filled with pride and envy, that no scheme was too cruel or bloody for him. But it is always, as it was with him, such wicked passions indulged are more injurious to those who allow them to govern them, than they are to the victims upon whom they are expended. *It is better to receive and endure an injury, than to inflict one.* Oh how dangerous is ambition in a narrow minded, ill-informed, headstrong man on the pinnacle of earthly grandeur! Seest thou a man wise in his own conceit, there is more hope of a fool than of him? If he be brayed in a mortar, he is still a fool. Prov. xxvii. How impossible is it for a man to have the spirit of Christ who is filled with malice and anger, and evil-speaking, and backbiting, and slander? How earnestly ought we to pray to be delivered from violent passions, and from unreasonable men; and how thankful should we be when God restrains us from the indulgence of wicked propensities?

But what if we have fallen; what if we are sinners? Is there no hope for us? O Israel, thou hast destroyed thyself, saith the Lord, but in me is thy help. There is forgiveness with God, not that we may go on in sin, but that He may be feared. Christ Jesus is exalted at His right hand, a Prince and a Saviour, to give repentance and remission of sins. I remember having read something like the following, in regard to a little boy, a white-haired lad of some six years of age. His mother was sick, and the little fellow left his playthings in the yard to stay with his mother, and in trying to amuse himself in her sick chamber, without making a noise, he employed himself sometime in painting his name, with a pencil, on paper. But suddenly his busy little finger stopped. He had made a mistake, and wetting his finger, he tried again and again to rub out the wrong mark, as he had been accustomed to do on his slate; but in vain. His mother having observed his distress, and his useless efforts, said: "My son, do you know that God writes down all you do in a book? Every naughty word and wicked thought—all your acts of wickedness, peevishness and disobedience? And do you suppose, my boy, *you can ever rub out these marks against you?*" His face grew red, and then pale. He was evidently much agitated with thoughts about his standing in the sight of God. His mother observed him affectionately, but said nothing. At last he came to her bedside and said, with great earnestness: "Dear mother, can not the blood of Jesus Christ rub them out?" Yes, dear boy, you have the secret now. A secret the whole world cannot give you without the Gospel: *The blood of Jesus Christ cleanseth us from all sin.*

CHAPTER XIX.

THE DAY OF SLAUGHTER.

"Thus the Jews smote all their enemies with the stroke of the sword, and slaughter, and destruction, and did what they would unto those that hated them."

Esther ix: 5.

"Just in the last distressing hour
The LORD displays delivering power,
The mount of danger is the place,
Where we shall see surprising grace."

Watts.

As the history now before us opens up, we find two royal edicts, just the counterpart of each other, left to war it out. Neither side are rebels, for both are to fight under royal authority. And since it must be so, may God protect the right.

We have found Haman hanging on the gallows which he built for Mordecai, and Mordecai coming into the possession of the honors, power and estates of Haman. And the queen undisputed mistress of the king's heart; but the decree of extermination, against the Jews, cannot be reversed. It can only be met by a counter-one, which it is hoped will practically render it null and void. Accordingly, two months after the first, and nine months before the time fixed for the execution of the first edict, the second one is issued, and expressed by the swiftest couriers throughout all the kingdom. Josephus, in his antiquities, (lib. xi: c. 6,) gives the words of the decree, which corroborate the truth of our text. But, contrary to the hopes of the Jews, and of the king and court, the day does not pass quietly. It is made, in spite of their wishes, a day of terrible vengeance. The Jews act strictly on the defensive. *To lay hand on such, and on such only, as sought their hurt. And no man could withstand them: for the fear of them fell upon all people.* The cause of this fear is easily seen. The Jews had powerful friends at court. The king was on their side. The queen, being of their own blood, was, of course, on their side. And, no doubt also, the more intelligent among the Persians were now acquainted with the most remarkable portions of Jewish history, and knew how their God had helped them in days of old. And then there was a prestige—a moral—with the Hebrews that made them all-powerful. According to the king's commandment and decree, on the thirteenth day of the twelfth month, which is Adar, the day that the enemies of the Jews hoped to have power over them, though it was turned to the contrary, and the Jews everywhere prevailed over their enemies: On this day, the Jews gathered themselves together in their cities, throughout all the provinces of king Ahasuerus, and smote all their enemies with the stroke of the sword, and slaughter and destruction, and did what they would unto those that hated them. And all the rulers of the provinces, and the king's lieutenants, and deputies, and officers, helped the Jews; because the fear of Mordecai fell upon them. See Esth. ix: 1, 11. In the history of the slaughter, we find, among the slain, Haman's ten sons. It appears that the number of the slain, in the palace and city of Shushan, was reported to the king in the afternoon, or evening, for the purpose of enraging him against the Jews; but it had quite a contrary effect. For as the king is made acquainted with what had been done in the royal city, he "said unto Esther, the queen, The Jews have slain and destroyed five hundred men in Shushan, the palace, and the ten sons of Haman; what have they done in the rest of the king's provinces? Now, what is thy petition? and it shall be granted thee; or what is thy request further? and it shall be done." As if he had said, I am grieved that this has turned out to be so bloody an affair, but it is all owing to the malice of Haman and his partisans; and, if there is yet anything more that can be done in behalf of the Jews, to protect them against their enemies, I am ready to have it done. And the queen said: "If it please the king, let it be granted to the Jews, which are in Shushan, to do to-morrow also according unto this day's decree, and let Haman's ten sons be hanged upon the gallows. And the king commanded it so to be done: and the decree was given at Shushan; and they hanged Haman's ten sons." A little examination of the case will exonerate the queen from wanton cruelty in her request of the king. Haman's retainers have turned out to be more numerous and powerful than was expected. They are also found to be as dangerous to the state as they were to the Jews. They are the enemies of the queen, and are ready for a new attack, which is to be apprehended the next day. Their cause is desperate. They must prevail or perish. Mordecai, no doubt, is fully informed of these facts, and has them communicated to the queen; and she knowing that many of Haman's friends have escaped the first day, and are only waiting for to-morrow, or for a good chance to attack and destroy the Jews, she desired the king to extend the decree another day; that is, that it might be lawful for the Jews to assemble and arm and defend themselves to-morrow, as they have done to-day, against those who may try to do them hurt.

But why must *Haman's ten sons be hanged upon the gallows?* Are these ten other sons, or the same tha have been slain? Probably the same whose names are given in the previous verses; why then are they to be hanged, seeing they are already dead? It was a custom, both among the Jews and Persians, to hang the bodies of malefactors after they had been executed in some other way. This was intended, of course, to add to their infamy, and to make them a more conspicuous example of terror to all others. And, in this case, the infamy was the more terrible because they were hanged on their father's gallows; that is, the same he had made for Mordecai, but upon which he had himself been hanged. In comparatively modern times, and in Christian countries, we have read of martyrs, for the truth, being dug out of their graves, and their bones being burned. And besides, no doubt, it was designed, in this way, to give publicity to the fact that Haman's sons were all killed—that they were actually dead—and that, therefore, if any one pretends to be one of Haman's sons, and to excite rebellion, it could be easily shown that he was an impostor; for all of his sons were not only dead, but consigned to the deepest ignominy, which would not have been done if his friends had been sufficiently powerful to have prevented it. The people must have been deeply impressed with the hopelessness of Haman's cause, when they saw all his son's killed, and then hung one above another, all at one time, on the same gallows. Little did their father imagine that it was for this purpose he erected so high a gallows. The *fifty cubits high* did, however, serve all the better to make the certainty of his sons' death, and their ignominy, known throughout the royal city, and the vast empire. The first day, five hundred were killed in and near the palace, and the next, three hundred more, making eight hundred of Haman's friends and fellow-conspirators that were killed during the two days of slaughter; and there can now be no mistake about the fate of his sons. There is no danger of any one of them again heading an insurrection.

And according to the king's decree, "the Jews that were in Shushan gathered themselves together on the fourteenth day also, and slew three hundred men at Shushan; but on the prey they laid not their hand. But the other Jews that were in the king's provinces gathered themselves together, and stood for their lives, and had rest from their enemies, and slew of their foes seventy and five thousand, but they laid not their hands on the prey." Verses 15 and 16 of the ninth chapter.

In regard to the *great number slain*, it must be remembered that the Persian empire was very large and populous, and that the numbers slain in battles in ancient times were very great.* And then it is also to be remembered that the king's officers, rulers of the provinces, lieutenants and deputies, throughout all the provinces, helped the Israelites. Hebrew writers also contend that all these seventy-five thousand were Amalekites, and that in this slaughter was fulfilled the prophecy of Balaam: "Amalek was the first of the nations, but his latter end shall be, that he perish forever." It is true, that the prophets foretold the utter destruction of this people, and I know not that they were ever heard of after this slaughter. Numb. xxiv: 20; Exo. xvii: 14. It is clear also from the history, that the Jews' enemies were the aggressors. They acted only in self-defence. They lifted their hands only against such as sought their hurt. Haman's faction were infatuated to their own destruction. They could not stand—not a man of them before the Jews. But if they had remained quiet, there is no probability that a hair of their head would have been touched. The Jews were conquerors, because they were on the right side, and God helped them. And though victory is often an accident, yet it is true that Providence helps the best disciplined and bravest troops. Trust in God does not excuse us from keeping our gunpowder dry. The Jews were numerous, and they were united. They stood together in all the cities for their lives, their wives and their little ones.

It is twice said in the text—*that on the prey they laid not their hands.* They were authorized by the decree to take the goods of their enemies that should be slain, but there is not a syllable to show that they

---

* See His. of ancient Persia published by Carters of New York.

took any spoil, or that they injured any one that did not first attack them. By abstaining from the spoil, they showed that they did not act from malice, or for the purpose of enriching themselves. They were neither selfish nor revengeful. They were ready to mix mercy with judgment, and were disposed to show that they could be more generous than their enemies would have been to them. The spoil, therefore, they touched not, either leaving it for the king's treasury, or for the children of those slain. Their motto was not that the spoils belong to the victors. Nor were they wanting in loyalty. They were faithful subjects.

The effects of the counter-decree in Shushan, were just such as we should have expected, when we remember how sad the royal city was at the promulgation of the murderous one of Haman. If they were grieved at that, they would rejoice at this; the calm came after the storm. Joy, peace, and security, were the fruits of their wonderful deliverance. The dark cloud that had so long hung over them, was at last dispelled, and sunshine again beaming upon them. And the Jews had light, and gladness, and joy, and honor! In the Bible *light* is often synonymous with *gladness*, because light is pleasant to the eyes; and it is also common to add terms explanatory of former ones, to add emphasis to the sentence. *Gladness and joy* here, are intended to explain what is meant by *light*, and the *honor* is put in contrast to the contempt heretofore felt for the Jews.

And throughout the empire the *Jews had joy and gladness, a feast and a good day. And many of the people of the land became Jews, for the fear of the Jews fell upon them.* It is characteristic of the nations of the East to this day! just as it is with the savage tribes of our own continent, to join themselves in alliance with the stronger party, or the winning side. Many of the people became Jews, that is, renounced their idolatry, were circumcised, and became worshippers of the true God. *For the fear of the Jews fell upon them.* The fate of Haman was before their eyes. They were quite convinced that no one could stand against the seed of the Jews, for whose benefit such stupendous miracles had been wrought in former times. Fear and self-preservation, as well as a regard for religion, conspired to make many proselytes. Such converts, however, were not likely to do much honor to the true religion, but the historian is faithful to record the fact. And it is still a proof of the weakness of human nature, that many are willing to join themselves to a congregation, or become professors of religion when it is fashionable so to do, or when the church seems to be prosperous, who are not to be found among her friends in the days of adversity. But our Lord's teaching on this subject is remarkably plain and emphatic. "Whosoever therefore shall confess me before men, mine will I confess also before my Father which is in heaven. But whosoever shall deny me before men, mine will I also deny before my Father which is in heaven. He that loveth father or mother more than me is not worthy of me; and he that loveth son or daughter more than me is not worthy of me. And he that taketh not his cross, and followeth after me, is not worthy of me. He that findeth his life shall lose it; and he that loseth his life for my sake shall find it. Math. x: 32, 39.

CHAPTER XX.

THE LIVING MONUMENT.

"My fame extends from West to East,
And always at the Purim feast,
* * * *
The wine it so elateth me,
That I no difference can see
Between 'Accursed Haman be!'
And 'Blessed be Mordecai!'"

Longfellow.

ANOTHER result of the Jews' victory over their enemies, and of the great favor in which the queen and Mordecai are held by the great king Ahasuerus, is that no man durst lay his hand upon a Jew, nor even frown upon him. They who had been considered as wretched captives are not only safe, but are made lords in the land. It is, then, natural they should have a national festival in commemoration of their deliverance. Accordingly, we find the feast of Purim instituted at that time, and observed, from that day to this, by their posterity, in every part of the globe.

"On the thirteenth day of the month Adar; and on the fourteenth day of the same rested they, and made it a day of feasting and gladness. Therefore, the Jews of the villages, that dwelt in the unwalled towns, made the fourteenth day of the month Adar a day of gladness and feastings, and a good day, and of rendering portions one to another, and gifts to the poor. Wherefore, they called the days PURIM, after the name Pur. Therefore, for all the words of this letter, and of that which they had seen concerning this matter, and which had come unto them, the Jews ordained, and took upon them, and upon their seed, and upon all such as joined themselves unto them, so as it should not fail, that they would keep these two days according to their writing, and according to their appointed time every year. And that these days should be remembered and kept throughout every generation, every family, every province, and every city; and that these days of Purim should not fail from among the Jews, nor the memorial of them perish from their seed. Then Esther the queen, the daughter of Abihail, and Mordecai the Jew, wrote with all authority to confirm this second letter of Purim. And he sent the letters unto all the Jews, to the hundred twenty and seven provinces of the kingdom of Ahasuerus, with words of peace and truth. To confirm these days of Purim in their times appointed, according as Mordecai the Jew and Esther the queen had enjoined them, and as they had decreed for themselves and for their seed, the matters of the fastings and their cry. And the decree of Esther confirmed these matters of Purim; and it was written in the book."

The unwalled towns (verse 19) are so specified to distinguish them from Shushan, and the great cities of the land—The *lesser villages*, as is intimated in the Hebrew. From the expression in the *twentieth* verse, that "Mordecai wrote these things," it has been said by some that we are to infer that the Book of Esther, up to this verse, was written by him, and that the remaining part of the book was written by some one else, Ezra, or the men of the Great Synagogue. All that is known, or, at least, considered as worthy of any reliance about the author of this book, has been already given in the *third* chapter of this work; and it seems to me very plain, that the meaning here is, that Mordecai wrote the book, and the king's decree, also, in favor of the Jews, and the letters to the Jews, ordaining and instructing them how to keep the feast of Purim. These interpretations are not contradictory; and that this is the meaning, is rendered more plain from the last verse of the ninth chapter, where the decree of Esther, concerning these matters of Purim, is said to have been *written in the book;* that is, among the statutes and observances of the Jews, who were to keep this feast, and their seed after them, for ever. The decree confirming these matters was, no doubt, also recorded in the Chronicles of the Empire, and it is not impossible, but it may yet be dug up from among the ruins of Shuster. A national festival was to be established, and its observance to be perpetual, which is according to history to this hour.

Let us then consider a little the institution, history and observance of this feast of Purim. And to do this, we have to go back to the *third* chapter and *seventh* verse, where we get the name for the first time. "In the first month, that is, the month Nisan, in the twelfth year of king Ahasuerus, they cast Pur, that is, the Lot, before Haman from day to day."

In the *Septuagint*, of Esther iii: 7, there is an addition to the text, which some interpreters think belonged originally to the *Hebrew*. The addition is historically correct, and makes the passage plain. The reading of the Septuagint is in the manner following: "In the first month, that is, the month Nisan, in the twelfth year of king Ahasuerus, they cast Pur, that is, the lot before Haman, from day to day, and from month to month, that they might destroy in one day the people of Mordecai; and the lot fell on the fourteenth day of the month Adar." The *first month* here refers to their civil year, and the month *Nisan* answers, say to March, and Adar corresponds to parts of February and March.

They cast Pur, that is, the lot. It seems probable, from the best authorities, that *Pur* is the Hebrew form of the Persian *pari*, which means *happening fortuitously*. This word comes to us through the Latin *pars*, from which we have PART.

Some have suggested that *Pur* signified a *game of chance*, that was played with Haman, or by his direction, from day to day, for the purpose of diverting his mind, until the favorable time should come for seeking his vengeance on the Jews; or that they cast lots to determine how they should divide the spoils to be taken from the wealthy families they were going to destroy. It is well known that the Persians and oriental nations were much given to divination. Even the ancient Hebrews were in the habit of casting lots, or of using a species of divination by which to find out the divine will. Lot-casting, as far as it seemed to me for edification, was considered in my little volume on "Achan, or the Wedge of Gold,"† to which I beg to refer without repeating or adding anything here. But we western nations and peoples are not wholly emancipated from similar superstitions. *Shakespeare* following the old chronicler *Hollinshead,* says, speaking of *Agincourt,* and of the evening before the battle :

> "Proud of their numbers, and secure in soul,
> The confident and over-lusty French,
> Do the low-rated English play at dice."
>
> *Henry V.*

Hollinshead says, the French were so sure of victory, that the captains had determined how they would divide the spoil; "and the soldiers, the night before, had *placed the Englishmen at dice.*" Similar things are said of the English on the eve of the battle of New Orleans, eighth January, 1815.

From Horace,* in several places, and from other classic authors, whom it is not necessary to name, it is seen that it was the custom of the ancients to choose a governor *arbiter bibendi*—by the cast of the dice, or as some translate it, to gain the dominion of the bottle by the vote of the dice. The allusion is, no doubt, to the practice mentioned in a preceding chapter, of having some one chosen to preside over their feasts, whom all were obliged to obey, and to drink as he directed. The manner of choosing was by throwing the dice, which had, on their different sides, the figures of

---

† Published in San Francisco, and also by the Presbyterian Board at Philadelphia. Chapter iii: p. 46, et seq.

* Non regna vini sortiere talis. Odes, 1 lib. 18.
——— Quem Venus arbitrum
Dicet bibendi? 2 lib. vii. 25.

Jupiter, Mars, Saturn, Apollo, Venus and Diana. He who first threw a Venus presided, was called the king of the bottle, or governor of the feast, as at the marriage in Cana of Galilee. John ii: 8, 9. This much is certain, ancient nations were in the habit of casting lots to find out whether they should do or forbear to do—go to war or refrain; and to find out what days were *lucky* for beginning an enterprise. The king of Babylon cast lots, or divined which way he should lead his armies, by arrows. For example, when, at the parting of two ways, and wishing to know whether or not to go against Jerusalem, two arrows were prepared, one commanding him to go and the other forbidding, and they were shot, drawn or touched in some way, and which ever was made to answer first was followed. In Haman's case, probably, the names of all the months were written on the dice, and when the month had been designated, then the day of the month was ascertained in like manner. Though wicked, Haman was superstitious, as were Samson's enemies, the old Philistines. And so are the heathen to this day; and so, also, are most ungodly men, even men renowned for learning and scientific knowledge, and boasting that they are unbelievers, have yet often shown symptoms of the most tormenting superstitions. It is not unusual for skeptics to turn out the most credulous of men, and for those who do not believe Moses and the prophets, Jesus Christ and his apostles, to be believers in table-turning and spirit-rappings and the such-like nonsense.

Haman's object, no doubt, was to get his gods enlisted on his side, and, if possible, prevent the Jews from having any aid from their God. He, therefore, resorted to lot-casting, to find out what month and what day would be the most unpropitious for the Jews. And, upon trial, he finds, as answer, that Adar was the unfavorable month, and, upon investigation, is confirmed in this opinion, by finding that they have no festival for that month. It was a month not sanctified or protected by any religious rites. This, therefore, he concluded was the most suitable month for his business. And, giving thanks to his gods, he sets about fixing the day, and it falls on the *thirteenth* day of the month. And he again drinks to Ahriman, and vows to fill his temple with offerings and votoes.

It is worth while to observe here, that Haman's object was not—could not have been—as *Le Clerc* and some others have said, to give time to the Jews to escape; to frighten them to flee away. Whither could they go? How much of the then known world was open to them beyond the provinces of the great king? No. The time was, indeed, too far off to please him, but it had been fixed by lot, and he was too superstitious to think of changing it. And how remarkable it is, that the lot fixed the time nearly twelve months off—as far off as the list of months allowed—thereby giving Mordecai and Esther full time to concert measures for Haman's defeat. Surely, the Lord maketh the wrath of man to praise Him, and the remainder of wrath He restraineth. The God of Abraham here begins to work Haman's confusion. If the time had been shorter, how would it have been possible to neutralize the murderous decree throughout all the provinces, as we have found was done, from India to Ethiopia, in time to save the Jews? It was not, then, as men say, a mere chance—nor was it the Persian gods that fixed the month and the day, but the God of the Hebrews, who remembered His covenant with their fathers. The last month of the year is fixed upon, in order that as much time as possible may be given to Mordecai and the queen to use the proper means for the deliverance of their people. The Almighty's hand is upon all the events of life. If the lot is cast into the lap, the whole disposing thereof is of the Lord. Prov. xvi: 33.

And though it is remarkable, as has been already observed, that the name of God is not found in the book of Esther; yet, surely JEHOVAH's presence is clearly to be seen in it, from beginning to end. Where, in the whole of human histories, can we find a chapter of such remarkable Providential interpositions as are here recorded in favor of the seed of Jacob, scattered as a captive people throughout the Persian empire? "What was it, or rather, Who was it, that kept the king's eyes from slumber on a night big with the doom of the Hebrew nation? Who moved him to call for the chronicles of his reign, and to summon the tale-reciter, or the minstrel, to beguile his waking hours? Who moved the reader to open at that part which related to the service of Mordecai in disclosing a plot against the king's life? Who quickened the king's languid attention and interest, and stirred him to inquire what rewards had been bestowed upon the man to whose fidelity he owed his life and crown? Who timed this so, that this glow of kindly feeling toward Mordecai, and this determination right royally to acknowledge his unrequited services, occurred at the very moment that Haman had arrived at the palace to ask leave to hang this very Mordecai upon a gallows fifty cubits high, which he had caused already to be set up, in the assured conviction that the king would not refuse him so trifling a request, and little thinking that he himself was destined to swing high in air upon it? Lastly, Who ordered it so, that, coming with this errand, in his wrath, he was only stopped from uttering it by an order to hasten to confer upon this Mordecai, with his own hands, the highest distinctions the king could bestow upon the man he delighteth to honor. God not in the book of Esther! If not there, where is He? To our view, His glory—the glory of His goodness in caring for, and shielding from harm, His afflicted church, shines through every page."—*Kitto.*

In the feast of Purim, which occurs, I believe, in February, we have a commemoration of the Providential deliverance of the Jews in Persia, more than two thousand years ago. During this festival business is carried on, and work done, as on other days. It is not, therefore, a Jewish Sabbath. And it is also, perhaps, true that there are differences, or varieties, in some of the minor usages, or customs, found connected with the observance of this festival. It were not strange if the manner of keeping it should differ, in a few non-essentials, in Europe from that observed in America. The Lord's supper is observed, by some Christians, literally in the evening, and by others, at noon. Some receive the elements as they sit in their pews; others sit around a table, as nearly as possible, in the way the disciples sat around our Lord; while others kneel around the pulpit, or what they call an altar. But such differences in the manner of keeping this sacrament do not, in any wise, take from its importance, nor lessen the historic evidence in its favor.

At the festival of Purim, the book of Esther—*Megillah*, as the Israelites call it, is read. The copy used is written on vellum, in the form of a roll; and it used to be so written, and is perhaps so still, that the names of Haman's ten sons could be pronounced in a single breath—written in order, one after another, after the manner in which their bodies were hung on the gallows.†

It was a good day, and a day for the sending of portions one to another. This custom of sending portions is common in the East, and especially in India, where many Bible customs have been retained with but little change. The Hindoos on the first of every month often send cakes, oil, clothes, spices and fruits, as presents to one another. And if a Prince invites to a feast those who cannot come, he sends them a portion of his banquet to be eaten at their own home in remembrance of his bounty.* *It was a day of feasting and gladness,* as well as of sending portions one to another, *and gifts to the poor.* Almsgiving is always a becoming method of expressing our gratitude for the divine favor. A Hebrew proverb says: Alms are the salt that season and preserve our goods; and as Esther was an orphan, it is peculiarly fit that a feast at which she is the Heroine should show special munificence toward the fatherless. Our Hebrew brethren are justly celebrated for their protection of their own poor, and for the education of their own children. Usually in the observance of this feast, much attention is given in supplying the poor,

† See Horne's Intro., iii vol., chap. iv.

* See Harmer's Obs. chapter iv.

and in showing delicate kindness to their religious teachers, and to make every one comfortable and happy. Nor should it be thought a strange thing that some abuses should have sometimes been observed in this festival. Purim seems to be very much like some of the festivals of the Pagans, or to resemble our *Fourth-of-July*, when men, women and children, indulge in diversions and in the foaming bowl more freely than at any other time. I have heard it said that it was a part of the duty of "a free born American citizen to imbibe freely of old Bourbon on the Fourth-of-July, though he were a son of temperance all the other days of the year." It were not unnatural, then, if the Israelites did excuse the free use of wine at the feast of Purim, saying, that all men, women and children, must drink of the "crowned goblet foaming with floods of wine," for all men and women and children were exposed to danger. But if it ever was true, as our gifted countryman makes Rabbi Ben Israel say, in the lines at the head of this chapter, that it was the duty or the custom of those who kept the feast of Purim, to indulge in wine so freely, as not to be able to know the difference between "cursed be Haman! and blessed be Mordecai," it is not so now. Israelites, I think, have always used wine as a good gift of the Almighty; but as far as my observation and historical researches go, and I have seen them in large numbers in all the four quarters of the globe, and I must say, and I am happy to say it, I regard them as the most temperate people I have ever known. I can say of them, what I cannot say of any other race or religion; I have never seen an Israelite drunken. It is well known that in the East at the present day, *drunken dogs*, are among the epithets bestowed on Franks and Christians, and with more truthfulness than it is pleasant to confess.

The feast of Purim then, is an annual commemoration of the deliverance of the Jews in Persia, Esther being the Queen, and Mordecai Grand Vizier. It was instituted at the time in the most solemn manner, and the Jews took it upon themselves, and ordained, with all the authority of the king and queen, that they and their seed after them, and all who should ever join themselves to them forever, should observe as a day of feasting and gladness, and of giving portions one to another, and gifts to orphans. "The truth of this whole history," says Dr. Lee, "is demonstrated by the feast of Purim, kept up from that time to this very day. And this surprising providential revolution in favor of a captive people, thereby constantly commemorated, standeth even upon a firmer basis, than that there ever was such a man as king Alexander the Great in the world, of whose reign there is no such abiding monument at this day to be found anywhere. Nor will they, I dare say, who quarrel at this, or any other of the sacred histories, find it a very easy matter to reconcile the different accounts which were given by historians of the affairs of this king, or to conform any one fact of his, whatever, with the same evidence which is here given for the principal fact in the sacred book, or even so much as to prove the existence of such a person, of whom so many great things are related, but upon granting this book of Esther, or sixth of Esdras, as it is placed in some of the most ancient copies of the Vulgate, to be a correct, most true and certain history."—*Dr. Lee's Dissentations on Esdras.*

It is according to the instincts of the human heart as well as according to the laws of the human mind, that some monument or memorial of past events that have been of great interest to us, or our race should stand out as their concrete history. This is the meaning of the columns, arches and pillars that have been erected, of some kind or other, in all ages and countries. The lion crowned mound of Waterloo, the monument of Bunker Hill, the plain of Marathon, and the mountains looking on it, are not more truly monuments of past realities, than is the feast of Purim. Nor is there any monument, unless it be the Church of God itself, that is so truly a living proof and demonstration of the truth of our Holy Scriptures as the Israelitish race. Every Hebrew face on earth is an epistle from the Almighty, proving the truth of Divine Revelation. Their writings are admitted to be ancient, and that they have been preserved with singular care and fidelity; and their personal, tribal and national histories, (and yet they are not a nation,) are according to their own writings; that is, a fulfillment of the threatenings and promises of JEHOVAH, made to them and concerning them. Their feast of Purim and their day of Atonement, are proofs of the reality of great past historic events, just as our Fourth-of-July is a proof of the truth of our Declaration of Independence. And as Americans are wont to have a feast and read the Declaration of Independence on the Fourth-of-July, so are the Israelites wont to have a feast and a good day, and read the Megilloth Esther on the thirteenth and fourteenth of the month Adar. And the length of time, the number of generations that have kept the Purim feast, only enhances its importance, without diminishing the certainty of its historic verities. If Americans should be perpetuated distinctively as such for two thousand years, and keep up without failure, the observance of the Fourth-of-July and the reading of the Declaration, would it not be an irresistible argument at that advance period of time in favor of the historic events commemorated thus on the Fourth-of-July, and which we know to be verities, and not fables or myths? An argument of the same kind is easily constructed out of our holy sacrament, but I need not dwell on it.

And finally, it is, in every way, proper to have our resting places in the wilderness—our monumental piles, in remembrance of God's mercies. It is thus that we honor Him, encourage His people, and strengthen our own faith. In traveling through the wilderness, or across a dreary desert, it is some relief to find signs, or traces, or proofs, that other human beings, like ourselves, have gone successfully through the same; just so, as we are journeying on through the world, we may draw great comfort from the monuments that God's people have left behind, proclaiming His faithfulness and loving-kindness. These monuments are stones of help—*Ebenezers,* where we should raise our notes of praise, and shout back encouragement to the weary and fainting that are behind—but all our way is not desert. Here and there a table is spread for us in the presence of our enemies. Here and there an oasis is found for refreshment and social intercourse. Here and there mountain hights are gained, from which we may see the promised land. The church of God is not always in storms. There are periods of gladsome sunshine.

Believers have some sweet interchanges of joy amid their warfare. The grapes of Eschol, in rich clusters, are sometimes found in the desert way, even before they enter upon their endless triumph.

"The men of grace have found
Glory begun below,
Celestial fruits, on earthly ground,
From faith and hope may grow.

The hill of Zion yields
A thousand sacred sweets,
Before we reach the heavenly fields,
Or walk the golden streets.

Then let our songs abound,
And every tear be dry,
We're marching through Immanuel's ground,
To fairer worlds on high."

CHAPTER XXI.

FLOWERS FROM THE TOMB.

"That nothing walks with aimless feet;
That not one life shall be destroy'd,
Or cast as rubbish to the void,
When God hath made the pile complete."

Lord Bacon had more confidence in the justice of posterity, and of distant nations, than in his own times. And time, that proves all things, has justified his confidence. It is a curious fact, and, in some degree, an illustration of his opinion, that we are much more indebted to the tombs of Egypt, than to the sculptures of its other public buildings, for a knowledge of the occupations, customs, and domestic life of its ancient inhabitants. The same remark is true of the ancient Persians. From themselves we have scarcely anything, except their monumental inscriptions, and they were lost—buried under the whirring sands and rubbish of centuries—until within a few years; yet it is to these inscriptions, and to foreigners, that we are indebted for our knowledge of the Persian Xerxes and Cyrus.

As life shows itself in living, so do true principles flower into practice. Every truth revealed in Holy

Scripture, has a practical tendency. The doctrines of the Bible are not mere abstract dogmas, to be retained, in all the clearness and coldness of moonlight, in the head, but warm, living, life-giving, like the grace of God, which teaches us to live godly, denying all worldly lusts. It is God's plan, in His word, to teach us principles—the system of Divine truth the most suitable for us to know—by examples. There are several ways of teaching moral and religious truth, namely: The dogmatic, or scholastic method; and the scientific, or inductive; and, thirdly, the illustrative method, or teaching by examples. If the first chapter of the Bible had begun with the proposition logically stated, after the manner of the schools: There is a Supreme Being, whose name is God; and then, if the proofs had been arranged in orders and classes, we should have had the existence of God stated and proved in a dogmatic manner. But this is not the method of the Bible. It begins by assuming that there is a God, and describes some of His works. So far, however, as we are taught, by the sacred writers, to argue from effect to cause, from the works and revelations of God, that there is a Supreme Being, just so far we are taught, in the Bible, to find the existence of God proven by scientific reasoning. But it is plain, to all who read the word of God, that its manner of teaching truth is chiefly by examples. The historical and inductive method of unfolding Divine truth, is the one chiefly pursued by the sacred writers, and, to most minds, this is the most interesting and convincing method that can be pursued. The scholar learns to write more easily by seeing his master write, and then by copying after him, than by hearing him read a lecture on chirography. Alexander the Great was much more inspired by studying the history of the exploits of Achilles and Cyrus the Great, than he was by the lectures of Aristotle on courage and heroism. Seneca says, the crowd of philosophers which followed Socrates, learned more of their ethics from his manners than from his discourses. And of Origen, it is said that, though he was one of the most learned men, and most voluminous writers of his or of any age, that he recommended religion more by his example than by all that he wrote. And this peculiarity of the human mind is duly provided for in the Sacred Scriptures. It is God's plan, in His holy word, to make His goodness, as it were, to pass before us in living forms, and then to have the record made and preserved for our instruction, warning and comfort. If it is faith that we are to be taught, then we have the lives of Abraham and Noah, and a host of worthies; and so, for meekness, Moses; and for patience, Job; and for zeal, Peter and Paul. There are illustrious examples in the Scriptures of every Christian virtue, and, in the Son of God, we have an example of perfect goodness. Nor is there any treatise on sin, that shows its odiousness so clearly, as the expulsion from the garden, the drowning of the old world, the overthrow of the cities of the plain, and the history of the Israelites, and the sufferings and "bloody passion" of our Lord, when He made His soul an offering for sin. It is thus that infinite wisdom has seen fit to teach us, namely, that truth and error, sin and holiness, should be lived out, and then the history written and preserved for us. This plan has been followed in our sacred writings, both as to nations and as to individuals, and it is certainly not without significance. It is, no doubt, true that historic preaching, or the communicating of religious truth by parables and narratives, was eminently fitted to rude or half-civilized nations; but it is equally true, that the most refined Greeks and Romans, as well as the most polished nations of the East, have been greatly delighted with precisely the same method of entertainment and instruction. And, I fancy, it were difficult now to find a man too highly educated, east or west, to relish a good parable, or a great truth, exhibited in its strength and beauty, in a living character. If history, and fable, and parable, are suited, in a peculiar manner, for the instruction of children, and the uneducated classes, it is no less true that they are also the most interesting and convincing methods of presenting truth to the aged and most cultivated intellects. Even philosophers prefer to have religious truth brought home to them in a simple garb. They desire consolation for grief, not on stilts, nor in abstract and stately phrases, but in a simple style. "When the great" and learned Bengel was ill, he sent for one of the students of his University, to impart to him some word of consolation. The youth replied, "Sir, I am but a pupil, a mere learner, I don't know what to say to a teacher like you." "What!" said Bengel, "a Divinity student, and not able to give a word of Scriptural comfort!" The student, abashed, contrived to utter the text: "The blood of Christ, the Son of God, cleanseth us from all sin." "That is the very word I want," said Bengel, "it is quite enough;" and taking him affectionately by the hand, dismissed him.

Grief, whether in the palace or in the cottage—whether in the university or the log-cabin, is always simple. A great man, bowed down under affliction, has no time, nor disposition, for learned investigations. He wants something to lean upon. His own powers of body and mind are relaxed; he wants comfort without toil. His own spirit is fainting; he wants relief, not learned abstractions; and where can he find comfort so easily, and with so direct an application, as in the looking-glass of reliable history? He may there find an example similar, or so nearly like his own case, that he has only to change the name, and it is himself.

We have found that the Persians were remarkable for their chronicles, and that it was fortunate for Mordecai, and the Jews, that they were; and, it is also fortunate for us, that we have so many documents that prove the truth of our sacred narratives. Even the *Tareekhs* of Persia, which are very numerous, and of great importance to this day, are full of illustrations of, and allusions to such facts, customs and past events, as throw light upon the Hebrew chronicles, as far as they are connected with the history of Persia. The Chaldee Targum is extravagant in praising Mordecai. It says: "All the kings of the earth feared and trembled before him: he was as resplendent as the evening star among the stars; and was as bright as Aurora beaming forth in the morning; and he was chief of the Jews." And our text says (Esth. ix: 4,) that "Mordecai was great in the king's house, and his fame went out throughout all the provinces; for this man, Mordecai, waxed greater and greater." Read also, the tenth chapter of Esther.

The great king, *Ahasuerus, laid a tribute upon the land;* that is, upon the one hundred and twenty-seven provinces; *and upon the isles of the sea,* probably "the isles of Greece," which were conquered by Darius Hystaspes. And *Mordecai was next unto the king*—was his prime minister, and, under the king, governor of his whole empire. And he was exalted to be a blessing to his people. It was his study to promote their prosperity: *seeking the wealth of his people, and speaking peace to all his seed, and he was accepted of his brethren.* This is a great eulogy. It means, that he sought to advance his brethren in wealth, he settled their disputes, causing them to live, as far as possible, in peace with their Persian neighbors, and among themselves; and he was accepted of his brethren. The basis of their prosperity was peace, and they had confidence in their government; it was likely, therefore, that their well-doing would continue a long time.

If Ahasuerus, Esther and Mordecai have not died, they must be somewhat ancient by this time. But our history does not tell us anything of their death. It is possible, then, I fancy, notwithstanding the skeptic's cavilling at omissions in the sacred writings, for some things to be omitted that must have happened, and are, therefore, in themselves true; and possible, also, for these same writings, in which omissions thus occur, to be credible. Omissions are not, necessarily, contradictions, nor are they sufficient to destroy our faith in the genuineness or authenticity of a record. We have some traditions—even some monumental proof —that Esther and Mordecai must have died; for we have their tomb, although this is not conclusive, for some men have built tombs for themselves which never contained their ashes. The sarcophagus, or coffin, of an Empress of Russia, made for herself, during her lifetime, and sent to the Convent of Mount Sinai, contains, instead of her Czarinian ashes, the reputed body of St. Catharine. The politics of Asia and of Europe would not permit a Russian Empress to take her last sleep at Mount Sinai. The Pharaoh who lies in the coral chambers of the Red Sea, built his pyramid-tomb in his day, as we found in our lectures on Moses, but another possessed it. But of Ahasuerus we have neither record of his death nor monument to mark his tomb. The grave of the absolute sovereign of one hundred and twenty-seven provinces, even from India to Ethiopia, is totally unknown. And so is the grave of Moses and of John Calvin. No man knoweth it to this day. The causes or the reasons why we know nothing of the grave of Moses, Ahasuerus or Calvin are, doubtless, very different, but the fact is the same.

It is a simple, and not wholly a useless custom, to plant flowers over the graves of our beloved dead, and sometimes to gather a flower from their grave, as a memento of affection. Now, we would have our readers, who have come with us thus far, visit the tomb of our Queen, and, while musing there, gather a few flowers, that we hope may bloom in beauty and fragrance many days.

It is believed by most travelers that the tomb of Esther and Mordecai exists to this day. At least, a tomb so called is still shown, near the city of Hamadan, in Persia, which lies on the route as one goes from Bagdad to the Caspian. The tomb is in the midst of ruins, believed to be those of Ecbatana, the old Median capital of the Persian Empire. The present city of Hamadan contains from 30 to 40,000 inhabitants, among whom are several hundred Israelitish families. The tomb is a square building, with a dome, such as is common over the tombs of holy persons, in Mohammedan countries. It is regarded, both by Mohammedans and the Jews of Persia, as a place of great sanctity, and pilgrimages are still made to it. It is spoken of in the days of Benjamin of Tudela. And Sir Robert K. Porter made a visit to it, and says it is the tomb of Esther and Mordecai, and has been carefully preserved from "the day of the holy pairs' interment." The keeping up of a pilgrimage among the Jews to this place, at the same time of year when the feast of Purim is celebrated, makes this monumental pile a kind of eye-witness of the event—"an evidence to the fact, more convincing, perhaps, than even written testimony." It is true that Timour sacked the city and the tomb was destroyed, but, soon afterward, another was built, on the same spot, by a Rabbi, called Ismael. The sarcophagi are of dark wood, covered with Hebrew letters, which is said to have been preserved from the ravages of the Tartars. It is certain that the tomb is now kept in the highest state of repair, and held in the highest veneration. It is, also, an admitted tradition that the Queen and Mordecai were buried in the same tomb. The following translation of the Hebrew inscriptions is given by Sir John Malcolm, and copied by me from the Gleaner: "At that time, there was in the palace of Susa, a certain Jew, of the name of Mordecai; he was the son of Jair, of Shimei, who was the son of Kish, a Benjamite, for Mordecai the Jew, was the second of that name under Ahasuerus, a man much distinguished among the Jews, and enjoying great consideration among his own people, anxious for their welfare, and seeking to promote the peace of all Asia."

And on this subject it is not irrelevant to introduce the following facts from the commissioners, on the part of England, Russia and Persia, who have been engaged in establishing the boundary line between Persia and Turkey. "In the prosecution of this work, the commissioners have come upon the remains of the ancient palace of Shushan, mentioned in the sacred books of Esther and Daniel, together with the tomb of Daniel the prophet. The locality answers to the received tradition of its position, and the internal evidence, arising from its correspondence with the description of the palace recorded in the sacred history, amounts almost to a demonstration." Col. Williams, of the British army, who is one of this commission says, that the pavement of the king's palace and court, as described in Esther, "of red, and blue and white and black marble," still exists in exact correspondence to the description given in the sacred history. And in the marble columns, dilapidated ruins, the sculpture, and the remaining marks of greatness and glory that are scattered around, the commissioners read the exact truth of the record made by the sacred penman." "Not far from the palace stands a tomb; on it is sculptured the figure of a man bound hand and foot, with a huge lion in the act of springing upon him to devour him. No history could speak more graphically the story of Daniel in the lions' den. The Persian arrow-heads are found upon the palace and the tomb. Glass bottles, elegant as those placed upon the toilet-tables of the ladies of our day, have been discovered, with other indications of art and refinement, which bear out the statements of the Bible." * It is generally believed that it was owing to the influence of Daniel, Esther and Mordecai, that the Persian rulers of this period were so favorably disposed toward the Jews. It is at least certain, that not only Cyrus, but his successors, granted great favors to the Jews, and materially aided in rebuilding the Temple. After the downfall and death of Haman, it is easy to see that the influence of Esther would be very great. It is not at all surprising that the king construed Haman's attempt to destroy all the Jews as an indirect way to get to the throne, and that, therefore, he considered the queen as having saved his life at this time, as Mordecai had done once before; and that on this account, as well as his love for her, there was nothing he was not willing to do for her and him. It is not then incredible that he should grant her request, and allow his palace to flow with the blood of eight hundred of Haman's friends and fellow conspirators, and that Haman's ten sons were hanged as well as killed, and that Mordecai should be promoted to the honors and place from which Haman had been removed. Nor does it appear that the king's favor was misplaced, or his confidence betrayed. Mordecai was faithful and worthy of the esteem not only of his brethren, but of his sovereign also. Nor did the queen betray any unworthiness of

* This extract of the report of the Commissioners is taken from the Boston Chronicle. And it is not the statement of "a fanatical, half-educated missionary," but of a scientific corps of the most enlightened nations of the world.

her great influence. Though exalted to the highest station a woman could then enjoy, and possessed of great beauty, she was neither vain nor haughty, nor did she forget her religion. "The same gentle, pure, and noble creature when queen, as when living in the lowly habitation of her uncle—generous, disinterested, and ready to die for others, she is one of the loveliest characters furnished in the annals of history."

1. The wide dispersion of the Jews in the time of queen Esther, though somewhat overlooked, is historically correct; and it is equally true that their tenacity of character was not less remarkable then than at the present day. It seems to be generally supposed that the wide-spreading of the Hebrews over the face of the earth begun at the destruction of the holy city by the Romans. This is indeed a marked epoch in their dispersion, but numerous Jewish colonies are known to have been settled in various and remote parts of the globe before the coming of Christ. Only a fragment returned from Babylon and aided in the rebuilding of the Temple. Jews are found in our day in the heart of Africa, in China and India, whose traditions are quite clear as far back as king Solomon. A writer in the "Revue des Deux Mondes," advances the opinion that the Jews in China are the descendants of those who settled there during the Assyrian captivity of the ten tribes. At least enough is known from authentic documents to prove the credibility of the dispersion of the Jews throughout the Persian empire, five hundred years before the Christian era; and enough is known to show that to this day, and from a very early period of their national history, the Israelites are distinguished for two

things, which seem almost paradoxical or antagonistic, namely: a wide spread dispersion, and yet a most remarkably distinct tenacity of character. There may be some resemblance to them in this last particular, though I think a minute examination of the point, would show but a very faint resemblance to the Jews, among some of the Hindoo or eastern races; and as to their dispersion, the Israelites are certainly without any parallel. They are now, as Haman said to the king of Persia, *a certain people scattered abroad and dispersed among the people; and their laws are diverse from all people.* They are scattered among all nations, live under all sorts of governments, speak almost all known tongues, pursue many avocations, and form parts of most nationalities, and yet never coalesce; nor have they a home as a nation anywhere on earth. They present the historical phenomena of a nationality that has resisted all change from time and contact with all other nations for at least three thousand years, and yet they are not a nation at all. It is only in the light of their own peculiar history, and of their own holy prophets, that a rational solution can be given of this phenomenon, and the solution when given, is to our mind, a perfect demonstration of the truth of the Scriptures of God, and of the Christian religion. This then is a flower we may gather at the tomb of Esther and Mordecai.

Again: 2. *How perishable is all earthly grandeur!* A winding sheet, said Saladin, as he looked upon his hosts from his pyramid of human skulls, is all that will soon remain of me! And how much more is remaining of the greatness and glory of Xerxes and Alexander, than the name; and, of Xerxes, even his own empire has not preserved his name; at least, not the name by which he is known to mankind. Persia was justly distinguished for her public works, cities, towns, roads, bridges and posts; and her Greek and Roman conquerors added castles, and acqueducts, and cities, and extended her roads, and increased her bridges; but still the remains of ancient Persian grandeur, and power, are very insignificant. The name Xerxes is not yet discovered in the chronicles of his own vast empire; nor is there any agreement, among historians, as to several of the chief events of the life of Cyrus the Great. Xenophon closes the exploits of Cyrus, with his conquest of Egypt, and says he spent the last seven years of his life in perfect peace, and, as the Persian chroniclers say, in devoting his days to God; for that he said he had spent a life long enough for his own glory. Xenophon says he died in his bed. Herodotus says he perished, and a great part of his army, in a war against the Scythians, which is the generally received account. The poets, Ferdusi and Mirkhond, say, however, that Cyrus, with a number of the most remarkable warriors of Persia, disappeared together, or at the same time, from a favorite spot selected by him for retirement; and will have us to believe they were carried up to heaven in a tempest, or whirlwind. His tomb is said to be at Pasagarda. Pliny, Arrian and Strabo, have described it. Alexander offered funeral honors to the shades of Cyrus, at his tomb, and then broke it open in hopes of finding treasures there; but in this he was disappointed, for all he found was a rotten shield, two Scythian bows, and a Persian scimitar.

Now, the omissions, discrepancies, and contradictions we thus find in the history of such renowned men as Xerxes, Cyrus and Alexander, are the more remarkable, when we remember how careful they were in taking every precaution to have their deeds embalmed for all coming ages. The Persians were extremely ambitious and vain. They seem to have taken more pains than any other people, except it be the Hebrews, to preserve their early history, and yet, beyond Cyrus, we have scarcely a reliable syllable of their history—almost left without any means of fixing their chronology; and for the life of Cyrus, and anything like a full or satisfactory history of some of their greatest men, we are indebted to the writers of contemporary nations. A few fragments only remain of their original documentary history. But, notwithstanding all this, what man is there, possessed of common sense, that doubts the personal existence, and the reality, substantially, of the deeds of Xerxes, or of Cyrus, because the name of the one is not found in the history of his own empire, as far as we are yet informed, and because historians are not yet agreed as to where, when, or how, the other died. It must certainly be admitted that men, known to us by the names Xerxes and Cyrus, did once live, and that they performed deeds that still live in history, and that they are both dead. Neither omissions, discrepancies, nor contraditions, in their memoirs, can destroy our belief in them as historic personages. They are not myths, nor are their histories fables. What then, if it be true that there are omissions, and apparent contradictions, in the history of Bible heroes? If we receive the history of Persian kings, much more may we rely upon the lives of Hebrew prophets and kings. And surely we may be allowed to hold to the WORD OF GOD until it fails us, or until we have a better book furnished us. But it never fails. The law of the Lord is perfect, converting the soul. And if all earthly honors and glory are so fleeting, let us lay up treasures in the skies, in a kingdom that passeth not away.

3. Another flower then, that we would gather from the tomb of Esther and Mordecai, is, *that our youug readers should learn to trust in the truthfulness of the Bible.* It is wonderful that, after the lapse of two thousand five hundred years, the records of Esther and Daniel should be thus verified by the scientific explorations and researches of our day, and that too by races and men from countries unknown in their times. Truly it is a vain thing for the heathen to set themselves against the Lord, or for them to rage against His annointed. His word is true, and must prevail. Heaven and earth may pass away, but God's word is a tried word, that endureth forever. It has been finely said, by Madame Dacier, in her notes upon the Iliad, that *Homer* appears greater by the criticisms that have been put forth upon him, from age to age, by the great minds of the world, than by the praises which have been bestowed upon him. Now if this rule be applied to the Bible, it would be impossible to fix the limits of the highth of the pyramid of its glory. It has been censured more than any other book. It has been burned oftener than any other book. It has provoked the opposition of hell, and of wicked men, more

than all other books. It has been opposed more uniformly, and more universally by the vicious and the ungodly, than any other, or than all other books; and yet no weapon that has ever been tried against it has prevailed. It still stands, like a great light-house, in the midst of the surging waves that dash around it and roll away, and leave it still perfect, shining over the darkness, and guiding the voyager to the haven of eternal rest.

"Mutter o'er your words of Power!
Ye can shatter the dwellings of man;
Ye can open the womb of the rock;
Ye can shake the foundations of earth,
But not the WORD OF GOD:
But not one letter can ye change
Of what His Will hath written!"

4. *The history of Esther teaches us to trust our orphans to God.* He who cares for the flowers of the wilderness, and feeds the birds of the air, and the mosses of the sea—will He not provide for his own children? We are of more value than many sparrows. The very hairs of our heads He numbers. It was God's plan, in furnishing a queen for the Persian throne, that none should please the king but the *orphan* Hebrew maid. And still we see it is His plan often to employ orphans as agents in great works. How many daughters of widows have been charmingly beautiful, and have become mothers in Israel? And how many widows' sons have risen to honor; and how many orphans have become eminently pious, and have been benefactors to the world? So remarkable is the goodness of God toward the fatherless, that it is an oriental

saying that " God takes care of orphans and fools." And we remember how our Lord had compassion on the ruler of the synagogue, and when He had raised his daughter, twelve years of age, from the dead, that He gave her to her parents, commanding them to give her something to eat; and how he restored Lazarus to the society of his sisters; and how, when he had raised the son of the widow of Nain from the dead, that He gave him to his mother. Now these instances show that our Lord exercised the tenderest and most considerate compassion toward the afflicted and bereaved, and we know that His tenderness is as great now as it was in the days of His humiliation. In making our children fatherless, therefore, we are not to conclude that God shuts them out from His compassion. On the contrary, one of the divine titles is, "The Father of the fatherless, and a Judge of the widows is God in His holy habitation." "Leave thy fatherless children; I will preserve them alive; and let thy widows trust in me." Ps. lxviii: 5; Jer. x: 4; ix: 11. If, then, Hadassah is left a little orphan, without father or mother, and in a strange land and a captive, still the God of her fathers will take care of her, and prepare her for the highest position that a woman could occupy. God was more to her than her parents could have been. The Almighty became her guardian, and had her carefully brought up. She was beautiful in person, but her wisdom and grace were her chief attractions—still her beauty was a blessing to her. It is an advantage even to a diamond to have it well set. Beauty and accomplishments are to be used as God's gifts, and not abused. If, then, we are deprived of our earthly parents, let us put our trust in our Heavenly

Father, whose eye is always upon us, and whose ear is ever open to our cry, and whose arm can reach and save us to the ends of the earth. What, then, if you are written orphan—if no noble-hearted father is left to smooth down your flaxen locks as his soul rises up in fervent benedictions on your head—what though you are without a mother's sleepless care, and there is no longer a bosom on which your aching head can lean with perfect confidence—no heart into which you can any longer pour your many grievances and the sad tale of all your youthful sorrows—yet you have a Father in heaven, whose heart is infinitely more kind than that of any earthly parent. Trust in Him. He ever liveth to bless. He will never disappoint you nor forsake you. And, my young readers, if God has raised you up friends away from home—tender and faithful guardians of your character and happiness, as He did for Esther in the land of her people's captivity, then be careful to own God's goodness. Such friends are sent of God. Learn, also, to be merciful as God is merciful. Do good to all men; but especially to widows and orphans in their affliction. There is no species of benevolence that repays with so much interest to the benefit of mankind as the care and education of orphans. God seems to take peculiar pleasure in making orphans a blessing to mankind, as an encouragement to us to show them kindness, and to commit our children, as orphans, to Him, if He sees best to take us from them.

5. And this suggests another thought, namely, that it is *by doing good that we build the most enduring monuments in the world.* The tomb of Moses, says

some one, is not known to this day, but travelers and pilgrims, from every land and for many generations, have thanked God for water, as they have quenched their thirst at Jacob's Well. Nor is it without significance that the splendid pile of hewn stone and marble, and gold and silk, ivory and cedar, erected by king Solomon, for the service of Jehovah, was burnt, and has, long since, been in utter, undistinguishable ruins, while his reservoirs and fountains and aqueducts are almost as perfect as they ever were. The golden house of Nero is a mass of ruins, and cabbage and garlic and onions are growing over the ruins of the palace of the Cæsars, but the aqueduct of Claudius still pours its limpid streams into the eternal city. The fountains of Tadmor in the wilderness still sparkle as freshly as when Zenobia was queen, but her Palace and the Temple of the Sun have fallen, and are known only in story and by a mound of rubbish. The marble floors and columns of Shushan and Persepolis are known as ruins, the dwelling-places of unclean beasts and birds; but the lessons of virtue and holiness, which Mordecai taught the orphan Jewess, have never lost their power. The harvest of benevolent doing is perpetual. It is not only a personal and immediate blessing to the doer himself, but every good deed is immortal. A good deed is so great a blessing that it is to be sought after and performed, because of the present happiness it bestows; how much more, then, since it is to live forever? The example of the patriarchs, the sufferings of martyrs for truth and liberty, and the principles enunciated and lived out by the great and good before us cannot die.

6. *Here then is encouragement to teachers, parents and guardians.* Mordecai toiling and patiently teaching Hadassah her catechism—does he know what destiny awaits her? By no means. He is only doing his present duty, hoping for the divine blessing. While he is diligently laboring and praying that he may do his whole duty to his cousin-ward, he has no revelation telling him she shall become the Queen of Persia. No, not a syllable like it. But he toils on, trusting the God of Jacob for the future. And just so it must be still. The importance of early education, it is impossible to estimate too highly. The infant in the nurses' arms has faculties which an angel cannot comprehend, and which eternity alone can unfold. That infant may sway listening Senates, or thunder home truth from the pulpit into the hearts of thousands, or wield the pen or the sceptre that is to govern millions; or that little girl may occupy a place as wife or mother that shall send forth an influence ever widening and traveling onward to the last day of the world. The workers, the thinkers, the orators, the writers, the statesmen, the heroes of the ages of the future, are these infants now carried about by our nurses; and as they are educated so will they be a blessing or a curse. I observe that many writers and speakers often dwell on the dangers to be apprehended to our institutions from foreigners, and especially from the Jesuits; now I will tell you a secret—tell you of a power in our midst much greater than that of all the followers of Loyola in the world. I mean the young women who are our nurses, helps or servants. They are chiefly from Ireland and Germany, and the most of them are conscientious and honest Catho-

lics, and it is my solemn conviction that there is more power in their hands than in all the Jesuit schools in America. I do not mean that anything is to be apprehended under our laws, from what they will say or do to the children, or in the families where they live as domestics. As a general rule, I do not believe there is anything wrong here; but I do mean, that the rhymes and tales the nurse tells our little ones, are to live forever. And I mean also that these women are to be the wives and mothers of thousands of citizens, in whose hands are to rest the destinies of the institutions of this country. It is confessedly from them the increase of the power of the Catholic Church in America is chiefly to be expected. These women are industrious and healthy. They generally make good, honest, hard-working economical wives, and it is no uncommon thing for their sons to be the men of money and influence in their day; and we need hardly say, that the sons are defenders of the faith of the mothers. It is the mother that moulds the man, the elector and the statesman. These mothers have more power over our institutions than all the armies of the Napoleons of Europe can ever wield. England's "Iron Duke" once said on visiting, in his old age, the place where he was educated, "the battle of Waterloo was fought in Eton School." He meant that the military discipline of thought, the manliness of character, the knowledge and virtue, that he acquired in his school-boy days, enabled him to fight successfully the battle of Waterloo against the conqueror of the continent. And he was right. The general makes the soldier, and the boy is father to the man-general. It is so—it has always been so—and it will continue to be so. The mind of the child is immortal, and yet it is plastic in the hands of the mother; and truth taught to the youthful mind, lodged in the infant soul, prepares it for the bosom of God. And as parents and teachers, and the guardians of youth—as members of society, there is no escape from responsibility as to the proper education of the young.

And *finally,* let me while we are yet musing over the tomb of the Hebrew orphan, whom God made a queen, say to all young people: *Confide in your parents.* Esther as Sultana, obeyed Mordecai, as when she was brought up with him. Your parents' love is sincere. No one can love you with an affection so disinterested as your father or mother. Many a daughter has dug the grave of all her earthly happiness, by receiving the addresses of a young man contrary to the wish of her parents. The pale and melancholy features, the hastening to the grave of the broken-hearted, a stranger and neglected, have, alas! too often told the sad story of a lovely and confiding one that married contrary to the wishes of her parents, and exchanged thereby sympathizing friends, able and judicious counsellors, and kind and devoted nurses in sickness, for a selfish, unfeeling companion, who sought only his own vanity or pleasure. *Young woman,* if you have an intelligent and godly father, never forget his counsels. He knows the world; he knows the hearts of men, and his advice is free from selfishness. Dishonor not his gray hairs by disobeying him. *Young man,* if you have an intelligent and pious mother on earth, you yet have a treasure worth more than all the mines of the mountains. A mother's love, even if all other things seem lost to you, will follow you through all the changings of life, and far beyond the portals of the tomb. Forget not the law of your mother. A mother's love!

> "O, potent love! that throws its tendrils wild
> E'en round the footsteps of an erring child:
> That still sustains the mother's broken heart,
> And bids her hope till life itself depart;
> Sweet is the bond, and dear the hallowed tie,
> Made perfect only in Eternity."
>
> *Miss Barnes.*

Thus nobly lived Queen Esther and Prince Mordecai; and having served their generation according to the will of God, they fell on sleep, and, being dead, yet live. Blessed be Esther! Blessed be Mordecai!

www.ingramcontent.com/pod-product-compliance
Lightning Source LLC
LaVergne TN
LVHW010153110826
845151LV00002B/507
9781425537135